Prai~~ ~~

'The word quantum means "how much". Orrell proposes that mon~~,~~
a quantum phenomenon that entangles us in relationships not dissimilar to
the particle entanglements of the subatomic domain. Here credit and debit
constitute a wave–particle-like duality enmeshing us all in a quantum-weave.
Beautifully written, inherently ethical, and often hilarious, this book is a
must-read for anyone wanting to understand the weird, and getting weirder,
world of modern finance.'

Margaret Wertheim, author of *Pythagoras' Trousers* and *The Pearly Gates of
Cyberspace*

'As money becomes more digital and diffuse, it also becomes more quantum.
In this timely and illuminating book, David Orrell brings us to the frontier of
where economics, physics and psychology intersect. You'll never look at money
the same again!'

Dr Parag Khanna, author of *Connectography: Mapping the Future of Global
Civilization*

'Reading David Orrell's *Quantum Economics* is equivalent to playing a game of
3-D chess against the concept of value itself. The book easily switches between
physical, economic and metaphysical conceptions of value, revealing their
hidden parallels and paradoxes. The result is at once an explanation of our
current economic predicament, a diagnosis of how we got there and a credible
guide to the sort of "out of the box" thinking that is likely to get us out of it.
After you've forgotten about the latest wheeze about the financial crisis, you'll
be returning to this book.'

Steve Fuller, Auguste Comte Chair in Social Epistemology, University of
Warwick, and author of *Post-Truth: Knowledge as a Power Game*

'Rich with suggestive insights on every page and written in an accessible style,
this book will both engage and infuriate its audience. For those of us who
feel trapped in the professional cocoons of the like-minded, this book offers a
chance to escape from the iron cages we have built.'

Peter J. Katzenstein, Walter S. Carpenter, Jr. Professor of International
Studies, Cornell University

'Forty years ago, I wrote a paper noting in analogy to quantum physics, the
order of determining the price and demand for a commodity would change the
quantities determined. It is delightful to see a book devoted to exploring another
analogy to quantum physics for economics, that money exists in a dual way.

Orrell has explained his ideas in a very lively style, providing the history and a basic explanation of the physics; and goes on to explore the various consequences of this dual nature, which neo-classical economics did not foresee. The book should be read, not only by economists but also by all decision-makers.'

Asghar Qadir, Professor of Physics, National University of Science and Technology, Pakistan

'On the cusp of an earlier revolution, Karl Marx said all that is solid melts into air and all that is holy is profaned. Constructing a less mechanistic and even more revolutionary science of quantum economics, David Orrell proves it so. Orrell does not dabble in metaphor or metaphysics: he intellectually, persuasively and corrosively transmutes money into a quantum phenomenon. In the process, classical economics is profaned to good effect and a quantum future glimmers as a real possibility.'

James Der Derian, Chair of International Security Studies, University of Sydney

Praise for *Economyths*

'A fascinating, funny and wonderfully readable take down of mainstream economics. Read it.'

Kate Raworth, author of *Doughnut Economics*

'This is without doubt the best book I've read this year, and probably one of the most important books I've ever read … Orrell exposes the rotten heart of economics … [S]hould be required reading for every politician and banker. No, make that every voter in the land. This ought to be a real game changer of a book. Read it.'

Brian Clegg, www.popularscience.co.uk

'Lists 10 crucial assumptions (the economy is simple, fair, stable, etc.) and argues both entertainingly and convincingly that each one is totally at odds with reality. Orrell also suggests that adopting the science of complex systems would radically improve economic policymaking.'

William White, former Deputy Governor of the Bank of Canada (Bloomberg Best Books of 2013)

'His background allows Orrell to reliably and convincingly question the claim of economics to quasi-scientific objectivity and mathematical accuracy, and expose it as a sales ploy.'

Handelsblatt (Germany)

'Consistently interesting and enjoyable reading ... A wide audience including many non-economists could benefit from reading it.'
  International Journal of Social Economics

'His ten economic myths should be committed to memory.'
  Monthly Review (US)

'[Orrell's] tone is engagingly curious, drawing on biology and psychology, and his historical view spans more than merely the past few decades. Orrell recommends an interdisciplinary approach to a "new economics", in which ethics and complexity theory might have a say.'
  The Guardian (UK)

'Required reading for anyone who deals with the economy.'
  Obserwator Finansowy (Poland)

'I urge you all to read [this book]'
  New Straits Times (Malaysia)

'A book that can help you appreciate economics in action, and also help make it less of a voodoo science.'
  Business Line (India)

'A book full of intellectual stimulation.'
  Toyo Keizai (Japan)

'One of the best books I've read this year.'
  Pressian (Korea)

'Highly readable and a great introduction to the dynamic thinking used in many natural sciences.'
  The Post-Crash Economics Society (UK)

'Read this book!'
  Indonesian Society for Social Transformation

'Terrible, willfully ignorant, deeply anti-intellectual ... there is nothing an interested layman could possibly learn from this book.'
  Professor of economics, University of Victoria

'Just random – sort of like Malcolm Gladwell without the insight.'

Professor of economics, Carleton University

'Must be good as I've had hate mails from economists for writing a positive review of it.'

Brian Clegg

Praise for *Truth or Beauty*

'Fascinating ... Orrell is an engaging and witty writer, adept at explaining often complicated theories in clear language.'

Ian Critchley, *Sunday Times*

Praise for *The Money Formula* (with Paul Wilmott)

'This book has humor, attitude, clarity, science and common sense; it pulls no punches and takes no prisoners.'

Nassim Nicholas Taleb

Praise for *The Evolution of Money* (with Roman Chlupatý)

'Perhaps the best book on money I have ever read ... A reasonable and benign dictator might demand that those engaged in activities relating to economic management should, as a condition of employment, be compelled to read *The Evolution of Money* and pass a written examination based on an understanding of its contents.'

Colin Teese, former deputy secretary of the Department of Trade, *News Weekly* (Australia)

Praise for *Soumrak homo economicus* (*The Twilight of Economic Man*, with Tomáš Sedláček and Roman Chlupatý)

'The reader has the sense of being a silent guest at a smart table talk in which earth-shattering things are discussed.'

Die Welt (Germany)

Quantum
Economics

Quantum
Economics

The New
Science of
Money

David Orrell

ICON

Published in the UK and USA in 2018 by
Icon Books Ltd, Omnibus Business Centre,
39–41 North Road, London N7 9DP
email: info@iconbooks.com
www.iconbooks.com

Sold in the UK, Europe and Asia
by Faber & Faber Ltd, Bloomsbury House,
74–77 Great Russell Street,
London WC1B 3DA or their agents

Distributed in the UK, Europe and Asia
by Grantham Book Services, Trent Road,
Grantham NG31 7XQ

Distributed in the USA by
Publishers Group West,
1700 Fourth Street, Berkeley, CA 94710

Distributed in Canada
by Publishers Group Canada,
76 Stafford Street, Unit 300, Toronto, Ontario M6J 2S1

Distributed in Australia and New Zealand by
Allen & Unwin Pty Ltd, PO Box 8500,
83 Alexander Street, Crows Nest, NSW 2065

Distributed in South Africa by
Jonathan Ball, Office B4, The District,
41 Sir Lowry Road, Woodstock 7925

Distributed in India by Penguin Books India,
7th Floor, Infinity Tower – C, DLF Cyber City,
Gurgaon 122002, Haryana

ISBN: 978-178578-399-9

Typeset in Minion by Marie Doherty

Printed and bound in the UK by
Clays Ltd, Elcograf S.p.A.

CONTENTS

For James, Vera, and Lenny

David Orrell is an applied mathematician and author of popular science books. He studied mathematics at the University of Alberta, and obtained his doctorate from Oxford University on the prediction of nonlinear systems. His work in applied mathematics and complex systems research has since led him to diverse areas such as weather forecasting, economics, and cancer biology. His latest books are *The Money Formula: Dodgy Finance, Pseudo Science, and How Mathematicians Took Over the Markets*, written with Paul Wilmott, and *Economyths: 11 Ways Economics Gets It Wrong* (Icon Books, updated edition, 2017).

Introduction

*You never change things by fighting the existing
reality. To change something, build a new model
that makes the existing model obsolete.*
R. Buckminster Fuller

*If there be nothing new, but that which is
Hath been before, how are our brains beguil'd,
Which, labouring for invention, bear amiss
The second burthen of a former child!*
Shakespeare, Sonnet 59

What is economics?

How about this for an exciting definition: economics is the study of transactions involving money.

Obvious, right? Economists talk about money all the time. Everything gets expressed in terms of dollars or euros, yen or yuan. The health of a nation is reduced to how much they produce, as measured by Gross Domestic Product; a person's value to society is expressed by how much they earn. Economics is about money, everyone knows that.

And yet – if you look at an economics textbook, it turns out that the field is defined a little differently. Most follow the English economist Lionel Robbins, who wrote in 1932 that 'Economics is a science which studies human behaviour as a relationship between ends and scarce means which have alternative uses.'[1] Gregory Mankiw's widely-used *Principles of Economics* for example states that 'Economics is the study of how society manages its scarce resources.'[2] Or as it is sometimes paraphrased, economics is the science of scarcity. No mention of money at all.

And if you read a little further in those same textbooks, you will find that economists do not talk about money all the time – in fact they steer clear of it. Money is used as a metric, but – apart perhaps from chapters to do with basic monetary plumbing – is not considered an important subject in itself. The textbooks are like physics books that use time throughout in equations but never pause to talk about what time is. And both money and the role of the financial sector are usually completely missing from economic models, or paid lip service to.

Economists, it seems, think about money less than most people do: as the former Bank of England Governor Mervyn King observed, 'Most economists hold conversations in which the word "money" hardly appears at all.'[3]

Believe it or not, defining economics in terms of money transactions is a rather radical statement. For one thing, it leads to the related question: what is money?

In this case, the accepted answer is to quote Paul Samuelson's 'bible' textbook *Economics* and say that money is '*anything that serves as a commonly accepted medium of exchange*' (his emphasis).[4] This certainly seems to be a good description of how we use money in the economy. But again, it doesn't give us a sense of how money attains this special status as a medium of exchange; and it implies that money's only importance is to act as a passive intermediary for trade. The economy can therefore be viewed as a giant barter system, in which money is nothing more than a veil, a distraction from what really counts. The exciting and sometimes disturbing properties of money, which have fascinated and intrigued its users over millennia, have been largely written out of the story.

This book argues that the textbook definitions – and the economics establishment in general – have it the wrong way round.

It makes the case for a new kind of economics, which puts money – and the question *how much* – at its centre. The time has come to talk about money – and the implications of this simple adjustment promise to be as significant in economics as the quantum revolution was in physics.

Talking about a revolution

People have of course been calling for a revolution in economics for a rather long time – and especially since the financial crisis of 2007–08. In 2008 the physicist and hedge fund manager Jean-Philippe Bouchaud wrote a paper in the journal *Nature* with the title 'Economics needs a scientific revolution'.[5] In 2014 Ha-Joon Chang and Jonathan Aldred of Cambridge University called for a 'revolution in the way we teach economics'.[6] A number of student groups around the world agreed, releasing their own manifestos demanding a more pluralistic approach from their professors. In 2017 the UK's Economic and Social Research Council let it be known that it was setting up a network of experts from different disciplines including 'psychology, anthropology, sociology, neuroscience, economic history, political science, biology and physics', whose task it would be to 'revolutionise' the field of economics.[7] And there have been countless books on the topic, including my own *Economyths* which called in its final chapter for just such an intervention by non-economists, when it first came out in 2010.[8]

The reasons for this spirit of revolutionary zeal are clear enough. For the past 150 years mainstream (aka neoclassical) economics has clung to a number of assumptions that are completely at odds with reality – for example, the cute idea that the economy is a self-stabilising machine that maximises utility (i.e. usefulness; the wheels fell off that one a while ago). It fails even in terms of its own scarcity-based definition: with social inequality and environmental degradation at a peak, mainstream economics doesn't seem up to the task of addressing questions such as how to fairly allocate resources or deal with natural limits.

While there have been many calls for a revolution, though, the exact nature of that revolution is less clear. Critics agree that the foundations of economics are rotten, but there are different views on what should be built in its place. Most think that the field needs more diversity and should be more pluralistic (though as revolutionary demands go this one seems a bit diffuse). Most also agree that the emphasis on economic growth for its own sake needs to be reconciled both with environmental constraints and with fair distribution. Many have pointed out that economic models should incorporate techniques from other areas such as complexity theory, and properly account for the role of the financial sector. And the idea of rational economic man – which forms the core of traditional models – should be replaced with something a little more realistic.

But what if the problems with economics run even deeper? What if the traditional approach has hit a wall, and the field needs to be completely reinvented? What if the problem comes down to our entire way of thinking and talking about the economy?

This book argues that we need to start over from the beginning, by considering the most basic feature of the economy, which is transactions involving money. Rather than treat money as a mere metric, or as an inert medium of exchange, we will show that money has special, contradictory, indeed magical properties which feed into the economy as a whole. We can no more ignore these properties than weather forecasters can ignore the properties of water when making their predictions. Rather than treat people as rational, computer-like agents, with a few tweaks for behavioural effects, as in traditional economics, we will take their complex, multi-faceted behaviour at face value. And instead of seeing the economy as a machine that optimises utility, we will show that it is better described as a complex, connected system with emergent features that reflect the contradictions at its core.

All of this will come from analysing the meaning of the simple phrase: *how much*. Or in Latin, *quantum*.

A quantum of money

The word 'quantum' of course has a lot of history. It was applied by physicists over a century ago to describe another kind of transaction – the exchange of energy between subatomic particles. And it eventually overturned our most basic assumptions about the universe by showing that, instead of a deterministic machine, it was something more complex, entangled, and alive.

Classical or Newtonian physics, of the sort that was accepted orthodoxy in the first years of the twentieth century, was based on the idea that matter was made up of individual atoms that interacted only by bouncing into one another. The motion of these particles could be understood and predicted using deterministic laws. Quantum physics changed all this by showing that quantities such as position and momentum were fundamentally indeterminate, and could only be approximately measured through a process which affected the thing being measured, and which furthermore seemed to some theorists to depend on the choices made by the persons carrying out the measurements. And the states of particles were entangled, so a measurement on one could instantaneously inform an experimenter about the state of another. As physicist David Bohm observed, 'It is now clear that no mechanical explanation is available, not for the fundamental particles which constitute all matter, inanimate and animate, nor for the cosmos as a whole.'[9]

One might think that quantum principles and techniques apply only to the subatomic realm, and are of no relevance to our everyday lives – and indeed this was long commonly believed. But in recent years, a number of social scientists working in everything from psychology to business have put ideas from quantum mechanics to new uses in their own fields. The area where quantum mechanics has perhaps its most direct application is in the rather technical area of mathematical finance. As we will see later, many of the key results of that field, such as the equations used by traders to calculate the price of an option (contracts to buy or sell securities at a future date), can be expressed using the mathematics of quantum mechanics. The aim of these researchers is not to prove that finance is quantum in a direct physical sense or somehow reduces to quantum mechanics, but that it has properties which are best modelled using a quantum-inspired methodology. This offers some computational advantages over the usual statistical approach, but also changes the way we think about the financial system, from being a mechanistic system with added randomness, to a world of overlapping alternative possibilities, in which uncertainty is intrinsic to the system rather than an extra added feature.

The emerging fields of quantum cognition and quantum social science, meanwhile, take broader inspiration from quantum mechanics to think about how human beings make decisions and interact with one another.[10] While most applications to date have been in psychology or sociology, these findings are also very relevant to the economy. In particular, researchers have shown that many of the behavioural quirks long noted by behavioural economists – such as our tendency to act in a less than rational way when interacting with money – may elude classical logic, but can quite easily be expressed using a version of quantum logic, which allows for effects such as context and interference between incompatible concepts (the cause of cognitive dissonance). As physicist Diederik Aerts notes, 'People often follow a different way of thinking than the one dictated by classical logic. The mathematics of quantum theory turns out to describe this quite well.'[11]

Instead of behaving like independent Newtonian particles, as assumed in mainstream neoclassical economics, we are actually closely entangled and engaged in a sort of collective quantum dance. As the feminist theorist (and trained physicist) Karen Barad puts it, 'Existence is not an individual affair. Individuals do not preexist their interactions; rather, individuals emerge through and as part of their entangled intra-relating.'[12] We'll get on to what that means in later chapters – some of which draw heavily on the findings of these scholars and scientists – but the upshot is that rather than being quite as weird and counterintuitive as we have been taught, many aspects of quantum behaviour are actually rather like everyday life (which can also be weird). We have more in common with the subatomic realm than we thought.

Nowhere is this more true than in our dealings with money and our own approach to the commonly-asked financial question *how much*. This is shown by another theory presented here – dubbed the quantum theory of money and value – which provides the central thread of the book and states that money has a dualistic quantum nature of its own. Money is a way of combining the properties of a number with the properties of an owned thing. The fact that numbers and things are as different as waves and particles in quantum mechanics is what gives money its unique properties. The use of money in transactions is a way of attaching a number (the price) to the fuzzy and indeterminate notion of value. It therefore acts like the measurement process in quantum physics, which assigns a number to the similarly indeterminate properties of a particle.

The act of money creation also finds a direct analogue in the creation of subatomic particles out of the void, as we will discover. One implication is that the information encoded in money is a kind of quantum entanglement device, because its creation always has two sides, debt and credit. And its use also entangles people with each other and with the system as a whole, as anyone with a loan will know. All this will be explored in more detail as we delve into the world of the quantum.

This view of money – which I have previously described for an academic audience in talks, papers and a book – was originally inspired as much by the dualities of ancient Greek philosophy, and the need to explain the emergence of modern cybercurrencies such as bitcoin, as by quantum physics.[13] But when combined with quantum finance and quantum social science, each of which were developed independently in different settings and for different ends, the result is what I am calling quantum economics – which is to neoclassical economics what quantum physics was to classical physics.

Don't mention the quantum

I should address a few concerns here. One is that, since the time quantum mechanics was first invented, it has been treated as a highly esoteric area that can only be understood by experts. Commonly attributed quotes from famous physicists state that quantum mechanics is 'fundamentally incomprehensible' (Niels Bohr); 'If you think you understand quantum mechanics, you don't understand quantum mechanics' (Richard Feynman); 'You don't understand quantum mechanics, you just get used to it' (John von Neumann). Einstein said it reminded him of 'the system of delusions of an exceedingly intelligent paranoiac, concocted of incoherent elements of thoughts'.[14] If even such luminaries can't grasp the meaning of 'quantum', then what chance does anyone else have?

Perhaps as a result, the word has also long been seen as a marker for pretension, pseudery, or worse. 'Where misunderstanding dwells', wrote physicist Sean Carroll in 2016, 'misuse will not be far behind. No theory in the history of science has been more misused and abused by cranks and charlatans – and misunderstood by people struggling in good faith with difficult ideas – than quantum mechanics.'[15] Physicist Murray Gell-Mann devoted an entire chapter of his 1994 book *The Quark and the Jaguar* to 'Quantum Mechanics and Flapdoodle'.[16] Economist Paul Samuelson wrote back in 1970: 'There is really nothing more pathetic than to have an economist or a retired engineer try to force analogies between the concepts of physics and the concepts of economics … and when an economist makes reference to a Heisenberg Principle of [quantum] indeterminacy in the social world, at best this must be regarded as a figure of speech or a play on words, rather than a valid application of the relations of quantum mechanics.'[17] (Though this didn't stop him from later writing a paper on 'A quantum theory model of economics' which as Philip Mirowski points out, 'has nothing whatsoever to do with quantum mechanics'.[18])

Speaking as a former project engineer I agree that translating concepts and equations in a literal way from quantum mechanics to economics smacks of physics envy. In my previous books, such as *Economyths* and *The Money Formula* (with Paul Wilmott), I have done as much as most people to argue against the idea that economics can be simply transposed from physics. However, metaphor is intrinsic to our thought processes, and neoclassical economics has long been replete with metaphors from Victorian mechanics – one of its founders, Vilfredo Pareto, for example said that 'pure economics is a sort of mechanics or akin to mechanics' – so perhaps it is time to expand our mental toolbox.[19] As we'll see, it isn't just quantum mechanics which has been 'misused and abused' – bogus claims for the efficacy of mechanistic economics have probably damaged more lives than things like 'quantum healing' – and while it is understandable that physicists are protective of their quantum turf, overly-reactive policing of it is one reason social scientists are stuck in an oddly mechanistic view of the world.

Also, while I did study quantum mechanics and use it in my work (my early career was spent designing superconducting magnets which rely on quantum processes for their function), my intention is not to further mathematicise economics – quite the opposite. Although a number of books and papers cited throughout do take a heavily mathematical approach, the core ideas of the theory proposed here are very simple, and do not require equations or sophisticated jargon. If, as I believe, the money system has quantum properties of its own, then one could imagine a historical scenario where things developed in a different order, and quantum physicists were using economics analogies to explain their crazy ideas (though it is hard to think of physicists being accused of economics envy, or of borrowing from the high prestige of social science).

Some of the remoteness of quantum mechanics has also worn down as the field is increasingly adopted by technologists and featured in the media. For example, the logic circuits of quantum computers – whose design is turning into something of a cottage industry in many countries – rely explicitly on quantum principles to make calculations far faster than a classical computer. And if the price of a financial derivative, such as an option to buy a stock at a future date, can be calculated more rapidly and efficiently using a quantum model running on a quantum computer, then a degree in quantum financial engineering may turn out to be a rather lucrative qualification – a 'quant' (short for quantitative finance) degree with bells on.

Quantum processes begin to seem even less remote when we consider the hypothesis advanced by a number of scientists such as the physicist Roger Penrose that the mind itself is a quantum computer.[20] While this hypothesis remains controversial, it is consistent with the impression, at least from some interpretations of quantum mechanics, that consciousness seems to be inextricably linked with quantum processes (not to mention the fact that we live in a quantum universe). It is also buttressed by recent findings in quantum biology, which show how quantum effects are exploited in everything from photosynthesis in plants, to navigation by birds.[21] If this is the case, then things like quantum cognition begin to seem less like metaphor, as it is usually treated, than physical fact.

I will also argue that, just as understanding quantum physics helps to understand economics, it also works the other way: understanding how money works in the economy makes quantum physics seem a lot more accessible. Consider for example the notion that a particle's position is described by a probabilistic 'wave function' which only 'collapses' to a unique value when measured by an observer. That sounds impossibly abstract, until you realise that the price of something like a house is also fundamentally indeterminate, until it 'collapses' to a single value when it is sold to a buyer.

The notion of entanglement between particles, where the status of one particle is instantaneously correlated with measurements on its entangled twin, also seems less bizarre when financial contracts such as loans enforce a similar link between creditor and debtor. And the idea that quantum particles move in discrete jumps, rather than continuously, sounds less mysterious and counterintuitive when you compare it to buying something with a credit card at a store, where the money goes out in a single jump rather than draining out in a steady flow like water. When these properties were observed in the behaviour of subatomic particles, they led to the development of quantum mechanics as we now know it – but exactly the same argument can be applied to say that we need a quantum theory of money. Perhaps the main difference is that in quantum mechanics, the underlying explanation for phenomena such as wave function collapse or entanglement is unknown, and the topic of much controversy; while in the economy, these are just what we are used to.

It is sometimes said that, in order to free ourselves from the mechanistic worldview imposed on us by society, we need to familiarise ourselves with the mysteries of quantum physics, which offer a radically different picture.[22] But we don't need a PhD in quantum physics or access to a particle accelerator to accomplish this. We just need to look more closely at money. When we compare quantum physics with our everyday notion of how objects exist and move around it makes no sense; but when we compare it with monetary transactions it all seems rather reasonable. Money therefore has much to tell us about the quantum world. (And perhaps money really does make the world go round.)

The approach here is therefore not so much to use quantum physics as an analogy for social processes, or to assert a direct physical link between the two, but instead to start with the idea that money is a quantum phenomenon in its own right, with its own versions of a measurement process, entanglement, and so on, of which we all have direct experience.[23] Nor of course is it to say that the economy obeys immutable laws. A mortgage entangles the debtor and creditor in a formal sense, but a default might be a negotiated process rather than a sudden event. A money object has an exact value within a certain monetary space, but depends on things like locally-enforced laws or norms. One way to interpret this is to say that the money system is our best attempt to engineer a physics-like quantum system; but another, as we will see later, is to say that money is embedded in a larger, more complex social quantum system with competing forms of entanglement. However, the quantum approach was initially adopted in physics, not for abstruse philosophical reasons, but for pragmatic ones, since it was needed in order to mathematically describe physical reality;

and from a similarly pragmatic viewpoint I will argue that the more pressing question is not one of how to interpret quantum ideas (a question which is still debated in physics), but of how they can be put to use in economics – and why it took so long for their relevance to be recognised.

While discussing these concepts with both economists and physicists I soon found that, while many were supportive or at least tolerant, a rather common initial reaction was a visceral resistance to my use of words such as 'entanglement' to describe the monetary system that went beyond normal scepticism. One economist insisted I was just introducing new words for things like contracts, as I would know if I had ever taken an economics course, while physicists (who sometimes confuse their equations with the underlying reality) tended to see these as technical terms unique to their own domain, subject to control and quarantine. But John Maynard Keynes for one spoke about 'economic entanglement' in 1933 (see page 305), before Schrödinger introduced the physics version in a 1935 paper.[24] As physicists Gabriela Barreto Lemos and Kathryn Schaffer noted in a 2018 essay for the School of the Art Institute of Chicago, 'scholars in the arts, humanities, and many interdisciplinary fields now write about the "observer effect" and "entanglement" – technical physics concepts – in work that has a distinctly social or political (that is, not primarily physics-based) emphasis'.* My own use of such terms is intended to carefully relate the money system to the broader findings of quantum social science, not to mention their other meanings in

---

* 'Many scientists simply object to the idea that scientific ideas could have meaning outside their original contexts.' Lemos, G.B., and Schaffer, K. (5 February 2018), 'Obliterating Thingness: an Introduction to the "What" and the "So What" of Quantum Physics'. Retrieved from: http://www.kathryn schaffer.com/documents/obliterating-thingness.pdf

the English language.* And I felt the objections seemed to be more about an instinctual response to some perceived transgression of boundaries on my part than about anything of substance. Words are themselves an entangling device, in physics or in economics, and in binding minds and ideas together they can also define limits and remove flexibility. So while the path of least resistance may have been to stick with neutral language and avoid such conflicts, why ignore the obvious connections? If physicists once felt fit to adopt a particular set of mathematical tools, why shouldn't social scientists do the same now? More deeply, is there something about quantum behaviour that repels some part of us? As we will see later, there is much to be learned by following these threads, even or especially when they lead to topics that are considered off-limits or even taboo in economics.

Finally, one may reasonably object that economics should not be just about money and finance; it should also be about quality of life, social justice, power, the environment, and so on, none of which lend themselves easily to a monetary description. If quantum economics doesn't address these issues, then how is it any better than the existing neoclassical approach, which at least claims to be about happiness? Yet I will argue that recognising the importance of money affects how we see all of these things, and that limiting the domain of economics can paradoxically make it more useful and relevant. And while finance employs relatively few people directly, my own motivation for getting involved in economics grew out of a response to the 2007–08 financial crisis which affected the lives of many people, and not just bankers.

---

* As the political scientist – and leader in the area of quantum social science – Alexander Wendt notes: 'money is not only a perfect illustration, but arguably (along with language) one of the most fundamental "quantum" institutions in all of society.' Personal communication, 2017.

The idea of *how much* – of quantifying value, of putting numbers on the world – goes to the very heart of what economics should be about, which is monetary transactions. Following this thread will reveal new ways of approaching our gravest economic issues including inequality, financial stability, and the environmental crisis, while giving fresh insights into the sources of economic vibrancy and energy. Instead of predicting an economy that is efficient, fair, and stable, quantum economics suggests one that is creative but tends towards inequity and instability – rather like the world we live in.

Quantum knitting

The aim of this book is to look at a very simple question – what we mean in economics by the expression *how much*. Following the spirit, but not the letter, of quantum physics, we start with the small and knit our way out to form a cohesive whole. The goal of the book is not to present a new vision of society or expand human consciousness – as desirable as those may be – but to make economics smaller but more grounded and realistic. The book is divided into two parts. The first part, Quantum Money, begins by tracing the history of quantum physics from its discovery at the start of the twentieth century, and explaining some of its key principles. We then relate these findings to the dualistic properties of money, a substance which is as important to the economy as water is to life. We show how money is produced in the modern economy; and reveal how the banking system exploits the magical properties of money to produce wealth, especially for the bankers.

In the second part, The Quantum Economy, we expand the picture to include the economy as a whole. We first delve into the field of quantitative finance. As we'll see, the equations behind these derivatives grew out of the project to build a nuclear bomb – economists who resist the idea of importing ideas from quantum physics might be surprised to learn that it already happened, if in a rather distorted way – and this connection to quantum mechanics has been rediscovered in recent years by experts working in the area of quantum finance. Similarly, the mathematics of game theory, which underlies much of mainstream economic theory, assumes rational behaviour; but rather than acting as individual atoms when making financial decisions, we behave more like members of an entangled complex system, and operate according to a kind of quantum logic which resonates in interesting ways with the quantum properties of money. We will see that many key aspects of the economy emerge as the product of our quantum money system. The book concludes by drawing these ideas into recommendations for the reform of economics.

Along the way we will explore topics including:

Money. During the gold standard, money was thought to be a real thing, while today it is more commonly seen as a number representing virtual government-backed debt, except for cybercurrencies which don't quite fit with either picture. We will show that money is both real and virtual, in the same way that light is both particle and wave.

Value. Classical economists such as Adam Smith believed that money was measuring labour, neoclassical economists that it measures utility. According to quantum economics, money is measuring – money, which is a form of information.

Pricing. In conventional theory, prices are thought to be determined by imaginary supply and demand curves, which – as we'll see – have no empirical backing. Quantum economics shows that price is an uncertain property which is in a sense *created* through transactions – just as a particle's position or momentum is inherently indeterminate until measured. This has implications for areas such as quantitative finance, but also for the dynamics of things like the price of your house or the value of your pension.

Debt. Mainstream economics treats debt as something that comes out in the wash – what one person owes, another is owed, so they cancel out. According to quantum economics, though, debt is a force that entangles people, institutions, and the financial system as a whole in ways that are difficult to understand and potentially destructive. This is a concern, given that global debt is now estimated at over $200 trillion.[25]

Risk. Mainstream theory assumes that markets are stable, efficient, and self-correcting. Quantum economics shows that none of these assumptions stand up, which means that the risk models currently taught in universities and business schools, and relied upon by businesses and financial institutions, are not fit for purpose (as many guessed after the last crisis). We need to update our approach to handling risk.

Decision-making. Mainstream models assume that consumers make rational decisions, with the occasional adjustment to account for behavioural factors such as 'bounded rationality' (i.e. the fact that we make decisions under informational and cognitive limitations).[26] Quantum economics admits no such bound, and treats things like emotion and entanglement as integral to the decision-making process.

Finance. Mainstream models downplay or ignore the role of the financial sector, which is one reason financial crises always come as a surprise. Quantum economics puts money in its rightful place at the centre of economics, and offers new tools for understanding the financial system. Only by acknowledging the dynamic and unstable nature of the system can we find ways to better control it. Nowhere is this more true than with the quadrillion dollars'-worth of complex derivatives which hang over the economy.

Inequality. Mainstream economics was inspired by classical thermodynamics and concentrates on optimising average wealth (like the average temperature) instead of its distribution. But the dynamics of money tend towards disequilibrium and asymmetry. This helps to explain why a group of people who could fit into the first-class cabin of a jet now control as much wealth as half the world's population.[27]

Happiness. Mainstream economics assumes that people act to optimise their own utility, which leads to maximum societal happiness. Quantum economics draws on the field of quantum game theory to show that the truth is more complicated, in part because people are entangled – and asks whether economics is the best tool for thinking about happiness in the first place.

Environment. As quantum cognition shows, context is important when we take decisions. The inbuilt biases of neoclassical economics have meant that for too long, we have been ignoring the wider environmental context, with very visible effects. Quantum economics points the way to an economics which can, not account for, but *make space* for fuzzy, uncertain quantities such as the health of ecosystems; while also addressing one of the main contributors to environmental damage, which is our money system.

Ethics. Just as money has been excluded from mainstream economics, so has ethics. One reason is that, as with classical physics, the economy has been treated as an essentially mechanistic system where things like will, volition, and personal responsibility seem to have no role. Another is the fact that, ironically, economics itself has been influenced by money. Quantum economics is the ethical alternative.

Modelling. Orthodox models of the economy used by everyone from economists to central banks to policy-makers are based on a Newtonian, mechanistic view of human interactions and emphasise qualities such as stability, rationality, and efficiency. Quantum economics starts from a different set of assumptions, and leads to models that exploit techniques developed for the study of complex, living systems. A word of warning: this area is new, so while I will concentrate on tested methods, not all of the ideas and techniques described here have been demonstrated yet in an economics context. I will make it clear when that is the case.*

*

Quantum economics will therefore provide a consistent and much-needed alternative to the mainstream approach: one which is rooted in recent developments in areas such as social science, information theory, and complexity; which radically challenges our most basic assumptions about how the economy works; and which leads to concrete recommendations for the reform of economics. We begin by showing what happened over a century ago, when a physicist working for a lighting company asked *how much* – and came up with a rather surprising answer.

---

* Readers interested in mathematical details are referred to: 'Introduction to the mathematics of quantum economics', available at davidorrell.com/quantumeconomicsmath.pdf

PART 1

QUANTUM MONEY

CHAPTER 1

THE QUANTUM WORLD

*The great revelation of the quantum theory was that features
of discreteness were discovered in the Book of Nature, in
a context in which anything other than continuity seemed
to be absurd according to the views held until then.*
Erwin Schrödinger, *What is Life?* (1944)

Natura non facit saltum (Nature makes no sudden leaps)
Epitaph of Alfred Marshall's 1890 *Principles of Economics*.
It remained there until the final edition of 1920

**Money, according to the media theorist Marshall McLuhan,
is a communication medium that conveys the idea of value.
To understand the properties of this remarkable medium, we
begin by looking at a different kind of exchange – that of energy
between particles. This chapter traces the quantum revolution in
physics which began in the early twentieth century, and shows
how its findings changed the way we think about things like matter, space, time, causality, and even the economy. As we'll see,
economic transactions have more in common with the quantum
world than one might think.**

How much? This was the question pondered by the German physicist Max Planck in the late nineteenth century. *How much energy
is carried by a light beam?*

Planck's employer was the Imperial Institute of Physics and
Technology, near Berlin, and his work was sponsored by a local

electrical company. Their interest was in getting the most light out of a bulb with the least energy. A first step was to figure out a formula for how much light is produced when you heat something up.

Anyone who has placed a poker in a fire knows that as the metal heats it begins to glow red, then yellow, and then – at very high temperatures – a bluish white. When you turn on a lightbulb the thin filament inside does the same thing, except that it skips quickly to the white.

Scientists at the time knew that light was a wave, and that both the colour and the energy were determined by the frequency (or the closeness of the wave crests).* When something is heated, it emits light at a range of frequencies which depend on the temperature. An object at room temperature emits light in the low-frequency, low-energy infrared range, which is visible only through night-vision goggles. At extremely high temperatures, most of the light is in the invisible, high-frequency, high-energy ultraviolet range, but the object appears to our eyes as white – which is a mix of all frequencies.

The problem was with conventional theory, which predicted that a heated object would *always* emit light at all frequencies. Since high-frequency waves carry a lot of energy, an implication was that the energy would be channelled into arbitrarily short wavelengths of unlimited power. The question *how much* was therefore giving a puzzling answer: infinitely much. Instead of warming us, a log fire would vaporise us.

Few people at the time were calling for a revolution in physics. When Planck was contemplating a career in physics, a professor advised him against it, saying that 'in this field, almost everything is already discovered, and all that remains is to fill a few holes'.[1] In 1894 the American physicist and future Nobel laureate Albert

---

* The frequency of a wave, in the usual unit of hertz, is the number of waves that pass a point in one second.

Michelson had announced that 'it seems probable that most of the grand underlying principles have been firmly established and that further advances are to be sought chiefly in the rigorous application of these principles to all the phenomena which come under our notice.'[2] And Planck was not setting out to disrupt the field when he found a way in 1901 to model the radiation distribution with a neat formula. He just needed to use a little trick, which was to assume that the energy of light could only be transmitted in discrete units. The energy of one of these units was equal to its frequency multiplied by a new and very small number, denoted h. To name these little parcels of energy, Planck chose the word *quanta*.

The only problem with this assumption was that it violated the time-honoured principle that *Natura non facit saltum*: nature makes no sudden leaps. Or as Aristotle put it in *Metaphysics*, 'the observed facts show that nature is not a series of episodes, like a bad tragedy'. But as Planck later wrote, he considered it 'a purely formal assumption … actually I did not think much about it.'[3]

Thus was launched what became known as the quantum revolution. It took a while for the waves of this revolution to lap onto the shores (let alone the textbooks) of academic economics, but as we'll see, it promises to have the same effect on that field as it did on physics.

A century after Planck, the Nobel laureate economist Robert Lucas, famous for his theory of 'rational expectations', echoed Planck's teacher when he told his audience in 2003: 'My thesis in this lecture is that macroeconomics in this original sense has succeeded: Its central problem of depression prevention has been solved, for all practical purposes, and has in fact been solved for many decades.'[4] All that remained, it turned out, was to fill a few holes – like the ones left by the great financial crisis that started just a few years later, when the economy took a sudden leap off a cliff. But we're getting ahead of ourselves.

The colour of their money

While Planck's quanta may have been intended as just a pragmatic technical fix, they soon proved useful in solving another problem, which had to do with the photoelectric effect. This refers to the tendency of some materials to emit electrons when light is shone on them. Physicists found for example that, if they placed two metal plates close together in an evacuated jar, connected the plates to the opposite poles of a battery, and shone a light on the negatively charged plate, then the light dislodged electrons which raced across to the other, positively charged plate, in the form of a sudden spark.

According again to the classical theory, the energy of the emitted electrons should depend only on the intensity (i.e. brightness) of the light source. Shine a bright light, get a bigger spark. But in practice, it turned out that what really mattered was the colour, or frequency: high-frequency blue light created a bigger spark than low-frequency red light. And each material had a cut-off frequency, below which no amount of light would work. In a 1905 paper – one of a stream of results including his famous formula $E=mc^2$ which would define the new physics – Albert Einstein showed that the photoelectric effect could be explained by use of Planck's quanta.

According to Einstein's theory, electrons were emitted when individual quanta of light struck individual atoms. Think of the metal plate as a marketplace of atoms, each selling electrons at a particular price, measured in energy; and think of the quanta of light as being the spending power of individual shoppers. Shining red light onto the plate is like sending a lot of low-budget shoppers into the market. No matter how many there are, if none of them have sufficient cash then no electrons are released – they can look but they cannot buy. High-frequency blue light, on the other hand, is an army of high-spenders. So what counts is not just the number of shoppers (the brightness) but how much each shopper can spend (the colour).

Einstein of course did not use this metaphor, and he gave his paper the careful title 'On an heuristic* viewpoint concerning the production and transformation of light'. But it was clear that unlike Planck, he saw these light quanta – which later became known as photons – not as mathematical abstractions, but as real things. As he wrote, 'Energy, during the propagation of a ray of light, is not continuously distributed over steadily increasing spaces, but it consists of a finite number of energy quanta localized at points in space, moving without dividing and capable of being absorbed or generated only as entities.'[5]

This sounds mysterious when applied to light, but again is similar to the way that we make financial transactions. When you receive your pay packet, there isn't a little needle which shows the money draining into your account. Instead it goes as a single discrete lump. The same when you use your credit card at a store, or when a bank creates new funds by issuing a loan. And it is impossible to make payments smaller than a certain amount, such as a cent.

Most physicists responded to these new ideas in the same way most mainstream economists react to disruptive ideas today, which was to ignore them totally and hope they went away. But the question *how much* soon proved useful in solving another problem, which this time went right to the heart of what we mean by things – the atom.

Atomic auction

In the early twentieth century it was understood, at least according to the classical model, that there were two basic kinds of phenomena: waves and particles. Light, for example, was a wave, an

---

* Here 'heuristic' refers to a kind of mental shortcut.

electromagnetic perturbation in the ether, which played the role of a background medium through which the wave moved (this substance was later dropped, as discussed below). Objects, on the other hand, were made of atoms, and these in turn were composed of negatively charged electrons circling a small, but heavy, positively-charged nucleus like planets around the Sun. The energy of an electron depended on the radius of its path. The simplest atom, hydrogen, had only one electron, but larger atoms had multiple electrons at different energy levels.

The solar system model, as it was known, did explain a number of features of atoms, for example experimental results which showed that they mostly consisted of empty space. Fire small charged particles at a thin foil, and most pass through as if there were nothing there, while only a few bounce back. Again, though, there were a couple of problems. One was that the model didn't spell out why atoms of a particular substance, say hydrogen, are identical with one another. What made electrons of different atoms always whizz round at the same radius? An even more serious issue was that, according to classical theory, a circulating electron should immediately radiate away all its energy and crash into the nucleus, like Mars colliding with the Sun.

In 1912 the Danish physicist Niels Bohr proposed a novel solution. If the energy of light was limited to discrete units, as Planck said, then so perhaps was the energy of the electron.[6] This would mean that electrons could not have a continuous range of energies, but would be limited to multiples of some lowest base amount. And the reason an electron couldn't radiate away all its energy was because it could only give it away in lumps, and it couldn't go to zero. Electrons could gain energy, for example from a passing photon, and move to a higher level; or they could lose energy, by emitting a photon, and go down a level; but the change in energy would again always be a multiple of the base amount. The process was like an auction in which the auctioneer sets a certain base price, and only accepts bids that are multiples of some amount. The price can never go below the minimum, and can only go up in discrete steps.

Evidence that Bohr was on the right track was provided by the fact that his model could help to explain another puzzle. It was known that atoms of different elements emit and absorb light at certain distinct, characteristic frequencies or spectra (this is the basis of spectroscopy, used to determine the chemical makeup of a material). This property was again inconsistent with classical physics, which predicted a continuous spectrum; but starting with the simplest case of hydrogen, Bohr showed that it matched his model rather well. The favoured frequencies just reflected the possible transitions from one energy level to another, as electrons absorbed or released photons.

In Bohr's model, the analogue solar system picture was therefore replaced with a digital one in which electrons could live only in certain layers arranged in concentric rings around the nucleus. The inner layer could hold at most two electrons. The next layer out could hold a maximum of eight. If the atoms of a particular element had a full outer layer, then that element was chemically stable. Helium, for example, has only two electrons, both in the inner layer. Neon has ten electrons, with two in the inner layer, and eight in the next layer, so again it is a full house. Sodium, however, has eleven electrons, with the extra one in the third layer, and is so reactive that it can explode in contact with water. Chlorine, a poisonous gas, has seventeen electrons – organised as 2-8-7 – so is one short in the third layer. The combination of the two is stable because sodium shares its extra electron with chlorine. This is a useful feature, since otherwise sodium chloride – aka table salt – would presumably be both explosive and poisonous, which would limit its attraction as a seasoning (the taste of salt is an example of an emergent property, which, as discussed later, implies that it is not the same as the sum of its parts).

Odd versus even

Quanta, it seemed, could explain much about the basic structure of matter, but Bohr's model still had a few problems. One was that it had little to say about the experimental observation that a material's spectral lines were split when it was placed in a magnetic field. To accommodate such effects, three more quantum numbers eventually had to be added; two which described the orbit's exact shape and orientation, and another number called the spin which was like a quantum version of a particle's rotation around its own centre. For photons, as discussed below, their spin is related to the polarisation of light.

The model seemed to be getting rather cumbersome, but in 1925 the young physicist Wolfgang Pauli realised that it could be used to explain why the electrons in an atom didn't all drop down to the ground state.[7] The reason was that the quantum numbers acted as an address, and no two electrons could live in the same place. The helium atom, for example, has two electrons in the same inner ring, but they differ in spin.

It was later found that Pauli's 'exclusion principle' applied only to the particles known as fermions, which include the basic constituents of the atom such as the electron and proton, and that have an odd multiple of the basic unit of spin.* Bosons, which are responsible for force transmissions and include photons, have an even-multiple spin. These are less stand-offish and can share the

---

* The term 'spin' is a little misleading since in quantum mechanics it doesn't make sense to think of a particle as a solid object, so it isn't clear what would be spinning. The basic unit of spin is defined as ½, so fermions can have spins of ½, ³⁄₂, and so on, while bosons have integer spins.

same space.* (In her 1990 book *The Quantum Self*, Danah Zohar describes bosons evocatively as 'particles of relationship' and fermions as 'anti-social'.[8])

A more basic question, though, was what it meant for matter and energy to be divided into quanta at all. After all, scientists knew that light was a wave. Thomas Young had demonstrated this fact back in 1801, in his famous double-slit experiment.[9] He shone a beam of light from a point source through two thin slits, and looked at the pattern projected onto a screen behind them. Instead of finding two distinct bright spots, which one would expect for streams of particles, he instead found that each light beam was diffracting as it passed through the slit, and then merging to form an interference pattern of alternating bright and dark bands, just like the ones formed in water when the crests and troughs of one wave add or subtract from the crests and troughs of another. In 1861 James Clerk Maxwell derived the equations which proved that this wave was nothing other than an oscillating electromagnetic field. But here were Einstein and the others saying that it consisted of photons – particles.

An answer of sorts was supplied in 1909 by Geoffrey Taylor, who tried the same experiment as Young, but this time using a very faint light source, so faint that individual photons were emitted one at a time.[10] What he found was perplexing – because even when the photons passed through the slits individually, the interference pattern was still reproduced. It was as if each photon was somehow interfering with itself. The wave crests now corresponded to places where there was a high probability of seeing a photon, while the troughs had a low probability.

---

* Fermions were named after Enrico Fermi, bosons after the Indian physicist Satyendra Nath Bose.

As Einstein told a German newspaper in 1924: 'There are therefore now two theories of light, both indispensable, and – as one must admit today in spite of twenty years of tremendous effort on the part of theoretical physicists – without any logical connection.'[11] The reason, as we'll see, was that matter wasn't based on classical logic – it was based on quantum logic.

The indeterminacy principle

The question *how much* had led to the idea that light waves were actually particles. But if that were true, then surely – if only for the sake of symmetry – particles could be waves as well? This was the idea suggested in his 1924 PhD thesis by a student at the Sorbonne called Louis de Broglie.[12]

Physicists had abandoned the idea of an ether, for both experimental reasons (the speed of light, denoted c, was the same in every direction, which made no sense if the planet was spinning through some invisible medium) and theoretical reasons (Einstein's relativity, which set this constant c as a universal speed limit), and they now thought of waves as some kind of free-standing entity. De Broglie combined Einstein's theory with Planck's quanta, plugged the results into the equation for a wave, and reasoned that the wavelength associated with a particle should be Planck's constant h divided by the momentum.

Experimental results soon proved De Broglie right: electron beams do indeed diffract like waves when they encounter matter (this is the principle behind modern electron microscopes). And the orbit of an electron circulating around an atomic core could be viewed as a standing wave, with an integer number of peaks corresponding to the quantum number of the energy level. The main difference between photons and other particles such as electrons is that electrons have mass, while photons don't.

Physicists were adept at computing the behaviour of waves,

such as those of a vibrating string, and within months Austrian physicist Erwin Schrödinger had come up with a detailed equation that could be used to model electron waves. He also showed, at least for simple cases such as the hydrogen atom, that the possible quantum states of an electron correspond to the harmonics of its mathematical wave function, just as musical notes correspond to the sound waves produced by a tuned instrument. These quantum states therefore 'occur in the same natural way as the integers specifying the number of nodes in a vibrating string'.[13]

It was less clear how to interpret what the wave equation – which was just an abstract mathematical formulation – actually *meant*. De Broglie had viewed it as representing a kind of pilot wave that guided the position of the electron. Schrödinger's colleague Max Born suggested instead that the wave was supplying probabilistic information, so the chance of finding an electron in a particular place depended on the amplitude (distance between peak and valley) of the wave squared.[14] Because the wave function is expressed in so-called complex numbers, whose square can be negative, this allows for negative probabilities. When waves interfere, as in the double-slit experiment, it is because one wave is subtracting from the other. As Paul Dirac noted, 'Negative energies and probabilities should not be considered as nonsense. They are well-defined concepts mathematically, like a negative of money'.[15]

This seemed a reasonable interpretation, except that waves and particles have very different properties. For example, a property of waves is that they tend to be leaky. Think about sound waves: you might be able to reduce most of the noise from your neighbour by putting insulation in the wall or wearing earplugs, but reducing it to zero is impossible. Similarly, the wave associated with a particle can leak through boundaries, and since this wave describes a probability of finding the particle at a particular location, it means that the particle can potentially appear on the other side. In fact, this is the principle of alpha decay, in which a radioactive substance such as uranium emits an alpha particle, which is a helium atom stripped of its electrons. According to classical physics, alpha decay shouldn't happen because the alpha particle could never escape the attractive force of the nucleus, which imposes an apparently insurmountable boundary. But in quantum physics, this only means there is a very small chance that the particle will escape, which is not the same thing at all (see atom bombs).

The diffuse nature of the wave equation meant that the true state of a particle could never be completely nailed down. The German physicist Werner Heisenberg argued that it therefore made no sense to speculate about what was going on inside the atom.[16] The true state of a particle was unknowable, and all we had were observations, which were subject to inherent uncertainty because of the wave equation. He quantified this with his uncertainty principle, which stated that the more accurately a particle's position was measured, the more uncertain was its momentum, and vice versa.

One way to think about this uncertainty is to note that, in quantum mechanics, the chance of finding a particle in a certain location is specified by the wave function; and it turns out the more you know about the location – i.e. the narrower the wave – the less you know about how fast the particle is moving. In general there is always a trade-off between position and momentum (defined as mass times velocity), so you can never know both perfectly. The same type of uncertainty relationship applies to other pairs of quantities, such as energy and time, where the latter refers to a characteristic time such as a particle's lifetime. This is why a so-called virtual particle can appear out of nowhere, exist a brief time, then disappear back into the void without violating conservation of energy.

As an example of the uncertainty principle, suppose that we wish to measure the position and momentum of an electron. One method, as Heisenberg noted, would be to shine light on it and use a microscope to look at the reflected light. To accurately measure the position we need to use the shortest possible wavelength of light, since otherwise the image will be fuzzed out. This equates to using photons with short wavelengths (or equivalently high frequencies). But such photons have high energy, so will deliver a kick to the electron and change its momentum: 'thus, the more precisely the position is determined, the less precisely the momentum is known, and conversely.'[17]

It is important to note, though, that the problem is not just a practical one of measurement. In quantum physics (or at least the standard interpretation – see below), the wave function means that quantities such as position and momentum have no real independent meaning until the moment they are measured, so are fundamentally indeterminate rather than just impossible to precisely measure. (As is often noted, a better name might be the indeterminacy principle.) Measurement is therefore not a neutral, passive process, but an active process which affects what is being measured. For example, it has been shown in the laboratory that the results of different measurements depend on the order in which they are made.[18] As we will see later, the same effects apply in human psychology.

To be, or not to be
The idea that matter had attributes of both waves and particles made sense from a purely mathematical standpoint, which as far as Heisenberg was concerned was all that mattered. Bohr argued, however, that it had a deeper meaning. According to his principle of complementarity, the mutually incompatible wave and particle descriptions each gave one aspect of a single, unified reality. Instead of wave or particle, it was wave *and* particle.

This collided head-on with the most basic principles of logic. In *Metaphysics*, Aristotle had written that 'it is impossible for anyone to believe the same thing to be and not to be, as some think Heraclitus says'.[19] (The dissident Heraclitus was ahead of his time.) As Heisenberg noted, 'it was found that if we wanted to adapt the language to the quantum theoretical mathematical scheme, we would have to change even our Aristotelian logic. That is so disagreeable that nobody wants to do it; it is better to use the words in their limited senses, and when we must go into the details, we just withdraw into the mathematical scheme.'[20] Less controversial was Bohr's principle of correspondence, which stated that at scales large enough that the effects of Planck's constant h could be neglected, quantum mechanics should converge to classical mechanics – although quantum effects can sometimes be scaled up, as discussed below.

The philosophical debate over the meaning of the wave equation has never been settled, but in 1927 a kind of compromise was presented to the luminaries of physics at a conference in Solvay, Belgium. The Copenhagen interpretation, as it later became known, asserted that until it is observed, a particle's state is given by its wave function, and is uncertain; but when a measurement takes place, the wave function somehow reduces or 'collapses' so that the attribute measured has a specific value.

The Copenhagen interpretation therefore retained some of the deterministic flavour of classical mechanics, with a couple of important differences. One was that the determinism now applied to probabilistic wave functions. Instead of particles obeying mechanistic laws, said Born, 'probability itself propagates according to the law of causality'.[21] The other was that uncertainty was inherent rather than statistical. For example, if a jar is filled with 50 red beads and 50 blue beads, and we choose one at random, then from statistics we know that there is a 50 per cent chance that it will be red. In quantum physics, there is a bead in a jar, which is in a superposition of two states. When we pull it out, it might be red, but it could just as well have been blue. Instead of having a fixed colour, the bead has a potential colour that is resolved only upon measurement.

This sounds mysterious and magical, but – to again use a financial example – when you put your house up for sale, you might have a rough idea how much it will fetch, but you don't know for sure, because your house has neither a fixed price tag nor a guaranteed buyer. A hundred people might show up for the open house, resulting in a bidding war and a magnificent winning offer. Or you might get zero offers and have to lower the price. Your house does not have a fixed price, any more than a quantum particle has fixed attributes such as position. Only when someone actually buys it does the uncertainty collapse.

Mind control

Not everyone was convinced by the Copenhagen interpretation. Einstein in particular couldn't accept the idea that random behaviour – or worse yet, some kind of agency – could be built into the fabric of the cosmos. 'I find the idea quite intolerable', he wrote in 1924, 'that an electron exposed to radiation should choose of its own free will, not only its moment to jump off, but also its direction. In that case, I would rather be a cobbler, or even an employee in a gaming house, than a physicist.'[22] He believed instead that such behaviour was actually the result of undetected processes, or hidden variables.

The process of wave function collapse was also unspecified. In 1935, Schrödinger came up with a famous thought experiment to illustrate the theory's flaws. This involved a cat locked up in a steel chamber along with a small amount of radioactive substance, which had a 50-50 chance of emitting a radioactive particle within one hour. A Geiger counter is set up so that, if radiation is detected, a 'small flask of hydrocyanic acid' is released, killing the cat.[23] The fate of the cat was therefore linked to the wave function of the radioactive particle, which in turn collapsed only when observed. Taken literally, the Copenhagen interpretation therefore seemed to imply that the cat would be both alive and dead at the same time, until the moment someone opened the door and observed what had happened.

Perhaps the most disturbing feature of quantum mechanics, at least for physicists such as Einstein, was that it seemed to hold out a role for mind. As the mathematician John von Neumann argued in 1932, the special ingredient in a measurement process was not the measuring device itself, which was just part of the physical system, but the presence of a conscious observer.[24] Schrödinger also wrote in 1935 that the process relies on 'the living subject actually taking cognizance of the result of the measurement'. But just as classical logic drew a firm line between being and not being, so it drew a line between mind and body, subjective and objective. The idea that just observing something could affect its behaviour was about as repugnant as believing that a magician can make a table levitate using his mind alone. Something was fishy – and Einstein was determined to figure out the trick. The same year as Schrödinger's thought experiment, he and two collaborators finally hit on an (animal-free) thought experiment which could disprove the Copenhagen interpretation, and reveal the hidden variables that were operating behind the scenes.

The so-called Einstein-Podolsky-Rosen (EPR) paradox arises when two quantum systems are related in such a way that information on one yields information on the other, in a manner which appeared to contradict the idea that quantum properties are fundamentally indeterminate.[25] For example, suppose we know that a particle decays into two particles, A and B, which by conservation of angular momentum – a law which here implies the spins will add to zero – must have opposite spin. The two particles are then entangled, as if bound by an invisible contract, because information about the state of one yields information about the other. More generally, as Schrödinger noted, whenever two systems interact, their wave functions 'do not come into interaction but rather they immediately cease to exist and a single one, for the combined system takes their place'.[26] If we measure A's spin, then we automatically know B's spin – it will be the opposite. So in other words we have successfully carried out a measurement on B without disturbing it in any way. This contradicts the idea that such properties are intrinsically uncertain quantities that are known only after the collapse of some mysterious wave function. It also implies that the notion of individuality breaks down, since A and B are effectively part of a single system.

The only way out of this would be to assume that A and B can communicate in some way – but for that to work within the formalism of quantum theory, the information would have to be transmitted instantaneously, even if the particles were light years apart. This would violate Einstein's theory of relativity, which showed that nothing – including signals between particles – could travel faster than the speed of light, an idea he famously mocked as 'spooky action at a distance'. Einstein therefore concluded that quantum theory was incomplete, and something else had to be going on. The theory was correct in the sense that it made many accurate predictions, but it was best seen as a statistical approximation to a fuller theory which would explain all of its apparent randomness with a more logical explanation.

Getting entangled

The EPR paradox remained a mental puzzle until in 1964 the Irish physicist John Bell worked out a way to actually test it. The first step is to get a pair of particles that are suitably entangled. This can be done quite easily in the laboratory by shining an ultraviolet laser through a particular sort of crystal; some of the ultraviolet photons get split into two entangled infrared photons of half the energy, and with opposite polarisations.

As shown by Maxwell, a light wave consists of electric and magnetic fields oscillating at right angles to one another. The polarisation refers to the orientation of these fields relative to the direction of travel of the wave. In unpolarised light, the light is a mix of all different orientations. When light is reflected, for example from the surface of a lake, it naturally becomes polarised. Polaroid sunglasses work by using polarisation filters to preferentially filter out this reflected light.

Just like light waves, individual photons also have a particular polarisation, which is associated with their spin. The difference is that, if you test whether the photon is horizontally polarised, for example by passing it through a filter which only allows horizontally polarised light to pass, you don't get some partial answer like 12 per cent horizontal for that photon – you just get a yes or a no. It is Aristotelian logic in action. Before being measured, the photon's state is a superposition of vertical and horizontal polarisation, but if it passes through the filter, it's like it was horizontal all along (see figure opposite).

Because photons A and B are entangled, if photon A gives a yes when tested for horizontal polarisation, then so will photon B, since it is horizontal too (but opposite). But now suppose you measure photon A's horizontal polarity, but photon B's polarity along another direction. If the two directions are at right angles to one another, e.g. horizontal and vertical, then the results will be uncorrelated – knowing the polarisation along one tells you nothing about polarisation along the other. But for intermediate angles the situation is more complicated. John Bell showed that, if quantum mechanics is correct – in which case the particle polarisations are indeterminate up until the time they are measured – then

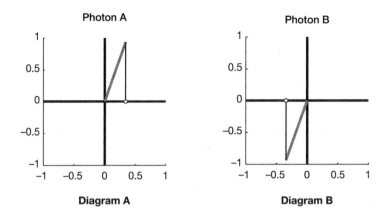

Figure 1. The grey line in diagram A describes the indeterminate spin state of a polarised photon, one of an entangled pair A and B, before measurement. The probability of the polarisation being measured as horizontal is given by the square of the projection onto the horizontal axis, indicated by the circle symbol. In this case the length of the projection is 0.35, which squares to about 0.12, corresponding to a probability of 12 per cent. Similarly the chance of the polarisation being measured as vertical is given by the square of the projection onto the vertical axis, which works out as 0.88 or 88 per cent (note the probabilities must add to 1 because the photon must be in one state or the other). The quantum state of photon B is shown in diagram B; the measured spin will always be in the same axis, but opposite in direction to that of photon A.

the correlation is as much as 50 per cent higher than if the particles are following some kind of deterministic plan.[27]

Bell's paper therefore supplied a way to test a deep philosophical puzzle about the nature of reality. Most physicists were too busy applying quantum mechanics to take notice, and the paper at first received little attention. But eventually interest picked up, and in the 1970s and 1980s a series of increasingly refined experiments managed to put Bell's ideas to the test – and established that the predictions of quantum mechanics did indeed hold. Even if the quantum state of one entangled particle is completely random, and only determined upon measurement, it is still linked to the quantum state of its partner; and a measurement on one entangled particle effectively acts as a measurement on the other. This would be the case even if the particles were located at opposite ends of the universe (experimentalists haven't managed to do this, but they can send entangled particles to satellites in space).[28] Since particles have had plenty of time since the birth of the universe to become entangled with one another, the implication is that space – or at least the concept of spatial separation – isn't quite as much of a barrier as we think it is.

Entanglement is not limited only to single particles. In 2001 a similar experiment was performed for individual atoms, and in 2017 scientists demonstrated quantum entanglement of crystals comprising up to a billion atoms. 'What this work shows us', noted physicist Vladan Vuletić, 'is that there are certain types of quantum mechanical states that are actually quite robust.'[29] Indeed quantum entanglement is one of the key features exploited by quantum computers (discussed in Chapter 6), quantum cryptology (using entangled particles as keys to a code), and quantum teleportation (sending information via entangled particles), which promise to revolutionise areas from finance to defence. It has even been suggested that similar experimental techniques could be applied to the quantum entanglement of the smallest living organisms, such as viruses.[30] Not quite Schrödinger's cat, but getting there.

In a 1985 article for *Physics Today*, physicist David Mermin wrote that 'The EPR experiment is as close to magic as any physical phenomenon I know of'.[31] However, while it may challenge our understanding of physical reality, the concept of entanglement will be quite familiar to anyone who has signed a contract or taken out a loan. Indeed, as we will see later, the process by which private banks create money by issuing a mortgage is rather similar to an entanglement experiment. Instead of photons with opposite polarity, the bank creates a negative credit for the customer, which is balanced in the bank's books by the positive credit of the underlying property. From that moment on, the customer and the bank are entangled, and an event on one side affects the other. As in quantum physics, these entanglements are not felt as mechanistic influences or forces, but as informational changes in state. For example, if the customer decides to default on a mortgage because they lost their job, and they return the keys to the bank, then that changes the state of the loan instantaneously, even if the bank doesn't find out until they open their mail. At least as far as the loan is concerned, the two parties can no longer be considered separate entities.

Back to the future

An even more graphic demonstration of quantum magic can be arranged by performing what is known as the quantum erasure experiment. As *Scientific American* showed in a 2007 article, a modern version can be done at home using readily available equipment such as a pen laser and polarising filters.[32] Instead of passing the light from a point source through two slits, you just point the laser at a screen about two metres away, and place a vertical wire directly in its path. The photons stream either side of the wire, diffract, and interfere with themselves to create an interference pattern on the screen, of the sort Young found in 1801.

Now, suppose that we want to analyse what is going on and find out which side each photon is taking. One way to do this is to attach oppositely-oriented polarisers on either side of the wire, so that for example only vertically polarised photons pass on the left, and horizontally polarised photons pass on the right. These filters effectively label each photon, and make it possible to distinguish which photon takes which path. What effect does this labelling have on the interference pattern?

Since the filters have no effect on the photons other than to stop them or not, we might expect that the interference pattern should remain unchanged. In fact, though, the effect is to make it disappear. The reason is that by measuring the photon's polarisation – or actually just making it possible in principle to measure – we have in effect collapsed its wave function and made it behave like a particle. And while the wave function can explore all possible paths, and so interfere with itself, the particle has to choose.

Note that what counts here is not whether we actually check the polarity of each photon and go through the exercise of determining which side it came from. The point is that the information has been made available by the labelling. To see this, we can repeat the experiment but this time scramble the labels so the information is lost. (One way to do this is to place a third polariser between the wire and the screen which is oriented *diagonally*. Both the left-hand and the right-hand photons then have a 50 per cent chance of getting through, and we can no longer tell which they are, so their labels have been erased.) The interference pattern then magically reappears.

To recap: photons form an interference pattern, but labelled photons don't. If we do something to scramble the labels and make them useless, then the interference pattern reappears. So the thing that controls the interference effect is the information in the labelling. Richard Feynman famously said that the double-slit experiment 'has in it the heart of quantum mechanics. In reality, it contains the *only* mystery.'[33] This therefore hints at a deep relation between quantum theory and information, which we return to in Chapter 8.

Another variation known as the delayed-choice quantum erasure experiment can also be carried out in the laboratory on pairs of entangled photons, by using the same apparatus but this time moving the detection equipment so that a measurement on one photon is registered only *after* the first photon has completed its path. Remarkably this doesn't change the result, implying that the behaviour of a particle is affected by what happens to its twin in the future – as if the system is entangled, not just in space, but also in time.

Not so strange

As Karen Barad notes, 'Quantum mechanics poses some of the most thoroughgoing challenges to our common-sense world-view'.[34] Quantum entities such as photons sometimes present as virtual waves, sometimes as real objects. Particles don't move continuously, like normal objects, but in sudden jumps. Quantities such as position or momentum are fundamentally indeterminate until measured. Particles can be entangled so that a change in one instantly affects the other. They can magically appear out of nowhere, and then disappear back into the void.

Obviously, this has nothing to do with the way things behave in the real world that we live in. A bottle of wine on the table doesn't suddenly disappear and rematerialise in the kitchen. The feeling that quantum mechanics was somehow alien to common sense was also cemented by physicists themselves. Textbooks such as Paul Dirac's *Principles of Quantum Mechanics* focused on 'unadorned presentation, the logical construction of the subject from first principles and the complete absence of historical perspective, philosophical niceties and illustrative calculations'.[35] The Copenhagen interpretation, with its emphasis on abstract mathematics, seemed particularly baffling; while other interpretations, according to the physicist John Clauser, were 'virtually prohibited by the existence of various religious stigmas and social pressures, that taken together, amounted to an evangelical crusade against such thinking'.[36] One result, as mentioned in the Introduction, is that the insights of quantum physics have been lost behind an intimidating wall of mathematics. A similar trend towards mathematisation was seen in economics.

At the same time, though, the quantum universe does not seem quite so bizarre or alienating when viewed from an economic perspective. As noted earlier, the emission of energy in terms of discrete quanta, as in the photoelectric effect, is similar to the transfer of money in discrete amounts. Money can present as real objects, like coins, or as a kind of virtual transmission, as when we tap a credit card at a store. It doesn't flow continuously, but is transmitted in sudden jumps. The quantised structure of an auction resembles the discrete energy levels of an atom; and while stock market investors haven't figured out a way to look into the future, they can buy futures contracts which depend on events that have yet to happen.

The quantity known as price is fundamentally uncertain, and is determined only during the measurement procedure, when things are exchanged for money. Like elementary particles, money objects can be created out of the void, for example when banks create money by issuing loans, but can also be annihilated and removed from the system. And while it is hard to think how one could perform something like a Bell's test on a loan agreement, this doesn't mean the entanglement is any less real.[37] Like a wave function, the loan contract is a virtual thing which in a sense exists outside the physical constraints of time and space.

One might object that effects such as the uncertainty principle or interference do not apply to money objects themselves. We know a ten-dollar bill is worth exactly ten dollars, and it doesn't interfere or cancel out if we put it next to a five-dollar bill in our wallet. But if we view a money object as an exact store of energy, then zero uncertainty in the energy translates, according to the uncertainty principle, to an indefinite lifetime – which just means that a ten-dollar bill is worth ten dollars for ever (even if that amount won't always buy you the same thing). Such fixed and stable quantities do exist in quantum physics, for example the charge of an electron. And while their fixed nature means that money objects can't interfere with one another, they can certainly produce interference effects in the human mind, as we'll see in Chapter 7 (though the mind can also do that by itself – see box below).

Quantum behaviour therefore isn't quite as alien as we have been led to believe – in fact we deal with it every time we go shopping or cash a cheque. The point is not just that quantum mechanics can be viewed as a metaphor for understanding money (though all models are metaphors, including quantum mechanics), but that the economy is a quantum system *in its own right*, with its own very real versions of measurement, indeterminacy and entanglement. (We therefore have to wrestle these words away a little from their subatomic context, while respecting their meaning – if it helps, set aside what you read in this chapter, and imagine that we are describing the money system from scratch. Or say that we will model the money system as if it followed quantum rules, and see where it takes us.) An advantage is that these concepts lack the obscure and confusing nature of their counterparts in physics. We don't need a Schrödinger wave equation to know that value is uncertain, or an obscure process of wave function collapse to understand transactions. Since metaphors are usually used to explain complex phenomena by comparing with something concrete and familiar, it actually makes more sense to use money as a metaphor for quantum physics than the other way round. After all, we may be able to calculate a particle's wave function, at least for certain cases, but we can actually *feel* a sense of value. According to one interpretation (there are many) of quantum physics, known as quantum Bayesianism (or QBism), the wave function represents an agent's subjective degree of belief, and its collapse represents the agent updating their beliefs in response to information, which seems to match the economic context quite well.[38]

The correspondence principle

Of course, even if money has quantum properties, does this mean that we have to change the way we do economics? After all, as Barad notes, 'It would be wrong to simply assume that people are the analogues of atoms and that societies are mere epiphenomena that can be explained in terms of collective behavior of massive ensembles of individual entities (like little atoms each), or that sociology is reducible to biology, which is reducible to chemistry, which in turn is reducible to physics. Quantum physics undercuts reductionism as a worldview or universal explanatory framework.'[39]

Indeed, it is often said that quantum physics is the foundation of all the sciences, just because it deals with the building blocks of matter; but when it comes to large-scale properties of materials it is impossible to derive much of anything directly from quantum mechanics. Instead it is more accurate to say that these properties *emerge* from quantum mechanics (which perhaps emerges from something else). They are therefore an example of what complexity scientists call emergent properties, which cannot be reduced to some lower level of explanation.[40] But on the other hand quantum-like behaviour does appear at the macroscopic scale. An example is sound waves passing through a metal bar. If these are weak enough, the sound becomes quantised into discrete pulses just as light does. The waves are equivalent to an 'emergent particle' known as a phonon, which has a well-defined momentum.[41] So the fact that a system cannot be reduced to quantum physics does not mean that it cannot have quantum properties of its own, or inherit those properties from lower levels. In the same way, the quantum properties of money are not limited to small transactions but are felt around the world.

Such macro-level quantum properties are also regularly exploited in engineered systems. It has been estimated that some 30 per cent of the United States' gross domestic product can be traced to technologies such as microchips, GPS, and so on which are explicitly based on properties that arise from quantum effects.[42] Quantum mechanics is also used directly in many areas of engineering, such as nanotechnology, drug design, and of course nuclear weapons. In economics, the closest thing to an engineered system (though as we'll see, it's not that close) is financial markets, which perhaps explains why 'financial engineering' was one of the first areas to explore quantum ideas.

Bohr's principle of correspondence, which is sometimes used to suggest that quantum effects at the micro level are no longer relevant at the macro level, or to everyday life, therefore doesn't always apply. Also, the fact that we cannot reduce a system to its quantum foundations, does not mean that we can reduce them to mechanistic foundations instead, as is commonly attempted in economics. The complex macro properties of water, for example, are ultimately the result of quantum processes at the molecular level. The same is true of living beings, which exploit such emergent properties in their own ways. As we will see in later chapters, this is why the most appropriate models for economics tend to be based on mathematical techniques such as complexity and network theory that have proved useful for the study of complex organic systems in general.

Quantum economics therefore reflects principles which have shaped other areas of science in recent decades, and is consistent with our understanding of the quantum universe. It could even provide a path for helping to understand the behaviour of subatomic particles. The fact that matter gives us weird answers when we try to put numbers on quantities such as position or momentum reflects the same kind of fundamental incompatibility or tension between number and the real world that we see when we try to put a number on the fuzzy quality of value. And even if the economy is not the same as the subatomic world, we certainly seem to have designed it to be as close as possible. This will become clearer in the next few chapters, where we study the properties of the mysterious, shapeshifting, polarising, and dynamic quantum entity known as money.

Fruit and veg

Quantum interference doesn't just apply to subatomic particles, it also seems a good description of the way that we order our thoughts. This was illustrated in a study led by the physicist Diederik Aerts.[43]

Aerts worked from a data set where experimental subjects were presented with a list of 24 fruits and vegetables, and asked to estimate the typicality of each being chosen as a good example of 'Fruits', 'Vegetables', and 'Fruits or Vegetables'. The complete list was: Almond, Acorn, Peanut, Olive, Coconut, Raisin, Elderberry, Apple, Mustard, Wheat, Root Ginger, Chili Pepper, Garlic, Mushroom, Watercress, Lentils, Green Pepper, Yam, Tomato, Pumpkin, Broccoli, Rice, Parsley, Black Pepper. Some of these fit neatly into one category or another, but several, such as mushroom, mustard or black pepper, don't. The results were then tabulated to calculate the probability of each being chosen.

If we think of the concept 'good example of a fruit from this list' as being represented by the conceptual equivalent of a wave function, then the probabilities of each choice correspond to the probability that the wave function will collapse to that state.

Consider for example the vexed question of whether a tomato is a fruit or a vegetable. To a botanist, a fruit is something that develops from a flower's fertilised ovary, while a vegetable is some other part of the plant. However, the word fruit is from the Latin *fructus*, meaning enjoyment, while vegetable is from *vegetabilis*, which just means growing; and many people associate the former with something that is typically eaten raw, like an apple, and the latter with something that you cook.

This all came to a head in New York in 1883 when tomato importers were slapped with a 10 per cent tax on 'foreign vegetables' even though, as they pointed out, it was a fruit. The case went all the way to the Supreme Court who ruled in 1886 that, even though tomatoes were *logically* a fruit, in the 'common language of the people' they were a vegetable because they 'are usually served at dinner in, with, or after the soup, fish, or meat, which constitute the principal part of the repast, and not, like fruits, generally as dessert'.[44]

In Aerts' study, 8.8 per cent thought a tomato was a good example of a fruit, 6.7 per cent said it was a good example of a vegetable, and 6.9 per cent thought it was a good example of a fruit or vegetable. So a slight majority disagrees with the Supreme Court ruling, no doubt because the 'common language of the people' has evolved since then. But the logic still doesn't quite add up.

According to classical logic, if the weighting of one selection is A, and the weighting of another is B, then the relative weighting of it being one or the other should be the average of A and B. For the tomato, this gives a probability of 7.8 per cent for fruit or vegetable, but the observed probability from the survey was only 6.9 per cent. The discrepancy is much larger for some other choices. For example, mushroom was rated 1.4 per cent for fruit, and 5.5 per cent for vegetable (it is actually a fungus, so neither). The average of these is 3.4 per cent, but the survey gave 6.0 per cent for fruit or vegetable – almost as high as tomato.

According to Aerts, this can be explained by assuming that the concepts of fruit and vegetable – which always have a probabilistic, uncertain element – interfere in our minds, so that asking each in turn is different from asking both at the same time. The situation is like a double-slit experiment, where one slit is labelled fruit and the other vegetable. The probability of a particle passing through the fruit slit with the other closed corresponds to the chance of being picked as a good example of a fruit, and likewise for vegetables; while the probability of fruit or vegetable is like having both slits open, which causes interference. Similarly, the statistics of word association experiments show that pairs of related words behave like entangled particles, and obey the linguistic version of Bell's inequalities.[45]

But really, tomatoes are a fruit. And don't let's get started on pronunciation.

CHAPTER 2

How much

All things are measured by money.
Aristotle, *Nicomachean Ethics**

*The growing differentiation of our representations
has the result that the problem of 'how much' is,
to a certain extent, psychologically separated from
the question of 'what' – no matter how strange
this may sound from the logical point of view.*
Georg Simmel, *The Philosophy of Money* (1900)[1]

**According to quantum physics, everything in the universe has
complementary wave/particle attributes. The same can be said
of one of our most powerful technologies: money. Money objects
such as coins, notes, or even bitcoins have dualistic properties
which rival those of photons or electrons. This chapter takes the
reader through a brief early history of money, and shows how its
twin aspects have shaped everything from Western philosophy
to the way we make decisions.**

How much? For many of us, our first experience of hands-on economics is buying a candy or a treat with a parent. In your hands are
a few metal coins with numbers on them. In the display case there
is the desired object – say, a chocolate-chip cookie. *How much is*

---

* Note that Aristotle is saying that in practice, things that are exchanged
are measured by money, not that all things are measurable by money.

that, you ask tentatively, gazing up at the sales person (or if you're in Italy, you might say 'Quanto?', which makes the link with quantum a little clearer). They tell you a number – say $2. Then you show them your coins – the colour of your money. Your parent might help you count them out. The numbers on the coins, you understand, must add to a sum which is greater than or equal to the cost of the item, in order for it to be released. The sales person puts the coins into the till, and gives you the cookie in a paper bag, along with any change. The transaction is complete.

The act of purchasing things soon becomes so automatic that we no longer think about it. Instead of counting out coins, we usually just swipe or tap a card. Purchases are made online – cookies are as likely to be the sort that vendors place on your computer as the sort you put in your mouth. The exchange of money has become increasingly virtual and invisible. We often don't think any more about it than we do about breathing.

Which of course is not to say that we don't think about money at all – indeed, surveys have shown that it is one of the greatest sources of stress.[2] Money has probably never been more important than it is today. And when we make a payment, there is still a sense that we are handing over something real – a kind of object – especially when we are short of the stuff. But the ebb and flow of money is largely taken for granted, as is the effect it has on our minds and our behaviour.

Even if you later enrol in an economics class, or go to business school, money is treated as little more than an inert medium of exchange, an intermediary for barter. But this obscures the fact that something else was going on when you bought that cookie as a child. In effect, you were making a measurement. You were discovering what the cookie was worth, in numerical units. You were putting a number on it. You were finding an answer to the question, *how much*.

In this case, of course, the answer was already provided, so it was a rather trivial exercise. The cookie had a firm price. The number was probably on a sign or a label nearby. The sales person didn't just pull a figure out of their head. But that is only because the procedure had been organised in a particular way. Later on, your parents might teach you to haggle or bargain at places like a yard sale, where the price is negotiable or you can get a discount if you buy more than one thing. And when it comes time to buy a house, the list price is often just a starting suggestion.

But even when the price is stated in advance, you are still performing a measurement when you purchase the cookie, because you are confirming the amount. Suppose for example that the sales person says they are all out of the preferred chocolate-chip flavour. Then the price is merely hypothetical. Perhaps they will have more in stock tomorrow, but for all you know the price may have changed by then because of large demand. Later on, you will have this experience when booking a hotel room or an airline flight online – only one available at this price, says the website, but by the time you have typed in your credit card details the price has already changed. If you are in a country suffering from hyperinflation, like Venezuela at the time of writing, price lists are constantly updated. If for some reason the entire financial system crashed, say because of a nuclear war, the price of that cookie would be pretty much undefined. And in general, the only way you truly know the price of something is at the exact moment you make the transaction.

So buying something with money is equivalent to putting a number on it. Which when you think about it, is a rather curious thing in itself. How can we put a number on something like a cookie? After all, numbers and things have rather different properties. It makes sense to think of two things, in the sense of counting, but it is less obvious how a cookie can be 2.

The transaction is rather like the measurement process in physics, where we measure – put a number on – the position of a particle, or record how far it moves in a certain time. Even there, we know from quantum physics that position and time are not simple, linear, external quantities. They warp and connect and break into small parts. In other words, they are not like number. Measurement is a far more complex procedure than appearances suggest – hence the uncertainty principle.

You may have wondered about this as a child. Money seems to be connected to value, but how does it work? Why are the cookies made by your grandmother free, but the ones in the store cost money? Or put another way: if money is measuring something, what is it measuring?

As described in more detail later, economists have long puzzled over this question. One answer (championed by classical economists such as Adam Smith) is that the price is measuring the labour required to obtain the ingredients and produce the cookie. Everything has a cost, except for grandma who works for free. But this raises a host of other questions about, for example, the mark-up of the store owner, the cost of renting the building, and so on, and in any case it just kicks the can further down the road – how do we decide how much to pay for labour?

Another answer (and a defining principle of neoclassical economics, which dates to the late nineteenth century and now dominates the mainstream) is to say that the price measures or reflects utility, which is loosely defined as the pleasure or satisfaction offered by the cookie. But again – how do you put a number on pleasure? It's not like sensations come with a price tag attached.

Finally, a third answer is to say that the price represents economic value.[3] But this is just a circular definition, since economic value is defined in terms of price. And all of these approaches assume that what counts is prices relative to other goods. Money itself is not important, other than as a score-keeping system.

In this chapter, I will argue that these approaches are mistaken and have led to much confusion. Measuring the price is like making a measurement of a quantum system. The result can't be reduced to labour, or utility, or anything else. Instead of grams or amperes, the units are units of currency. When you buy something, you are measuring – money.

To see why this statement is more than a tautology – and why the consequences of viewing the economy this way are actually rather exciting – we need to look more closely at those things you handed over as a child in exchange for the cookie. Just as the quantum revolution came from analysing the properties of energy exchange by subatomic particles, so the secret of money is to be found residing in coins and other such money objects, whose pedigree dates back thousands of years.

Ur-money

The Sumerian city states of ancient Mesopotamia were responsible for many important innovations which we still enjoy today: the wheel, beer, the 24-hour clock. Even the concept of a city state. But perhaps their most remarkable invention was an early version of money. It wasn't quite a quantum computer, but as we'll see, the money system as a whole, in concert with the human mind, does some of the same jobs.

Cities such as Ur, located in modern-day Iraq, were home to many thousands of people, and were surrounded by farms that supplied them with agricultural produce. The temple bureaucrats whose job it was to oversee this complicated society were faced on a daily basis with versions of a single, but very difficult, question: *how much*? If a man does a month's labour for the temple, how much grain or beer should he receive in return? If he rents a room or a wagon for a day, how much should he pay the owner? And if he harms another person in some way, or damages their property, how much should he give in compensation?

For smaller villages, such problems could be addressed perhaps by sharing out produce equally, and coming to agreements on an ad hoc basis. But for the modern and highly-centralised city state, a more organised solution was required. A first step in this direction was clay tokens that represented rations. Later, the tokens were replaced by clay tablets known as cuneiforms, on which instructions were inscribed with a reed (the Sumerians also invented writing). One such tablet from about 3000 BC is a pay stub, about 10 cm across in size, specifying an amount of beer to be paid in exchange for labour. As the British Museum notes, 'Writing seems to have been invented not for letters, literature or scripture, but for accountancy.'[4]

It was around this time that the temple accountants began to use a shekel of silver, about 8 grams, as a standard unit. The word shekel means 'weigh', so a shekel of silver literally represented a weight of value. Other units were based, like the Sumerian number system (they also invented arithmetic), on multiples of 60, so for example one mina was 60 shekels, or about half a kilogram. Prices for other things were then reckoned in terms of these shekels. One shekel would pay about a month's labour, which in turn would buy one gur (or bushel) of barley, or two rations a day.

The fact that prices were reckoned in terms of shekels did not mean that people carried out daily transactions using weights of silver. The shekel was just an accounting device. If someone needed to pay the palace, they could use wool or barley or some other commodity. And many dealings outside the palace were carried out on the basis of credit, so for example a farm worker might be paid in barley at harvest time.[5]

Larger debts were recorded on cuneiforms, which were put inside clay envelopes marked with a seal, and kept by the creditor until the debt was repaid. Sometimes the debt was made payable to whoever held the envelope, meaning that the creditor could sell it on to another person. Such cuneiforms therefore resembled modern paper notes, which promise to pay the bearer on demand a certain sum. But in general terms, the economy ran on credits which were periodically paid off by the delivery of some commodity.

On the surface, then, it might look like the shekel-based monetary system had little effect on trade, other than as a convenience for temple accountants. But in fact the invention of money would go on to have an even bigger impact than the wheel – because it didn't just transport things over roads, it could transport them virtually through space.

The money object

But where was this money, exactly? We have just seen that silver was not widely used for spending. Sure, there was lots of silver in the temple vaults. But how much exactly? If everyone had tried to cash in their rations for hard silver at the same time – a run on the temple instead of a bank – would there really have been enough to go round? Was the worth of a shekel really measuring a weight of silver, or was it more trust in the state, or both?

And how did the system differ from barter? What was the difference between someone paying a worker at a fixed rate of barley measured in shekels, and paying the barley without the mention of shekels? And even if you do pay with silver shekels, isn't that just a different kind of barter?

According to mainstream economics, the answer would be that nothing had really changed. Any barter exchange has to be expressed in terms of some ratio – x kilograms of this for y kilograms of that. All that had happened was that the shekel was being used as an intermediary, so the barter ratio could be determined from the price of each commodity in shekels. As the economist William Stanley Jevons noted in his 1875 book *Money and the Mechanism of Exchange*, 'Knowing how much corn is to be bought for a pound of silver, and also how much flax for the same quantity of silver, we learn without further trouble how much corn exchanges for so much flax.'[6]

Again, though, this emphasis on money's convenience misses what was really going on – which was that for the first time in history, people had worked out a consistent way to answer the question *how much*.

With barter, this question doesn't make sense except in a very limited way. Imagine that you are back as a child wanting to obtain a chocolate-chip cookie, but this time it is in the playground at school, from a friend. When you ask how much it is, instead of giving a price, your friend asks to look through your bag for something to trade. Maybe they settle for your slightly used pencil case. You now know that in that playground, with that friend, you can get a cookie for a pencil case. Except tomorrow that won't work, because they already have your pencil case. You will have to give them something different. The same is true for any kind of barter, because the prices of goods are always shifting relative to one another. The question *how much* does not give a single answer, it gives a cacophony of different possibilities.

By standardising their accountancy system around this thing called a shekel, the Sumerians had therefore worked out a way to put a number on value. They had found a method to collapse the plurality of possibilities down to a single number – just as a physicist does when they measure the position of a subatomic particle.

But by inventing this answer, they had done something else as well, which was to create a new kind of quantum entity – the money object.

Virtual versus real

It seems strange, in the era of bitcoin, to talk about 'money objects' as if money could somehow be reduced to a physical thing. Today of course we usually make payments electronically, by tapping a credit card or through a bank transfer, so they don't seem to involve objects at all. Even in ancient Sumeria, as we've seen, people might have reckoned prices in shekels but they didn't actually hand over small lumps of silver. Indeed, it has become almost a cliché among some economists and social scientists to point out that money is not a thing.

But one teaching of quantum physics is that objects are not as clearly defined as they were in classical physics – things aren't really things either, at least as we usually think of them. Entities which we perceive with our senses as solid objects – such as a coin, or a book – are really a virtual web of quantum interactions which happen to convey certain attributes such as mass and colour. You see this page because photons scatter off its force field in a particular way. Other particles don't see it at all, such as neutrinos from the Sun – many trillions of which pass through a page in the time taken to read this sentence. The electromagnetic force, which has the rather important role of holding atoms and molecules and objects of any sort together, is transmitted through the exchange of ghostly virtual photons, which are perhaps better described as ripples in the electromagnetic field. And any particle, as we have seen, has complementary wave/particle aspects.

In this quantum spirit, we can define money objects to be transferable entities, created by a trusted authority or body, which have the special property of a defined monetary value, specified by a number and a currency unit. They therefore combine the mental idea of a numerical quantity of money – the virtual wave attribute – with the physical idea of an object that can be possessed or transferred – the real particle attribute. These are numbers that you can keep or spend. So in a quantum framework, it makes sense to see a money transfer of any sort as representing the transfer of an object, real or virtual, from one party to another. Buying a book online might feel different from paying for it by counting out coins and notes at the store, but the net effect is the same. And even bitcoins aren't as virtual as they seem, as we'll see in the next chapter. Conversely, when money objects are used in transactions to purchase something, they collapse the wave-like idea of value down to a single particle-like number. Money objects are therefore a way of mediating between the real and the virtual. While they are naturally suited for use as a medium of exchange or a store of value, and their units are useful for accounting purposes, these properties are a consequence of their design, rather than a defining feature.

When the ancient Sumerians created the shekel as an account-ancy device, they were also creating the shekel as a money object. As we saw above, a shekel was a particular weight of silver – a thing that could be exchanged for something else. These shekels could be real – i.e. made of silver – but mostly they were virtual. Either way, the exchange of shekels had the effect of putting a price on value – of reducing it to number.

Sumeria was of course not the only early civilisation to have come up with the idea of money, but it is the best-documented. In ancient Egypt value was expressed in terms of *deben*, which originally referred to a measure, not of metal, but of grain; wheat was deposited in centralised, state-owned warehouses that func-tioned as banks, and used for payments of debts and taxes.[7] In pre-imperial China, which was relatively less centralised, the most common form of money was cowrie shells, though other instru-ments such as knotted strings, or notched pieces of bamboo, were also used.

One of the appeals of using a precious metal such as silver as a basis for money is that, unlike most commodities, it has many properties in common with number. Precious metals are stable (they don't rust, rot, or go off), fungible (one ounce can be substituted for another), and easily divisible. This natural correspondence or affinity between number and precious metal led to the next monetary innovation, which represented perhaps the most expressive embodiment of money's intrinsically dualistic nature – the coin.

Electrum

When economics textbooks describe the history of money, if they cover it at all, they usually skip the Mesopotamia phase and go directly to the first coins, which date to the seventh century BC, in the nearby kingdom of Lydia. These were made of a gold-silver alloy called electrum, and were fabricated by placing a blank round of the metal on top of a die, and hammering it down with a punch. The die was embossed with a design such as the head of a lion that certified the coin.

The story goes that the use of these coins grew out of using precious metal in barter. As Aristotle noted in *Politics*, 'the various necessaries of life are not easily carried about, and hence men agreed to employ in their dealings with each other something which was intrinsically useful and easily applicable to the purposes of life, for example, iron, silver, and the like. Of this the value was at first measured simply by size and weight, but in process of time they put a stamp upon it, to save the trouble of weighing and to mark the value.'[8]

Aristotle's explanation of the origins of money was highly influential, and in fact versions can be found in modern textbooks with remarkably similar wording.[9] In this view, the only thing that matters is the barter value of the metal – the stamp is just a convenience to 'save the trouble of weighing'. However, there are a few problems with this picture. One is that it misses earlier credit systems, including the well-documented Sumerian version, which is understandable in the case of Aristotle, less so for modern academics, since it has been known about for a while now. The British economist Alfred Mitchell-Innes made this point when he wrote that 'modern research in the domain of commercial history and numismatics, and especially recent discoveries in Babylonia, have brought to light a mass of evidence which was not available to the earlier economists'.[10] That was in 1913.

Another problem with the barter model is that it is based on the assumption, as one such textbook puts it, that 'If there were no money, goods would have to be exchanged by barter.'[11] But schoolyard swaps and the like aside, barter has never played a big role in commerce. In fact, according to anthropologist Caroline Humphrey, 'No example of a barter economy, pure and simple, has ever been described, let alone the emergence from it of money.'[12] Barter is a form of transaction that is common between groups that may be hostile or have little trust of each other, and in places where people are accustomed to using money but there is no money, such as jails. But money-free societies are usually organised around communal arrangements where goods are distributed by centralised councils; social currencies involving tokens that are used to signify status, arrange marriages, and so on; or gift economies, in which transactions are framed as gifts.

A third problem with this account is that the first coins were worth a very large amount of money. Denominations ranged from one stater (a translation of shekel), which weighed about 14 grams, down through various fractions to as small as 1/96th of a stater. A stater coin was worth about a month's salary, and the commonest coins, which were a third of a stater, would fetch about ten sheep. Even the smallest coins would have fed a person for a few days. So it didn't seem they were intended as a convenient substitute for day-to-day barter.

The biggest problem with this origin story, though, is that it treats the stamp as nothing more than an extra added convenience – when in fact it was the entire point.

Paying with stamps

As typically portrayed in textbooks, the invention of coinage 'created an important role for an authority, usually a king or queen, who made the coins and affixed his or her seal'.[13] So the monarch was acting here as a glorified notary. This viewpoint was well expressed by the Austrian economist Carl Menger, who wrote in 1892 that while 'Money has not been generated by law ... the establishment and maintenance of coined pieces so as to win public confidence and, as far as possible, to forestall risk concerning their genuineness, weight, and fineness, and above all the ensuring their circulation in general, have been everywhere recognised as important functions of state administration.'[14]

This idea that the state only plays a kind of certifying role in the process jars somewhat with the historical fact that money has traditionally been designed, created, and distributed by the state. And that it was mostly used, not as a lubricant for barter, but as a way to help the army. Quantum physics found its first applications in building bombs, and in an intriguing parallel the quantum power of money was first applied to the business of conducting war.

Coins in ancient Greece were produced by battling city states, whose largest expense by far was the military. A traditional way of motivating troops, mercenaries or pirates is to promise them a share of the plunder, and coin money was a way of codifying this.[15] An army would invade an enemy, confiscate its wealth, enslave the local population, and put them to work in mines, digging up more precious metal which was then turned into coins to pay the army. This process was perfected by one of Aristotle's more famous students, Alexander the Great. With an army of over a hundred thousand soldiers, his salary spend during his conquest of the Persian empire amounted to about half a ton of silver per day. Most of it came from Persian mines, with the labour supplied by war captives. Alexander later went on to invade the Babylonian empire in Mesopotamia, where he eliminated the existing credit system and insisted that taxes be paid in his own coins.

Coin money also helped with the related logistical problem of how to provide for the army. The state simply demanded coins from the population as payment for taxes. People therefore had to get their hands on coins, and the easiest way to do that was to supply the army with things like food or lodging. To say, as in economics textbooks, that the need to certify coin money 'created an important role for an authority' is therefore a massive under-statement. Really it was the other way round: the state created a need for money through the use of military force. Today, it is no coincidence that the world's main reserve currency is backed by the world's largest military.

Rather than emerging naturally from barter, then, it is more accurate to say that coins were imposed on the population by force – just as the stamp signifying the might of the state was forced into the soft metal. The reason for this is that the stamp is far more than a convenience or a formality. Instead, it is exactly what gives money its association with number, and turns transactions into a tool for consistent measurement. It is a specific, carefully designed form of ordered numerical information.

We discuss the relationship between order, information, and energy further in Chapter 8, but the main point now is that information can be viewed as a kind of energy. By stamping the coins, and asserting its power of ownership, the state was therefore doing a kind of work, which in a sense was as valuable as that of the slaves who dug up the metal in the first place. It is this work which fuses and engineers the two sides of money – the real thing and the virtual idea – into a single money object. A coin, with its abstract stamp embedded in earthly metal, is therefore a graphic representation of the dualistic, quantum properties of money.

While coin money may have been designed primarily for military purposes, it of course had what historian Michael Crawford calls the 'accidental consequence' of boosting the development of markets – and eventually the world economy.[16] And it had other effects as well. By putting a number on things, it turned everyday transactions into a mental accounting exercise – which had profound consequences for our mental development as a species (and even perhaps on the wiring of our brains, as discussed later). The development of money also shaped Western philosophy, with profound implications for the way that we think about – money.

The value of value

The first Greek city to produce its own coins in the sixth century BC is believed to have been Miletus, a city state located in what is now Turkey, adjacent to the kingdom of Lydia. But the city is known just as well for being the 624 BC birthplace of the philosopher Thales, with whom, according to Bertrand Russell, 'Western philosophy begins'. His mathematical discoveries include using geometry to figure out how to compute the height of the pyramids or the distance of a ship at sea. Thales also came up with an early version of a Theory of Everything, arguing that everything was made of water (today, physicists think everything is made of higher-dimensional strings, which will probably also sound pretty funny a couple of millennia from now).

When Thales was an old man, he was visited (it is said) by a young man in his twenties called Pythagoras, from the nearby island of Samos. Pythagoras would go on to found his own school of philosophy which also had a theory of everything, but with a twist. The unifying substance was not a physical material like water, but an idea: number. According to the Pythagorean creation myth, the universe began in a state of unity, which then divided into two opposite components: the limited (*peiron*), which was good, and the unlimited (*apeiron*), which was not ('Evil belongs to the unlimited, as the Pythagoreans surmised', wrote Aristotle in *Ethics*, 'and good to the limited'[17]). These combined to form numbers, which made up the structure of the cosmos (a word invented by Pythagoras).

The emphasis on number was no doubt largely due to Pythagoras' discovery that musical harmony – and the correct spacing of frets on a lyre or today a guitar – is based on mathematics (he would have appreciated Schrödinger's comparison of quantum states with the 'nodes in a vibrating string', or for that matter string theory). But according to the classicist W.K.C. Guthrie, it was probably also influenced by applications in commerce: it is likely that Pythagoras was involved in the design of coinage for his region in what is now southern Italy, and the impact of the new monetary economy 'might well have been to implant the idea that one constant factor by which things were related was the quantitative. A fixed numerical value in drachmas or minas may "represent" things as widely different in quality as a pair of oxen, a cargo of wheat and a gold drinking-cup.'[18]

The dualistic view of the Pythagoreans was summarised in a list of ten pairs of antitheses, documented in Aristotle's *Metaphysics*, which represented what they believed were the fundamental organising principles of the universe. In many respects their list resembles the similarly ancient Chinese concepts of yin and yang, with the left column being yang and the right yin; however, there is an important difference, which is that while the Chinese saw yin and yang as complementary, the Pythagorean list has a preferred direction, with one column labelled Good and the other Evil.[19] As seen in the box below, this distinction provides an interesting clue about the nature of money.

Pythagorean dualism was tremendously influential on Greek philosophy, and appears for example in the broader split in Greek thought between mind and body, which Plato took to its logical conclusion with his theory of forms. According to Plato, any real-world object is an imperfect version of an abstract form. Unlike real things, which change and decay, forms are static and unchanging and can be known only through the intellect. Numbers live in the world of forms, while measurable physical events and objects live in the real world.

Given that Western science grew out of this dualistic approach – its aim after all is to express the real world by using abstract numbers and equations – it is unsurprising, as I have argued elsewhere, that Pythagorean fingerprints can be found all over it.[20] One reason quantum physics came as such a shock was because it challenged this ancient good/evil dualism, by seeing opposing qualities not as ranked pairs but as complementary aspects of a unified dynamic whole, as in yin/yang. In fact, while Bohr's principle of complementarity was said to be inspired by the idea from psychology that we can hold opposite ideas in the mind at the same time, another influence was Chinese philosophy.[21] When the King of Denmark conferred on him the country's top honour (the Order of the Elephant) Bohr designed his own coat of arms, which featured a yin-yang symbol and a motto in Latin: *contraria sunt complementa*, 'opposites are complementary'.

As we have seen, money is inherently dualistic by design, because it combines the attributes of a number with those of an owned object. This duality is captured in the different senses of the word 'value' as applied to exchange (rather than to principles or standards of behaviour, which are not supposed to be for sale). We value something not just because it serves some mechanical purpose, but because it means something to us. Only a conscious entity can value something else. However, value also has a mathematical definition that refers to a particular number, such as the reading on a gauge, or the value of a parameter in an equation. Money is a way of mediating between these two types of value, the subjective meaning and the objective number. In classical economics, prices had meaning because they represented labour; in neoclassical economics because they represented utility. In quantum economics, prices and meaning are two sides of the same coin, and the same word.

Like a magnet, money therefore encompasses twin poles with opposite properties, and neither is ever seen in isolation; but as with Pythagorean dualism it also has a fixed polarity, because – like science – the whole point of money is to put numbers on things. It is a way to find the value of value. These dualistic properties feed into other financial instruments: the numerical debt owed on a loan is virtual, but the treasured possession supplied as collateral is real.

As noted in my previous book *Economyths*, the same dualism has also shaped the discipline of economics. Mainstream neoclassical economics – with its emphasis on stability (At Rest), symmetry (Square), linearity (Straight), and so on – never strays too far from the first or 'Good' side of the Pythagorean list (see box below), while heterodox approaches tend to take a more left-handed approach. Of course, this is not to suggest that the Pythagoreans somehow intuited the quantum nature of the universe, or that their descendants continue to populate economics departments. However, their number-based philosophy was influenced by the development in Greece of the monetary economy; and as already argued, the economy is a quantum system in its own right, with money having a special role in the measurement process; so in a way they were the first quantum economists. This is why their insights into the dualistic nature of the universe continue to resonate today – and why we still live in a world shaped by Pythagorean duality. As we'll see in the next chapter, nowhere is money's dualistic nature more evident, but also least understood, than in the act of its creation.

Quantum opposites

The tension between the two sides of value – subjective worth and numerical price – resonates in interesting ways with the Pythagoreans' list of opposites (in bold below), which again was created at a time when these concepts were being juxtaposed and brought into conflict by the advent of the market economy.

Limited versus **Unlimited**. A measured price (e.g. an amount that you just paid) represents a fixed, limited quantity. Value is a fuzzy, non-numerical quality that is essentially unbounded (economists may assign numbers to a human life, but a parent could put no price on the life of a child).

Odd versus **Even**. A measured price is stable and unique, while value is more diffuse. (In particle terms, the former would be an odd-spinned fermion, and the latter an even-spinned boson – see Chapter 1.) According to his biographer Iamblichus, Pythagoras similarly asserted that, while even numbers were associated with 'that which is dissolved', odd numbers were associated with stability and unity. One reason is that summing their sequence gives a square number, so for example 1+3+5+7=16 or 4 squared, and the sides of a square always have a fixed ratio of 1.

One versus **Plurality**. A price is a single unified concept. Value depends on viewpoint and is therefore inherently pluralistic.

Right versus **Left**. Numerical prices appeal to our left-brained computational and analytical abilities (see box in

Chapter 4). Value is more of a right-brained, context-driven attribute. (Note the left brain controls the right side of the body and vice versa, hence the polarity reversal.)

Male versus **Female**. A price is a virtual symbol (from Latin *virtus* for 'manliness'), while a valued object is a material thing (from Latin *mater* for 'mother') that can be owned and possessed. The gendered language relates to the classical association of ideas and numbers with the male principle, and real-world things with the female principle.[22] An updated version for money would be Virtual versus Real.

At Rest versus **In Motion**. A measured price is fixed and stable, while a valued object mutates and decays.

Straight versus **Crooked**. Numbers are linear and additive by definition, which is why they teach the number line at school, and so are prices. In the real world, when you add two things, or work twice as many hours, the value might not double.

Light versus **Darkness**. Prices are objective, susceptible to the light of reason, and mean the same thing to everyone. Value is more subjective and obscure, so depends on the person and the context. Subjectivity gets a bad rap in science – the political scientist Alexander Wendt (named in 2015 as 'the most influential scholar in international relations over the past 20 years') for example notes that 'in most of contemporary social science there seems to be a "taboo" on subjectivity' – which is awkward since according to some interpretations at least, the individual consciousness plays a key role in quantum physics (not to mention everyday life).[23]

Square versus **Oblong**. The Pythagoreans thought about numbers by arranging pebbles in patterns. They saw square numbers such as 4, 9 and 16 as stable and symmetrical, since they can be arranged to form a square. Prices or costs are symmetrical too, in the sense that positives and negatives cancel out, as in a square deal. A key difference between a monetary economy and a gift economy is that the former is based on symmetric exchange where the accounts always balance, while a gift is supposed to be asymmetric.[24]

Good versus **Evil**. Because the Pythagoreans wanted to reduce the world to number, they aligned themselves with only one set of these principles – the Good, which is consonant with number. Similarly, money has a polarity because its function is to put objective number on subjective value, not the other way round. It is Pythagorean dualism in action.

CHAPTER 3

QUANTUM CREATIONS

*I am afraid the ordinary citizen will not like to be told
that the banks or the Bank of England can create or
destroy money. We are in the habit of thinking of money
as wealth, as indeed it is in the hands of the individual
who owns it, wealth in the most liquid form, and we do
not like to hear that some private institution can create
it at pleasure. It conjures up a picture of an autocratic
and irresponsible body which by some black art of its
own contriving can increase or diminish wealth, and
presumably make a great deal of profit in the process.*
Reginald McKenna, former UK Chancellor
of the Exchequer (1915–16)

Quantum mechanics is magic.
Daniel Greenberger

One of the more mysterious predictions of quantum physics,
which has since been amply confirmed by experiment, is that
particles can spontaneously appear out of nowhere, and then
disappear back into the void. Indeed, such quantum eruptions
might explain the sudden appearance of the universe itself.
Central bankers have managed a similar trick, through the
magic of 'fiat money', which is ushered out of the void at the
press of a button. This chapter explores the quantum processes
of money creation and destruction, from ancient coins to modern bitcoins.

Where does money come from? In ancient Greece, the answer would have seemed rather obvious – the ground. Coins were made of precious metal, and their value – in terms of both weight and quality – was certified by the stamp. But even there the answer wasn't quite so clear-cut. For example, an Athenian drachma coin would by definition be worth exactly a drachma within Athens, but outside of the city its value would gravitate towards whatever the metal could be traded for locally – normally a little less. The value of a coin depended not just on the weight of the metal, but also on the weight of the state. Money objects may be *designed* to have well-defined numerical quantities, but (unlike with subatomic particles) those qualities tend to deteriorate unless actively enforced.

While neoclassical economics tends to view money as an inert chip, which apart from its made-up nature is not fundamentally different from any other tradable good, money is a complex entity and control of its production has always been loaded with social, political, cultural and economic implications. This can be seen from its history, where its essential features rearrange themselves in a constantly shapeshifting manner while somehow remaining the same.

The word 'money' is named for Juno Moneta, the goddess in whose Roman temple the first coins were minted. The Roman monetary system was a scaled-up version of the Greek: the army conquered foreign lands, put slaves to work in mines, and stamped out coins to pay themselves with. The state demanded that the conquered populations pay taxes in those same coins, which ensured their circulation.[1] In the mid-second century AD, when a denarius coin contained roughly £1 sterling-worth of silver at today's price (as opposed to an actual pound of silver), imperial spending reached an estimated 225 million denarii per year, with about 75 per cent going to supply the military.[2]

Money played a key role in building the Roman empire, but it was also one of the factors leading to its collapse. A disadvantage of having a currency linked to precious metal is that the quantity of money in circulation depends on the amount of metal being mined. When the empire was expanding, the growing economy was matched reasonably well with the growing supplies of metal. In the third century AD, though, the number of new foreign conquests began to dry up. Rome produced very little itself, so money was continuously draining away to foreign lands, especially once its citizens acquired a taste for exotic goods from India and China. At the same time, the army ballooned in size to 650,000 soldiers, which required more cash (it is always easy to pay people more, rather harder to pay them less, especially when they are armed).[3] The only way to square the circle was to debase the currency – a measure which proved to be quite addictive.

When the denarius, the common coin which was the equivalent of the Greek drachma, was first minted around 211 BC, it contained about 4.5 grams of nearly pure silver, and would pay a day's wages for a soldier or unskilled labourer.[4] Emperors progressively reduced the silver content until 500 years later all that was left was a silver coating on a copper core which tended to rub off with use. Such debasement was popular with emperors because they could pocket the difference between the stamp value and the metal value of the coin, but the increased quantity of money sloshing around the economy also led to runaway inflation. During a spell of just one year in 274–5 AD, prices multiplied by a factor of a hundred.[5]

Symmetrical versus asymmetrical

The dynamics of inflation were nicely explained, though a little late for the Romans, by the Renaissance mathematician and astronomer Nicolaus Copernicus in his 1526 treatise *Monetae cudendae ratio* (On the Minting of Coin), where – in an early version of what economists today call the quantity theory of money – he wrote that 'money usually depreciates when it becomes too abundant'.[6] In one sense, the Roman episode seems proof that money's value is an intrinsic quality, which eventually boils down to the metal content. Remove the bullion, and the currency falls apart. But after the fall of the Roman empire a curious thing happened, which is that the money survived for centuries without any metal at all, in the sense that debts were still calculated in units such as the denarius.

At the same time that the empire was shrinking, and Rome's population of a million people crashed to about 30,000 by 550 AD, the religions of Christianity and Islam rose in power and influence. Metal previously used for coins ended up in religious establishments. But even if the economy was smaller, and more closely regulated by religious authorities, this didn't mean that money was destroyed completely. It was just that the virtual symbol (i.e. the number) took priority over the real material (the metal). Money was returning to its virtual roots – and the region leading the change was the Islamic world, centred again on Mesopotamia.

Markets here flourished, but rather than based on cash transactions they relied, as in ancient times, on credit instruments such as the promissory notes known as *sakk*, or 'checks'. As today, Islamic finance forbade usury but allowed a range of fees, so it was still possible for financiers to make money. And just as the ancient Mesopotamians invented mathematics to keep track of payments, so mathematicians invented a new kind of number to keep track of debts.

As discussed in the previous chapter, a basic property of both numbers and monetary transactions is that they are symmetric, in the sense that for every positive there is a negative. If you exchange one currency for another at the market rate with no commission, then the net gain is zero, because what is gained (a positive amount) in one currency is cancelled by what is paid (a negative amount) in the other. However, until the seventh century AD only positive numbers were recognised. Negative numbers made no more sense than negative coins.

The rules around how to deal with negative numbers appeared for the first time in a book called *The Opening of the Universe* (628 AD), by the Indian mathematician Brahmagupta, who thought about them in monetary terms: positive numbers were 'fortunes', negative numbers were 'debts', and adding a positive with its negative gave zero, which was a number in its own right. These concepts were adopted in the Islamic world through translations of Brahmagupta's work, but took centuries to spread to Europe. They eventually led in the fifteenth century to the development of double-entry book-keeping, in which every transaction was entered in two different accounts, once as a debit and once as a credit. The method helped detect errors, since the sum of credits over all accounts should be balanced by the sum of debits, and also gave a quick picture of profitability.[7]

The invention of negative numbers also revealed a side of money which until then had remained unarticulated; which was that, just as money has real and virtual sides, so it has a positive side and a negative one – the first is owned, while the second is owed. In accounting, this symmetry is expressed numerically through the sign of the number. In ancient Greece or Rome, only the first side of money would have been obvious, but even there, the fact that coins were handed out by the state, but then demanded back as taxes, hinted that debt was involved.

Indeed, it is never possible to talk about 'inherent value' in an absolute sense, because monetary value is always relative and transactional. A lump of gold only takes on value for a person when that person exerts ownership over it, and when others recognise its value. As seen throughout history, the importance of a stamp on a coin is not really to indicate the weight. Instead it is to establish the crown's ownership over the object, and locate its value in a particular monetary space which is maintained by the crown. But where there is ownership, there is its negative, which is debt. The importance of virtual, mathematical debt – and the symmetry at its heart – became clearer still when the state switched to giving out money made of wood.

Wood

During the Early Middle Ages, Christian Europe operated under a feudal system in which the ultimate source of power was the crown, which was God's representative on Earth. The king granted land to his lords, and they in turn granted plots, and a portion of the land's agricultural yield, to their vassals in exchange for loyalty, work on the estate, and (for those in the warrior class) military service.[8] Feudal estates were largely self-contained, so money played little role except as an accounting device. Rents and taxes were usually paid in kind or through labour, rather than in cash.[9] The use of coins was further restricted by the fact that there was little coordination or centralisation. Each king and lord wanted to produce their own version, so that like Roman emperors they could collect the 'seigniorage' (from the Old French *seigneur* meaning lord) which is the difference between the face worth of the coin and its cost of production.

An exception to this lack of centralisation was England, where shortly after ascending the throne in 1100, King Henry I – son of William the Conqueror – introduced a payment system that was based on wooden sticks, known as tallies. The sticks, which were about ten inches long and made of polished hazel or willow wood, were notched to indicate their worth, and split lengthwise into two parts – the stock for the creditor, and the stub or foil for the debtor. The width of the notch varied from 'the thickness of the palm of the hand' for a thousand pounds, down to 'a single cut without removing any wood' for a penny.[10] The stock was also made slightly longer, to differentiate it from the part held by the debtor, who literally had 'the short end of the stick'. When the debt was repaid, the two sides were matched – comparing the grain of the wood made it easy to detect fraud – and destroyed. The tallies therefore functioned as a physical symbol for the debt, which was important when the population was mostly illiterate. A similar technique was used around the same time in China, with the difference that the tallies were made of bamboo.[11]

As with coin money in ancient Greece, but without the need for metal, tallies encoded numerical information whose context depended on the power of the state. Use of the tallies took off in England after King Henry began to use them for the purposes of tax collection. This expanded their use and made it easier for the stocks to circulate as money objects. For example, suppose the state held a stock representing a debt owed to it from a local tax sheriff. Then it could use the stock to pay a supplier, who could either collect from the tax sheriff, use it to pay their own taxes, or sell it at a discount to a broker who would collect the debt when it came due. The foil meanwhile was a kind of negative money object, in the sense that you had to pay to get rid of it.

An interesting thing had therefore happened to money – it had somehow physically bifurcated into two parts. As we have seen, coin money is inherently dualistic in the sense that it combines the properties of numbers and valued objects, but the two aspects come combined in what appears to be a single package. Coins were created by digging up metal from the ground, stamping them with a symbol, and enforcing their value locally through the power of the state. In fact, even here money has two parts joined by an invisible thread – the coin, which circulates as money, and the die for the stamp, which is engineered and controlled by the mint. But with tallies there was no valuable material, only a stick of wood; and together the two parts represented, not a single value, but a positive credit and a negative debit, which sum to zero. The situation is again analogous to quantum physics, where entangled particles with opposite spin can be produced from a single source. In this case, the holders of the two parts of the stick were entangled in the sense that whatever happened to one had implications for the other. For example if the stock was destroyed in a fire, there was no longer a record of the debt; if the monarch debased the currency, then both sides would lose their value.

Of course, this entanglement was not an invention of King Henry or any other ruler – an IOU does the same thing. But tallies also illustrated another feature of money, which is that its creation is not a zero-sum game. Tallies were money objects with a numerical price, just like coins, and their validity was backed by the state. Their creation therefore added to the money supply, even if the effect lasted only until the debt was cancelled. As seen later, this type of money creation can lead to inflation as surely as the debasement of coins, although it tends to look a little different.

Paper

The use of tallies in England peaked in the second half of the seventeenth century, and they were still in use into the nineteenth century, by which time wood had been taken over by paper. Europeans first learned about paper money from the Venetian explorer Marco Polo, who on returning from China in 1295 wrote of how the government of Kublai Khan used money made from sheets of paper, which were signed and stamped with the royal seal.[12] Inspired by this example, European bankers and goldsmiths began issuing paper promissory notes in exchange for deposits. These were tallies for the literate class of bankers and merchants, where they soon began to circulate as the predecessors of modern banknotes (the term originates from the fourteenth-century 'nota di banco').

In place of two physical objects that needed to be matched together in order to cancel the debt, as with tallies, there was now a piece of paper which could be redeemed for a deposit. In a sense, then, the stock had been replaced by the banknote, and the foil by the gold which was held on loan by the goldsmith. With tallies, the stock represented a credit to the crown; with banknotes, they represent a credit to the person who deposited the gold. Tallies were matched and cancelled only after the crown was delivered what it was owed; banknotes were cancelled when the gold was returned to its owner.

As with tallies, banknotes are two-sided instruments, which entangle debtor and creditor like particles with a shared wave function. An important difference, though, is that there is more scope for fraud or deception, in part because gold is fungible so harder to keep track of (referring to the quantum erasure experiment described in Chapter 1, tallies are like labelled photons, while gold is effectively unlabelled). For example, suppose a goldsmith had a certain amount of gold on deposit in its vault. It could let it sit there until the owner came to collect. Or alternatively, it might be tempted to loan some of the gold out at interest in the meantime. Or rather than lending out the physical gold, it could loan out a banknote giving someone the right to collect that gold – at which point, the backing for the note had less to do with gold than with the goldsmith's ability to juggle its liabilities. Indeed, accounts from the time suggest that goldsmiths typically maintained reserves of only about 10 per cent and loaned out the rest at interest.[13] We may have designed the money system to obey strict accounting laws, where each debit is balanced by a credit, but as always in human affairs the exact terms are open to interpretation.

A more specialised type of credit instrument was the bill of exchange, which was simply a letter instructing a banker or agent, perhaps in another country, to make a payment on the writer's behalf. These became sufficiently popular that trade fairs, like the quarterly one in Lyon, could be carried out on a nearly cash-free basis.[14] Because bills of exchange could be traded, if still only within a select group of international bankers and financiers, they again acted as money objects and boosted the money supply. Money objects could therefore be created not just by monarchs, but also by bankers. At a time when a growing commercial class was distrusting and resentful of monarchs whose financial literacy was weak to say the best – France, for example, saw 123 currency debasements in the period 1285 to 1490 – this led to a power shift from the state to bankers, which was epitomised by the rise of the Medicis in Renaissance Italy.

To be sure, the debts were finally settled in terms of local currencies. In medieval France and Italy, prices were reckoned according to the livre system. The main coin was the silver denier, denoted 'd', whose name was derived from the Roman denarius. Twelve deniers made up one sou, and twenty sous made up a livre (lira in Italy), which was nominally equal in value to one pound of silver (though inflation meant that it was worth much less). The system was later emulated by a number of European countries; in Britain the local version of the denier was the penny, again denoted 'd'. However, while the units of account related in theory at least to weights of metal, the money creation process still didn't require access to a mine.

Public and private

As discussed in Chapter 2, money has two sides, the real and the virtual, the object and the idea. Money was born in ancient Mesopotamia as part of a state-run credit system, so the virtual side

was in the ascendant. The invention of coin money, and its enthusi-
astic adoption by the armies of Greece and Rome, brought the real,
physical side of money to the fore. The fall of the Roman empire,
and the shortage of metal, meant that money again returned to its
virtual roots with the invention of credit instruments such as tallies, banknotes, and bills of exchange. As in Mesopotamia, prices
were once more reckoned in terms of theoretical weights of silver,
but the metal itself did not circulate widely.

This again changed rather abruptly in the sixteenth century,
with the Spanish discovery of new sources of metal in the New
World. From 1500 to 1800, its mines produced about 150,000 tons
of silver and 2,800 tons of gold.[15] A single mountain in Peru known
as Cerro Rico (rich hill) gave the Spanish some 45,000 tons of pure
silver.[16] As in Greek or Roman times, the labour was supplied by
local slaves.

Church-sponsored ideas about the dangers of money seemed
to go out the window as soon as the conquistadors first set their
eyes on Aztec gold. As recorded in the Florentine Codex: 'They
picked it up and fingered it like monkeys. It was as if their hearts
were satisfied, brightened, calmed. For in truth they thirsted might-
ily for gold; they stuffed themselves with it; they starved for it;
they lusted for it like pigs.'[17] (While it's hard to imagine anyone
getting so excited over wooden tallies, we should note that money
has a similar effect whatever form it takes, and not just on conquistadors.) The influx of metal certainly enriched many people,
but following Copernicus' quantity theory of money (which was
prompted by this episode) it also led to a huge level of inflation.
The Spanish economy in particular fell victim to what has become
known as the resource curse (similar to the 'trust fund curse' but
for countries rather than children).

The lust for gold was the organising principle behind
the doctrine known as mercantilism, as first championed by

Queen Elizabeth I in England. While England was not blessed with an abundant local supply of precious metal, this was no more a problem for the English than it was for Alexander the Great – it just meant that they had to conquer places which were. The task was largely carried out through private companies, with the largest being the British East India Company. But the true quantum power of money was only unleashed in 1694 with the founding of the Bank of England – which announced a new way of merging the two sides of money, and inverted the relationship between money and the state.

As mentioned above, a problem with metal money was that it was controlled by monarchs who had a tendency to debase the currency or default on their debts. After military defeat by France in the Battle of Beachy Head in 1690, King William III was in urgent need of £1.2 million to rebuild the navy; but his credit was so poor that he found it impossible to raise the money by the normal means. He therefore decided to set up a public–private funding vehicle called the Bank of England. The way it worked was that the bank – acting like a very large goldsmith – gave the government a permanent loan of gold, in return for notes against this debt. As compensation it would receive 8 per cent interest in perpetuity on the original loan, plus a service charge of £4,000 per year, plus whatever it could make from banking services. The subscription was quickly sold out.

The bank's original charter didn't actually mention banknotes, but like other banks of the time – such as the Amsterdam Exchange Bank (since 1609) or the Swedish Riksbank (since 1656) – it gave notes in return for deposits, and also lent them out at interest. Such notes included a promise to pay the bearer the sum of the note on demand, so anyone could redeem them in full or in part for metal coins. Supported as they were by royal approval, they soon began to circulate as money objects. As with the banknotes issued by goldsmiths, the principle behind the Bank of England notes was again similar to that of tallies, in that the notes represented the stock, or a claim on the debt. But now the direction of the debt had changed: as anthropologist David Graeber puts it, 'money was no longer a debt owed to the king, but a debt owed by the king ... In many ways it had become a mirror image of older forms of money.'[18]

The founding of the Bank of England also represented a different kind of bifurcation for money, in the sense that it involved a kind of public–private splitting of functions between the state and the bank. The state was responsible for the symbolic stamping of the money, while the private sector was responsible for stumping up the actual gold (though in fact subscribers also contributed wooden tallies, which muddied the waters somewhat). The success of this arrangement meant that money achieved a new stability and reliability, and the Bank of England became the model for similar central banks around the world.

In the end, money always comes down to a confidence trick. We value something like a banknote because we trust that it can be exchanged or redeemed, which will only be the case if other people also trust in it. Money is therefore a way of entangling people into a kind of belief system – and this level of entanglement reached a new high as banknotes became widely adopted, as the driving force behind the British empire.

Symmetry breaking

As mentioned above, one difference between banknotes and a more straightforward credit system such as tallies is that tallies represented particular verifiable debts which were designed to be cancelled, while the new banknotes were viewed more as a receipt for something tangible that existed in a vault somewhere. They weren't gold, but they served as pointers to gold. But because the gold wasn't physically matched to the note in any way – unlike wood sticks with their distinctive grain, one gold bar is as good as another – this made it easy to loan out the same gold many times over. Goldsmithing was a profitable business, and not because of the actual smithing part.

This system was formalised under the Bank of England as fractional reserve banking, which is traditionally described in economics textbooks as follows. A central bank buys a government bond (e.g. fronts a monarch some cash). The state then spends the money (e.g. on rebuilding the navy) and the money enters the larger economy. But this is just the first stage.

Suppose one such payment to a supplier is for £100. The supplier deposits the amount in their own bank. But that bank doesn't just let it sit there – it holds on to £10 (corresponding to a reserve requirement of 10 per cent) and loans out the other £90 to someone else. That money in turn gets deposited in another bank, which keeps 10 per cent or £9 and loans out £81. When you add up the chain of transactions, the amount of new money in the economy is £100 plus £90 plus £81 and so on, which sums in the limit to £1,000, meaning that the original payment has been scaled up by a factor ten.

According to the textbook picture, money creation is therefore initiated and controlled by the central bank. Private banks play a role as well, by issuing new loans, but the amount is limited by the fractional reserve requirement, which was 10 per cent in the above illustration. As discussed in Chapter 5, this picture is rather misleading, since in reality it is private banks that control the money creation process, with central banks playing more of a reactive role, loaning money as necessary to banks to top up their reserves. But it seems a reasonable interpretation of how things functioned under what became known as the gold standard, where banknotes supplemented the use of coins, but were valued in terms of precious metal and, in principle at least, could be exchanged for coins if requested.

One advantage of the fractional reserve system was that it added flexibility, so for example the money supply could be ramped up by issuing more banknotes during times of economic growth, even when the supply of gold lagged behind. It also made deposits more valuable to banks, which meant savings accounts could earn interest. But there was also an obvious structural problem, which was that if everyone wanted to withdraw money at the same time, there wasn't enough to go round. An important symmetry had been broken, between what is owned and what is owed. Just as physics has its conservation laws, which are subject to the uncertainty principle, so the economy has accountancy rules, but these are subject to human uncertainty. Tallies could be redeemed and the stub and stock destroyed together, but with banknotes it wasn't so simple. In principle, each loan and each note is backed by a corresponding asset, but during a crisis – when the link between real and virtual comes under stress – there can be a collection problem.

Central banks therefore increasingly found themselves to be what the nineteenth-century journalist Walter Bagehot called the 'lender of last resort', responsible for bailing out smaller banks that were subject to such bank runs. Instead of being backed by gold, banknotes were backed by the central bank. After the crisis of 2007–08, the lender of last resort was the taxpayers who bailed out the financial system.

Entangled money
As we have seen with the brief history so far, the dualistic, quantum, shapeshifting nature of money is manifested in the historical record through its myriad forms, including clay tablets, cowrie shells, metal coins, wooden sticks, and paper notes, not to mention the many other forms of money identified by anthropologists,

which alternate in emphasis between the real and virtual (see box below). But money has some constant features. One is that money is transmitted by the exchange of money objects, which are inherently dualistic in the sense that they combine the properties of owned objects with the properties of numbers. They are a way of stamping numbers onto the real world, and putting an objective numerical value on subjective social value, through a process similar to measurement of a quantum system.

We return to this measurement process in more detail later, but one thing to note is that because numbers have no inherent scale, it is possible to have an economy function with one set of prices, and also function at a set of prices which is exactly twice (or some other multiple) that of the first. In fact this kind of thing happens all the time because of inflation. This led economists from Adam Smith onwards to think – mistakenly, I will argue – that what counts is relative prices, with money just a distraction.[19]

Another common property, related to the first, is that money creation is based on the concept of ownership (and its negative, debt) which is signified by the stamp. When the ancient Greeks forced slaves to mine silver and turned it into coins, the stamp did more than just serve to certify the weight of the metal, as described by Aristotle and modern textbooks. Instead it was a stamp of ownership, which signified that the gold belonged to the state – and because ownership is relational, a gold coin represents a debt to the state which can be cancelled out by providing a service. With tallies, the role of debt was more transparent, since the stock was literally a receipt for money owed. In modern economies, central banks create money by issuing bonds which are sold to the private sector, and private banks create money by creating loans against assets. Money objects therefore entangle debtor and creditor at the moment of their creation. When the Bank of England loaned the king his money for his war debt, it was like handing him the short end of a tally stick. The stick was then metaphorically shaved off into many thousands of sheets called banknotes. If the state ever repaid the loan, all that money would disappear back into the void. This is one reason governments need to run deficits, because without the debt there wouldn't be money.

The creation of money always involves asserting ownership over a tradable object. This means that every money object has two parts: the object itself, and a record asserting the status of that object (which may in itself be tradable). In every case, there has to be a way of matching the two parts – the object and the record – to test whether the money is counterfeit. For a tally, this was done by literally matching the grain of the wood; for a coin or banknote, it is done through the design of the object; for a bitcoin, it is through cryptography.

In, say, eighteenth-century England a money object might have started off as a tally stick, been exchanged with a broker for gold coin, and then been swapped for a banknote. Money can therefore change its host from wood to metal to paper, even before it is used to buy anything. However, while gold coins and banknotes were backed directly or indirectly by metal, the tallies were produced out of thin air. How did this happen?

The obvious explanation is that with coins or banknotes, it isn't necessary for the sovereign to apply so much force to make the money work, because they are backed by metal – with coins physically, and with banknotes by contract. The hard labour was done by the slaves when they dug the metal up, and the army who controlled the process. But tallies are a different thing, because the sovereign is creating two money objects – the positive stock and the negative foil – and the stock is only worth something if he or she can force or cajole someone into accepting the foil. In the same way that energy can be transformed into mass or vice versa in nuclear reactions, so the sovereign's energy can be used to forge new money objects out of the void. Money objects therefore store a kind of potential energy.

With fractional reserve banking, though, the situation becomes more complicated because deposits can be loaned out multiple times and earn interest for the depositor in return, while banks can charge interest on loans. This means that some of the sovereign's power to create money objects – the seigniorage – has passed to the private banking system. This fact has not been widely advertised: as economist Norbert Häring observes, 'Central bankers never, ever talk about the hugely profitable privilege that the ability to create legal tender means for commercial banks.'[20] Another implication is that the amount of money in the economy has to build over time in order to pay off the interest. The money supply therefore tends to expand in an exponential fashion, and not just because of real economic growth, as discussed further in Chapter 5.

In medieval England the stock half of a tally stick became a money object representing a credit, made up by the king, that could be collected. With the founding of the Bank of England, the direction reversed, so that money was now based on the state's debt to the private sector. With modern fiat currencies* that are backed only by the word of the state, the central bank goes a step further and creates money not by loaning real assets to the state, but by loaning made-up funds, produced magically at the press of a button. Of course, this raises a couple of questions. One is that, since anyone can initiate a debt, it isn't clear why the state needs to be involved at all. Bitcoin believers would argue that it doesn't. Another question is, rather than the government borrowing fiat money from the central bank at interest, couldn't it just issue the money as a debt to itself? We return to this in the final chapter.

---

* From the Book of Genesis: *fiat lux*, let there be light.

To summarise, we have seen in this chapter how the creation of money objects always involves two entangled entities which reflect money's dualistic nature: a tradable object which is worth a fixed amount, and a virtual record of that amount. The record – which can be in the form of a government stamp, a tally, or a secure entry on a computer – guarantees that the money object which tallies with it is genuine and belongs to a specified monetary space. The strands which link these separate aspects of money objects braid together to form the complex web of entanglements that characterise the quantum system known as the economy (the quantum properties of this entanglement will be explored further in Chapter 7). According to mainstream economics, money is just a kind of commodity with no special properties, but in fact responsibility for its creation is the most important and sensitive role in an economy. In the next chapter, we show how economists drew a veil over this process – by saying that money itself was a veil.

Virtual gold

The debate over whether money is a real commodity (e.g. bullionism), or a virtual token which is created and granted value by the state (chartalism, from the Latin *charta* for record), has been around probably since the technology was invented. During the gold standard, most people would have agreed with the US banker J.P. Morgan, when he testified in 1912 that 'Money is gold, and nothing else'.[21] Few would have paid attention to the dissenting voice of British economist Alfred Mitchell-Innes, who wrote the next year that 'Credit alone is money. Credit and not gold or silver is the one property which all men seek.'[22] Today the popularity of these positions would be reversed (though most economists don't worry about the properties of money since it's not in their models).

From a quantum perspective, though, it makes more sense to say that money objects are quantum entities which are both real and virtual at the same time. The debate over money therefore resembles the debate over whether light was a wave or a particle. Democritus believed light was made, like everything else, of atoms, while Aristotle argued it was a wave in the ether. In the seventeenth century Newton saw it as a stream of corpuscles, while physicists on the continent preferred the wave option. In 1801, Thomas Young's double-slit interference patterns seemed to show it was a wave; but, as we saw earlier, when his experiment was repeated by Geoffrey Taylor in 1909 using only a single photon at a time, it was concluded that, rather than light being a wave *or* a particle, it had the characteristics of both. Most people just worried about keeping the lights on. So it is with money.

The dual nature of money can be seen clearly with cybercurrencies such as bitcoin. According to either bullionists or chartalists, bitcoin is not money because, as the *Globe and Mail* noted, it is backed by 'nothing tangible – no bar of gold, no promise from a central bank'.[23] This was confirmed by the Bank of Canada's Stephen Poloz, who said that since cybercurrencies cannot act as a reliable store of value or be spent easily, 'they do not constitute 'money'.[24] Agustín Carstens, general manager of the Bank for International Settlements, agreed that 'While cryptocurrencies may pretend to be currencies, they fail the basic textbook definitions'.[25] Economist Eugene Fama similarly said that bitcoin is 'not a store of value', which, according to his efficient market theory, discussed later, suggests its price should be zero.[26] Or as Pan Gongsheng of the People's Bank of China put it: 'There is only one thing left to do: sit on the river bank and see bitcoin's body pass by one day.'[27] It has been interesting to see how mainstream economists and central bankers, who are loath to describe explosions in stocks or real estate as irrational greed-fuelled bubbles, have been so quick to apply the label to cybercurrencies.

Yet bitcoin does seem to have established itself as a form of money. It has its drawbacks, such as huge price volatility – it has been through a massive boom and crash just while writing this book – and currently seems to be more hoarded than spent, but it has built a large following, is relied on for sending remittances to countries such as Zimbabwe where cell phones outnumber bank accounts, and has carved out a niche in areas such as overseas money transfers, buying stakes in obscure financial technology (fintech) companies, and various illegal activities (though cash still seems to be king here). And the fact that every transaction is recorded pseudonymously on a ledger known as the blockchain, which is maintained by constant network surveillance, gives it unique advantages – for example in fraud prevention – which are being eagerly if nervously investigated by banks.

In a 2015 interview discussing how cybercurrencies illustrated the quantum properties of money, I ventured that 'Bitcoin will continue to make inroads, with new fintech companies on the one hand and mainstream banks on the other hand, competing to take advantage of it. A less certain prediction is that bitcoin will shoot to prominence in a country because people lose trust in the main currency. Could be Greece, but it will probably be somewhere more left-of-field like Venezuela, which has some of the highest inflation in the world (and subsidised electricity)'.[28] Bitcoin transactions in Venezuela took off in 2017, with *The Atlantic* reporting that 'thousands of Venezuelans have taken to *minería bitcoin* – mining bitcoin'.[29] In late 2015 the largest note in circulation was worth 100 bolivars, which on the black market was worth about 0.5 mBTC (thousandths of a bitcoin); two years on, that fraction of a bitcoin was worth about two suitcases-worth of the same notes, which should give pause to anyone who thinks only state-backed currencies or gold can hold value.[30]

For those of an empirical bent, one could say that bitcoin's continued existence falsifies the theories of bullionism and chartalism. Even if it implodes of its own accord or because of regulation, cybercurrencies as a class are unlikely to go away. So where then does the backing for bitcoin come from, if not a weight of metal or the authority of the state or the legal system? The answer is – itself. Or rather, its network.

The first 43,000 bitcoins – the so-called 'Genesis' block – were produced or 'mined' using open-source software by a person going by the name of Satoshi Nakamoto on 3 January 2009. To timestamp the code, Satoshi included a headline from that day's London *Times* newspaper which hinted at his (or her, or their) motivations: 'Chancellor on Brink of Second Bailout for Banks.' The value of the coins was zero, so he handed some out for free to interested parties he met online, along with a paper explaining how they could mine more coins by running the cryptographic code used to maintain the blockchain and keep the network secure.

A community of users began to develop, and in October that year someone set up a website quoting the value of a bitcoin as being equal to the cost of electricity required to mine a coin, which seemed reasonable. At the time it was about 0.08 cents, so a thousand bitcoins was worth about 80 cents. Each time a user was added, the code took a little longer to run, but the price also went up. And up. According to an empirical equation known as Metcalfe's Law, the worth of a network scales roughly with the number of users squared, which seems to work quite well with bitcoin.[31]

So is this money real? Is it a *thing*? And how can value be produced out of nothing? Well, if those 43,000 bitcoins were held in a single bitcoin wallet – say on a detachable drive – and it was lost, then they would be gone for good. So the money would certainly feel real.[32]

As with all forms of money, the real value of the currency is in the network – the power to buy and sell within a community of users. With coin money, the network is maintained by the sovereign, but with cybercurrencies the power is distributed among its users. So bitcoins are a kind of virtual gold adapted for the network age. Its price might be a bubble, susceptible to swings in sentiment, but so is the price of gold – the latter is just a bubble that has lasted a very long time. Now we just need to update our ideas about money for the quantum age.

CHAPTER 4

THE MONEY VEIL

*I don't care who writes a nation's laws
– or crafts its advanced treatises – if
I can write its economics textbooks.*
Paul Samuelson

Neoclassical economics is based on a Newtonian picture of the economy as a mechanistic system, made up of self-interested, atomistic individuals who interact only by exchanging goods and services. Money has no important role and acts primarily as an inert medium of exchange. These assumptions allowed economists to build elaborate physics-like models of the economy. But just as Newtonian physics fails at the quantum level, so this mechanistic approach breaks down when we consider the complex dynamics of money.

In previous chapters we have considered the question of what money is, and where it comes from. The next question would be, what does money do?

For most economists, the answer has long been very simple – nothing special. Money is just an inert chip with no special properties of its own. To understand the economy, economists should not focus on money – in fact, they should do the opposite, and ignore its bewitching and distracting activities. As John Stuart Mill remarked in his seminal nineteenth-century textbook *Principles of Political Economy*, 'There cannot, in short, be intrinsically a more insignificant thing, in the economy of society, than money.'[1]

Of course, this isn't to say that economists omitted money altogether (for example, it was obviously needed as a metric) – only that it was deprived of any kind of life. This attitude was born in part from the Aristotelian creation myth that money evolved as a substitute for barter, so it was just another commodity that could be exchanged like any other. As Paul Samuelson wrote in *Economics*, 'if we strip exchange down to its barest essentials and peel off the obscuring layer of money, we find that trade between individuals and nations largely boils down to barter'.[2] But it also reflected a Newtonian view of the economy as a mechanistic system, in which the two sides of money were collapsed down to a single point, and money became no more than another inert particle to be held or exchanged.

The founding father of economics is usually considered to be the classical economist Adam Smith, who was much impressed by 'The superior genius and sagacity of Sir Isaac Newton' and aimed to put the study of the economy onto a similarly scientific plane. A first step, in his *Wealth of Nations*, was to assert that the value of money was determined only by its weight in precious metal, rather than by the stamp which was rather unreliable: 'Six shillings and eightpence, for example, in the time of Edward I, I consider as the same money-price with a pound sterling in the present times; because it contained, as nearly as we can judge, the same quantity of pure silver'.[3] Similarly the price of goods was equal to 'the quantity of pure gold or silver for which they are sold, without any regard to the denomination of the coin'.

This put economic trade onto a reassuringly Newtonian basis, since everything could be expressed in terms of weights of metal. But in order to complete the mapping from the physical to the economic sphere, Smith needed some kind of social analogue for mass, which he found in stock (i.e. goods or possessions) and labour. Following philosophers such as John Locke, Smith asserted that 'The real price of every thing, what every thing really costs to the man who wants to acquire it, is the toil and trouble of acquiring it.' Value is labour, and money is just a medium of exchange.

Of course, these prices were only relative. The exchange value of labour in terms of metal was not fixed, because it would depend on the cost of obtaining the metal, which in turn would depend on factors such as the 'fertility or barrenness' of mines. But this didn't matter, because what counted was relative prices – or what Smith called 'real' as opposed to 'nominal' prices – which stripped out these confusing effects. The economist Jean-Baptiste Say, who popularised Smith's work in France, summed this up in his statement that 'money is a veil'. According to Say's law, for example, production is the source of demand – when something is sold, the money is used to buy something else – so markets clear and money comes out in the wash.[4]

Finally, Smith needed a rule to specify how prices map onto the specified quantity. He found this with his most famous invention, the invisible hand.

Hard labour

Smith himself used the phrase 'invisible hand' only once in his book, in a section on trade, but it was later popularised by Paul Samuelson as the name for Smith's idea about how markets work. According to this rule, which eventually came to be viewed as the social science version of a Newtonian law, the price of an asset will be guided towards its 'natural price' (i.e. that which corresponds to labour value) by market mechanisms. If a particular good is too expensive, then more suppliers will enter the market, and competition will drive the price down. If the price is too low, then suppliers will go broke or leave the market, and the price will go up. So as Samuelson paraphrased, 'Every individual, in pursuing only his own selfish good, was led, as if by an invisible hand, to achieve the best good for all.'[5]

The invisible hand therefore closed the Newtonian loop between weights of metal, labour, and price. The answer to the question *how much* was simply the relative market price, which represented labour. The labour theory of value was highly influential among philosophers and economists such as Karl Marx, who wrote in his 1867 *Capital* that 'The greater the productiveness of labour, the less is the labour time required for the production of an article, the less is the amount of labour crystallised in that article, and the less is its value; and vice versa, the less the productiveness of labour, the greater is the labour time required for the production of an article, and the greater is its value.'[6]

However, a first thing to note is that, unlike something like mass, labour isn't easily measurable. For example, Smith equated the cost of gold with the labour required to extract it – but how did that square with the fact that most of the gold in circulation had been mined by slaves? For more sophisticated goods – say, an iPhone – it is even less clear how to add up the various sources of labour. Obviously there are the company's employees, its suppliers, and so on, but where do you draw the line? Many of its technologies (such as internet capability, GPS, touchscreens, cryptography) were based on government-funded military technologies, so how do you factor that in? What about the basic science behind those technologies? What about the free websites such as Wikipedia, or open-source software, or digital information in general, which add value to the iPhone? And so on.

Labour is also subjective in other ways. How do you compare the labour value provided by a CEO who has just received a multi-million-dollar payoff in return for leaving a money-losing company (there is no shortage of examples) with the hard graft provided by an undocumented farm worker, or for that matter someone assembling iPhones? As one trader said of his $10 million bonus, awarded after helping his firm to a multi-billion-dollar profit during the financial crisis: 'I guess it depends on your perspective of what's fair, right? If you're a steelworker you probably think I got paid pretty well. If you're a hedge-fund manager you probably don't.'[7]

Because labour is not directly measurable, one consequence is that the theory as a whole, including the invisible hand mechanism, is unfalsifiable in the sense that it can never be disproved by experiment. A broader point is that, as already mentioned, there is no direct mapping between numbers and value. Money objects are unique in that they are defined to be objects with a fixed numerical value. For other things, including labour, the price is determined through a measurement procedure involving transactions. As we'll see, even carefully designed markets are subject to a kind of uncertainty principle, in the sense that taking a measurement affects the thing being measured.

Smith's labour theory of value was useful in that it seemed to put economic calculations on some kind of hard, solid ground – it provided a sense of meaning. But its arbitrary quality meant that it could be swapped for something completely different, while leaving the rest of the theory effectively untouched, as the neoclassical economists next showed.

The mechanics of utility

In the second paragraph of his *Theory of Political Economy* (1871), the English economist William Stanley Jevons announced that 'Repeated reflection and inquiry have led me to the somewhat novel opinion that *value depends entirely upon utility.* Prevailing opinions make labour rather than utility the origin of value; and there are even those who distinctly assert that labour is the *cause* of value. I show, on the contrary, that we have only to trace out carefully the natural laws of the variation of utility, as depending upon the quantity of commodity in our possession, in order to arrive at a satisfactory theory of exchange, of which the ordinary laws of supply and demand are a necessary consequence.'[8]

The concept of utility was first proposed in the late eighteenth century by Jeremy Bentham, the English philosopher and social reformer, who defined it as that which appears to 'augment or diminish the happiness of the party whose interest is in question'.[9] Society's purpose, Bentham argued, was to satisfy the 'greatest happiness principle' – i.e. provide the greatest happiness to the most people. The goodness of an action could be assessed by adding together its positive and negative effects on the people involved.

Bentham's aim was to put social policy on a rational, enlightened basis. Neoclassical economics promised a way to do this, by expressing utility in terms of mathematical laws. Of course, utility was completely subjective, and even harder to measure than labour – but again that didn't matter. The aim of utility theory was not to incorporate subjectivity; it was to replace it with numbers, which is not quite the same thing.[10]

As Jevons argued, if utility is equated with value, then it can be measured through price. He wrote: 'I hesitate to say that men will ever have the means of measuring directly the feelings of the human heart. A unit of pleasure or of pain is difficult even to conceive; but it is the amount of these feelings which is continually prompting us to buying and selling, borrowing and lending, labouring and resting, producing and consuming; and it is from the quantitative effects of the feelings that we must estimate their comparative amounts. We can no more know nor measure gravity in its own nature than we can measure a feeling; but, just as we measure gravity by its effects in the motion of a pendulum, so we may estimate the equality or inequality of feelings by the decisions of the human mind. The will is our pendulum, and its oscillations are minutely registered in the price lists of the markets.'[11]

The economy could therefore be modelled using what Jevons called 'a mechanics of utility and self-interest', similar to Newtonian mechanics.[12] More precisely, exchange prices were determined by marginal utility, which took into account a person's current state – you will pay less for a loaf of bread if you already have as much as you can eat. When the transaction is complete, both parties 'rest in satisfaction and equilibrium, and the degrees of utility have come to their level, as it were'.

As the British economist Lionel Robbins wrote in 1932, such findings were based on 'deduction from simple assumptions reflecting very elementary facts of general experience' and as such were 'as universal as the laws of mathematics or mechanics, and as little capable of "suspension"'.[13] Today, economists often prefer to work instead with preferences, which simply rank things or desires in order, but utility is still seen as a mysterious, unmeasurable, subjective quantity which individuals aim to maximise (a word invented by Bentham) through economic exchange, subject only to budgetary constraints. Perhaps the most famous description of this process is supplied by what Jevons called 'the ordinary laws of supply and demand'.

The lines and the unicorn, redux

The law of supply and demand is usually illustrated by a figure based on an 1870 version by the English polymath Fleeming Jenkin, who went to school in Edinburgh with James Clerk Maxwell and went on to invent the cable car. The figure was later popularised by Alfred Marshall, and remains a fixture of not just textbooks, but also the models used by economists to simulate the world economy.

The figure consists of two intersecting lines, with a downward sloping demand curve and an upwards sloping supply curve, so basically an X. The vertical axis is price, so the figure says that consumer demand decreases with price, while producer supply increases with price. The two lines intersect at a single point, which represents the unique market-clearing price at which 'objective' supply and 'subjective' demand come into equilibrium. Economists think of these two lines as representing separate forces which balance out.

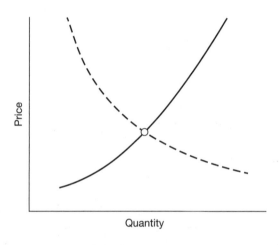

Figure 2. The law of supply and demand. The solid line shows supply, which increases with price. The dashed line shows demand, which decreases with price. The intersection of the two lines represents the point where supply and demand are in balance.

The law (or laws, as it is sometimes called to distinguish the two components) of supply and demand is therefore a graphical representation of Smith's invisible hand. If the price of some commodity is too high for whatever reason, then more suppliers will enter the market, while at the same time demand will fall. The result will be a surplus of supply, which will bring the price down. Conversely, if prices are too low then the combined response of supply and demand will push them back up again.[14] In fact, the only real difference is that utility has been substituted for labour as the presumed source of value. Since neither can be measured directly – only inferred from prices – this has no effect on the equations. Money has no role, other than as a book-keeping device for things like prices or budgetary constraints, so has dropped out of the calculations altogether, with any increase in budget leading only to increased consumption.[15] Genuine subjectivity has also been removed; individuals are treated as a black box, in the sense that the reasons for their motivations are left alone, but at the same time their actions are reduced to the maximisation of an equation.

According to Gregory Mankiw's *Principles of Economics*, as rote-learned by millions of students around the world, 'To analyze how any event influences a market, we use the supply-and-demand diagram to examine how the event affects the equilibrium price and quantity ... In market economies, prices are the signals that guide economic decisions and thereby allocate scarce resources. For every good in the economy, the price ensures that supply and demand are in balance. The equilibrium price then determines how much of the good buyers choose to consume and how much sellers choose to produce.'[16] (I'm not sure how this analysis applies to Mankiw's highly expensive textbook, since the demand is enforced by professors, and the money often comes from government-subsidised student loans.)

Another textbook by Yoram Bauman explains that: 'A good way to think about the market equilibrium is to imagine that the demand curve is blue, that the supply curve is yellow, and that the only color we can see in the real world is green. The market equilibrium comes at the point where the two curves intersect, and the punch line – yellow and blue makes green! – carries an important lesson: the green dot has no independent existence of its own, and it doesn't move unless either the yellow line or the blue line moves.'[17] Indeed, this seems to be the way that the subject is commonly taught, but really it is the lines that have no independent existence of their own, as I found while researching my 2010 book *Economyths*. Even though textbooks routinely claim that these lines have been empirically measured, and people have certainly tried, it is in fact impossible to properly measure a 'supply curve' or a 'demand curve' – all we can do is measure transactions at a particular price (the green dots) and the result we obtain will include the effects of both supply and demand.[18] We are therefore trying to tease out the values of two variables – supply and demand – from a single number, which doesn't work (in mathematics this is known as the identifiability problem).* And in fact there are plenty of reasons to believe that it makes no sense to view supply and demand as stable (for a time) and separate entities, rather than as parts of a coupled dynamic system.

One is that people's preferences and behaviours are not static, but as discussed in Chapter 7 are affected by other things such as the influence of other people, or changes in market conditions, or context in general. There is also cross-talk between supply and demand. This is seen clearly with luxury goods, where supply is deliberately restricted in order to help stoke demand.

Another problem is that what counts is not just price, but also change in price, or momentum as it is known. An example is supplied by a report on the UK housing market from May 2017, when the effects of Brexit were starting to sink in. 'As house price growth has slowed, and the market is buffeted by political and

---

* This is why when economist Stephen Levitt went looking for a suitable empirical example of a demand curve for a textbook he was working on, he couldn't find one either, according to a 2016 Freakonomics podcast. 'What I'd really say is that we completely and totally understand what a demand curve is, but we've never seen one.' Dubner, S.J. (7 September 2016), *Why Uber Is an Economist's Dream*. Retrieved from: Freakonomics.com: http://freakonomics.com/podcast/uber-economists-dream/

economic uncertainty, transaction levels have fallen and buyers have increasingly gone into retreat'; while at the same time, 'Many homeowners who might have put their house on the market to take advantage of rising prices are now drawing in their horns, leading to a drop in the number of available houses on the market.'[19] If only price mattered, then at a time when prices are near an all-time high one would expect supply to be high and demand low. Instead, supply is low, and demand is dropping not so much because of the price but because of worries that it will no longer increase.

A third problem is that the demand curve is usually supposed to represent the demand of some representative consumer. In macroeconomic models of the economy as a whole, a single demand curve might represent a country's demand for some basket of products. Yet if you add up the (fictional) demand curves of many different people, you are likely to arrive at a very complicated shape, if it can be defined at all. The reason is that in a heterogeneous population, a shift in the price for a commodity will benefit some groups more than others, so their demand curves will shift as a result, which in turn changes the net demand.[20] Similarly, the supply curve is supposed to represent a large (preferably infinite) number of suppliers, who are all competing with one another on price, which of course is not generally the case and neglects power imbalances.

The classic defence against such arguments is to assert that the law of supply and demand holds *ceteris paribus* (other things being equal), so if you hold supply constant, at least for a while, in your mind, then the demand curve makes sense. Lionel Robbins wrote in 1932 that 'Nobody in his senses would hold that the laws of mechanics were invalidated if an experiment designed to illustrate them were interrupted by an earthquake.'[21] But the point is that in economics, nothing is held constant. As the philosopher

Hans Albert et al. noted, the *ceteris paribus* clause 'here produces something of an absolute alibi, since, for every apparently deviating behavior, some altered factors can be made responsible. This makes the statement untestable, and its informational content decreases to zero.'[22]

The importance of these curves in mainstream economics cannot be overstated, not just because they form the basis of the large-scale macroeconomic economic models used by policy-makers, but also because they enshrine and justify a view of how markets work. In particular they underpin the assumption of equilibrium, since if the curves exist, then they can be used to argue that prices will be driven towards a unique and stable intersection. Economists sometimes try to modify them, for example by accounting for 'market failures' like imperfect competition, missing information, or behavioural effects of the sort discussed in Chapter 6 – as Paul Krugman wrote, 'We start with rational behaviour and market equilibrium as a baseline, and try to get economic dysfunction by tweaking that baseline at the edges' – but this is like the ancient astronomers adding epicycles (small circles that move around the circumference of larger circular orbits) to their geocentric models of the cosmos in order to get a better fit with observations.[23] Phrasing such effects as market failures and dysfunctions also makes them seem like one-off issues, while holding up the abstract vision of the perfect market as an ideal.

Any mathematical model involves simplifications and abstraction. Even in quantum physics it is debated whether the quantum wave function is 'real' or just a useful modelling device.[24] The problem comes when economists take these curves literally, and use them to deduce things like the existence of a stable equilibrium, for which there is no evidence either. The lines of supply and demand are like the crystalline spheres which were once believed to hold the planets in place. To make these models more realistic, we need to concentrate on something much more basic, that we can actually see: transactions.

House shopping

To get a sense of how transactions work, let's start with the largest purchase that most people make, which is a house. When you go to view a house for sale, the first thing you will notice is that the market hasn't cleared – because the house is still for sale. You will also notice that there is not an infinite number of suppliers – in fact there is only one, though a few similar houses may also be available in the same area. Finally, you don't have a demand curve specifying how many houses you will buy as a function of price – you have a budget, with maybe a bit of flexibility.

If you like the house, then you can submit an offer. The amount will depend on your assessment of the house's worth, not just now but also in the future. So you care about the current price – i.e. what the house will fetch now – but also the price momentum – how it is changing, and whether it will fetch more or less in a year's time. Your estimate of the current price will probably be based on comparison with similar properties, though you might also take other factors into account such as the ratio of price to rent, which gives an idea of how the house price relates to what you could earn by renting it out. This is similar to the price-earnings ratio for a stock. Your estimate of the price momentum will be based on a general sense of whether the market is hot or cold, informed perhaps by statistics showing how prices in the area have changed over time.

These estimates for price and momentum will also depend on what you see when you view the house – and not just the state of the roof or the quality of the kitchen counter. If you are the only person to show up for the open house and the owner appears eager to sell, then you might submit a lower offer; but if the open house is a crush, then you may get caught up in the excitement and submit a much higher offer. Finally, if you are borrowing money to make the purchase, then the maximum amount at your disposal will also depend on perceptions about the housing market, since banks are more willing to extend credit during boom times.

Suppose now that you do submit an offer. If it is rejected outright, then all you know is that, rightly or wrongly, the owner values their house more highly than you do. If the offer is accepted, perhaps after some negotiation or a bidding process, then – at least at the instant the transaction is completed – the price of the house is a known quantity. This information will have an impact on the prices of similar houses in the area, and therefore on their price momentum. For example, if your low-ball offer is accepted, then that might spur other realtors working in the area to suggest clients lower their prices; if you pay over asking, then in some countries at least, a sign reflecting that fact will soon adorn the house's front yard.

The house purchase does not therefore represent some neat intersection between two set lines. Instead, it is something more akin to a delicate measurement of a quantum system. The process may not be quite so tidy – for example, one party might later decide to try to pull out, leading to legal complications – but if all goes according to plan, what was vague and uncertain will be reduced to a single number. This is seen more clearly when we look at an institution which has been specially designed to facilitate such measurements – the stock market.

Taking stock

The word 'stock' originally came from the valuable part of the tally stick. It later came to refer to a financial security – also known as shares or equities – that signifies ownership in a corporation and entitles the owner to part of the corporation's assets and earnings.

Stocks are traded in stock markets by matching buying and selling orders, sometimes through an intermediary such as a stockbroker. The ask prices are the prices that sellers are advertising for immediate purchase, while the bid price is the price that buyers are advertising. The difference between the two is called the bid-ask spread.

The table below shows a sample order book for a hypothetical stock, with offers to buy shares on the left, and sell on the right. So what is the price of the stock?

Bid price (buyer)		Ask price (seller)	
Price per share	Number of shares	Price per share	Number of shares
$15.70	1,000	$15.90	1,000
$15.55	2,000	$16.00	1,000
$15.40	2,000	$16.20	7,000
$15.25	8,000	$16.25	1,000
$15.10	1,000	$16.30	2,000

The first thing you notice is that the bid prices are $15.70 or lower, while the ask prices are $15.90 or higher, so they don't intersect. There isn't, for example, someone trying to buy the stock for $16.00. This makes sense, because otherwise that transaction would presumably already have occurred, and it would no longer be in the order book. So for a sale to take place, either a seller or a buyer has to adjust their price.

A typical estimate for the stock's price would be the average of the highest bid and the lowest ask, which in this case is $15.80, with some random uncertainty to reflect the fact that the actual price will depend on the details of the transaction. But the correct answer is to say that there is no well-defined price, until the moment that a transaction actually takes place. All we have is a range of possible prices. As an extreme case, if a sudden piece of news about the company emerges, then offers to buy (or sell) might suddenly disappear, in which case the price is completely uncertain. During the 'flash crash' of 2010, Apple shares were briefly quoted at $100,000, which just meant that no one was selling. The real price of the stock can only be determined through transactions, which act as measurement events.

The order book also gives information about the stock's momentum – for example, if there are many more buyers than sellers, then one might predict that the price is likely to rise – but again this is not confirmed until a transaction occurs. The situation is therefore analogous to the measurement process in quantum physics. Indeed, it can be argued that the correct way to model the system mathematically is to evoke the formal structure of quantum physics.[25] Instead of the conventional approach of treating asset price as a random variable, which is well-defined but subject to random fluctuations, it makes more sense to model the price with a quantum wave function. We return to this in Chapter 6, but for now let us just see how the transaction process works in practice.

Suppose that you are an investor who is considering whether or not to purchase shares. If you are a 'value' investor, then what you care about is price. You have studied the company, pored over its business plan, earnings statements, corporate updates, and so on, and think you have a good idea of what it is worth. On the other hand, if you are a 'momentum' investor, then what you care about more is the direction of the price. If the price is ascending, then you want to hop on for the ride, but if it is falling, you keep away. Or perhaps you take a combination of these approaches, trying to guess whether the stock has peaked or is in danger of collapse. Today many trades are carried out by computer algorithms which make such predictions based on patterns in data. Or perhaps you are purchasing the stock because you like the name of the company, or because it is part of an index, or any other reason.

Different traders (human or otherwise) will therefore come to different conclusions about the stock; indeed, it is this difference which makes markets work, because otherwise the price would never change and there would be no one wanting to buy or sell. At the same time, though, traders influence each other's decisions. You might be buying the share because of a tip in a newspaper, or from a friend. Algorithms also share the same strategies and copy what others are doing. Momentum investors will buy exactly because everyone else is buying. As seen in Chapter 6, it isn't just wildebeest that suffer from a herd mentality.

In any case, suppose that you decide to buy a small number of shares in this company, say 100. You see that the best selling price for that number of shares is $15.90. The cost of the transaction is therefore $1,590.00 (plus commission). However, if you want to buy 10,000 shares – perhaps you represent an institutional investor – then the situation is more complicated. According to the order book, and working from the best price down, you can buy:

1,000 shares at $15.90 = $15,900
1,000 shares at $16.00 = $16,000
7,000 shares at $16.20 = $113,400
1,000 shares at $16.25 = $16,250

… for a total of 10,000 shares for $161,550, which gives an average price of $16.16 per share (though again this price is only hypothetical until the purchase is complete).

The average price is therefore higher if you choose to buy many shares than if you only buy a small number (unless of course you can use your institutional clout to obtain lower prices). The reason is that you are getting a more accurate measurement of the true stock price. When you only want a small number of shares, it might be easy to find someone to sell you them at a low cost; but if you want to buy a lot of shares, then you involve more sellers, and are therefore conducting a much better poll of the true state of the market. At the same time, though, the act of purchasing is changing the momentum of the stock, because it is acting as a new price point in its evolution. This in turn will affect the decisions of other investors, and therefore the price at the next transaction.[26] As in quantum physics, a measurement of the system affects what is being measured.

Of course this is a simplified picture, because the order book itself does not stay still, but changes and adapts as transactions take place. Firms acting as 'market makers' act as intermediaries between buyers and sellers, taking their cut from the price difference. Many high-speed trading algorithms work by what amounts to queue-jumping: sensing interest in a stock, they insert themselves into the order book, make a purchase, and sell it on quickly to the next in line, like a ticket scalper. The emergent result can be highly complex, nonlinear behaviour, epitomised by the sudden and extreme flash crashes which such algorithms occasionally inflict on markets.

Right versus left

The process of measuring a stock price is therefore similar to the process, described in Chapter 1, of measuring an electron's position by bouncing photons off it, which changes its momentum. The difference in finance is that, instead of firing photons, we are firing electronic money objects. Heisenberg's solution to this problem was to give up on the idea that things like a particle's position and momentum have some independent meaning when they are not observed: all we have are particular observations, such as the vapour trail left by a particle passing through a cloud chamber (an early kind of particle detector). Even here, though, the measurements have an intrinsic uncertainty: 'We had always said so glibly that the path of an electron in the cloud chamber could be observed', Heisenberg wrote. 'But perhaps what we really observed was something much less. Perhaps we merely saw a series of discrete and ill-defined spots through which the electron had passed.'[27] The same could be said of the price gyrations of a stock: all we observe is a sequence of transactions, never the stock itself.

Money therefore acts in markets as a measurement device: a means to collapse the estimate of an asset's value down to a single point, akin to the process of wave function collapse which occurs during quantum measurement. Rather than measuring labour, or utility, it is measuring money, which in quantum economics is treated as a fundamental quantity (it might be made-up, but so is the economy, and money at least has well-defined units). Like a photon, a money object is not an inert particle, but a quantum entity in its own right which affects what is being measured.

This measurement process is most obvious for assets traded on relatively open markets, such as stocks, which is why finance was one of the first areas to experiment with the quantum formalism. However, it applies to every single transaction, including the cookies you bought as a child: the store had an ask price, and the coins you held in your hand were the offer, but only in purchasing the cookie was the price confirmed. A union asks for one pay rise, the employer offers another. The economy as a whole can be viewed as a giant market where producers' asks are being reconciled with consumers' offers. As individuals we may usually feel like price-takers, paying whatever our budget can afford, but as a group we act also as price-makers. Our bids are constrained and channelled by price lists and conventions, but nothing is set in stone, and there is always an element of uncertainty. And supply and demand cannot be neatly separated, but are two aspects of a coupled system.

The quantum approach therefore challenges our ontological basis for understanding the economy. Reductionist models always try to express a system in terms of some elementary unit, which is acted on by known forces. In classical physics, the basic unit was the atom, which was a solid object with a well-defined mass and location. In classical economics, it was the atomistic individual, with value determined by labour. Neoclassical economics substituted utility for labour, but otherwise retained the same framework. What counted in this picture was not money but the exchange of goods and labour in a barter system, with price acting as a unifying metric. In quantum economics, however, the only things that have a well-defined numerical value are money objects; prices in contrast are seen as the emergent result of transactions, their uncertain nature reflecting the fluid and sometimes unstable link between number and value which is at the core of money.

This is unsettling, because it seems to imply that the economy has no solid underpinning; but on the other hand, it could be very liberating. One of the side effects of the quantum revolution in the early twentieth century was to inspire artists such as Wassily Kandinsky, who wrote that 'the collapse of the atom model was equivalent, in my soul, to the collapse of the whole world. Suddenly the thickest walls fell. I would not have been amazed if a stone appeared before my eye in the air, melted, and became invisible.'[28] He went on to found abstract art. The work of surrealist artists such as André Breton, Salvador Dalí, and Marcel Duchamp – whose 1912 painting 'Nude Descending a Staircase, No. 2' graced the cover of one of Heisenberg's books – was also influenced by the new physics.

Whether the quantum viewpoint applied to economics will push economists, or for that matter artists, to these heights of creativity remains to be seen, but it certainly has implications for the way we model the economy. Curves of supply and demand are not real, but at the same time they are much more than some kind of useful fiction; instead they are imaginary entities that were designed to represent a picture, or aspirational vision, of how markets, when properly competitive and free from external distortions, drive prices to a stable and optimal equilibrium. They also allowed economists to build up elaborate models of the entire economy based on so-called microfoundations, which represent the actions of individual economic agents. The models acknowledge uncertainty to an extent, but simulate it by making random perturbations to the parameters, while assuming that they follow a known and well-behaved statistical distribution. (As Samuelson explained in 1969, this neutered version of uncertainty was required in order for economics to be considered a 'hard science'.[29]) And they exclude or downplay money – a step typically described as an 'intellectual jump' or an 'intellectual strategy' as if it is a brilliant masterstroke.[30]

These models reflect the general desire, going back at least to Adam Smith, to reduce the economy to a set of Newtonian, mechanistic rules.[31] They are a creature of the left-hemisphere view of the world (see box below), which is characterised by the scholar and psychiatrist Iain McGilchrist as 'rigid, rarified, mechanical, governed by explicit laws'.[32] And allegiance to these rules, even as they collide with empirical data such as the failed forecasts discussed in Chapter 8, is maintained by confabulation – again a specialty of the left hemisphere, which when isolated in experiments will not only 'insist on its theory at the expense of getting things wrong, but it will later cheerfully insist that it got it right'.[33] The quantum world view, in contrast, is more aligned with the right hemisphere's affinity for uncertainty and complexity. Mainstream economics makes much of its microfoundations, but when you look at them closely they disappear into the mist.

Of course, one could argue that the whole point of economics is to reduce the economy to a set of mechanistic laws in order to make predictions. The thing that makes economics different from the other social sciences is that it deals directly with numbers, which is an advantage in this regard, but as we will see later, the predictive track record of such models is poor. Our focus here on the importance of money and transactions suggests a couple of alternative approaches. One method that has become increasingly popular since the crisis of 2007–08, known as agent-based modelling, is to model individual agents separately. Each agent – which could represent a person, a group, or a firm – has unique preferences, which are not static but can vary with time or include a random component, and furthermore agents can influence each other's behaviour, not based on but still mirroring the collective dance of quantum particles. The economy therefore emerges indirectly as a result of agent behaviour. Agent-based models of stock markets and housing markets have managed to reproduce, for example, the characteristic boom-bust nature of such markets, as heterogeneous agents representing individual investors interact and influence each other's decisions. It is therefore not very meaningful in these models to speak of pure independence or average behaviour or set supply and demand curves.

Another option is to take a top-down approach which takes emergent properties at face value. Instead of trying to produce a realistic economy by simulating agents, one can just concentrate on a few key variables. Or one can go 'full quantum' and model markets using the formalism of quantum mechanics. We return to these topics of economic modelling in Chapter 8. But whichever technique is used, one always needs to remember that the economy is an uncertain, dynamic system which is not automatically driven to a stable equilibrium. This is illustrated in the next chapter, when we turn to another kind of supply/demand problem – that of money itself.

Split brain

One of the most obvious physical features of the human brain is that it is divided down the middle into two hemispheres, the left and right, which are joined by a bundle of nerve fibres known as the corpus callosum. In the 1960s, psychologist Roger Sperry and others discovered – through experiments on split-brain patients whose corpus callosum had been severed as a treatment for epilepsy – that the two hemispheres could be addressed separately, and that when they were, they seemed to have completely different specialties: those of the left were 'highly verbal and mathematical, performing with analytic, symbolic, computerlike, sequential logic', while those of the right were 'nonverbal, nonmathematical and nonsequential in nature. They were largely spatial and imagistic, of the kind where a single picture or mental image is worth a thousand words.'[34]

This discovery led to the popular meme that, for instance, artists are 'right-brained' and accountants are 'left-brained'; which in turn led to the picture being debunked because the situation is far more complex, given that both sides of a healthy non-divided brain are in constant communication with each other, and tasks are usually shared. However, experimental evidence continued to accrue showing, not only that the two hemispheres had different roles in cognitive processes, but that they were involved in a kind of competition or power struggle. Furthermore, according to Iain McGilchrist, a major shift in 'hemispheric balance' appeared to have occurred in Western society along with the widening use – thanks to those Mesopotamian accountants – of both writing and money, with the result that the left hemisphere was now firmly in charge.[35]

As McGilchrist notes, 'Money changes our relationships with one another in predictable ways.' For example, it reduces things like gift exchange to monetary transactions where 'the exchange is instantaneous, based on equivalence, and the emphasis not on relationship, but on utility or profit'.[36] This is compatible with the viewpoint of the left hemisphere, for which 'space is not something lived, experienced through the body, and articulated by personal concerns as it is for the right hemisphere, but something symmetrical, measured and positioned according to abstract measures'.[37] But as McGilchrist notes, it also suggests a comparison with the wave/particle aspects of matter: the left hemisphere searches for closed, fixed answers, while the right hemisphere takes an open, holistic stance, and deals in possibilities: 'it needs to be "collapsed" into the present, as the wave function "collapses" under observation.'[38]

Money, as shown in this book, is therefore the left hemisphere's way of reducing the fuzzy, indeterminate notion of value to a single number that it knows how to work with. It is a tool for our own mental version of wave function collapse.

CHAPTER 5

THE MONEY BOMB

So how do banks create money? The answer to that question comes as quite a surprise to most people. When you borrow from a bank, the bank credits your bank account. The deposit – the money – is created by the bank the moment it issues the loan. The bank does not transfer the money from someone else's bank account or from a vault full of money. The money lent to you by the bank has been created by the bank itself – out of nothing.

Jon Nicolaisen, Deputy Governor of the
Bank of Norway, in a 2017 speech[1]

Neoclassical economics views the economy as an inherently self-stabilising system. Maybe the reason is because it doesn't take money into account. This chapter draws on the work of dissident economists such as Frederick Soddy and Hyman Minsky to explore the creative, dynamic, but also fragile nature of our modern financial system; and asks why the quantum power of money in the economy has been suppressed in mainstream economics.

As discussed in Chapter 3, money is created when banks issue money objects – be they coins, sticks, paper notes, or electronic cybermoney. This is obviously a very important, not to mention lucrative, business – after all, the best way to make money is literally to make it. But because mainstream economics sees money as little more than a passive intermediary for exchange, it has

traditionally paid little attention to the process of money creation
– and it is exactly this neglect of the power of money that makes
it potentially so dangerous. An early illustration was provided by
John Law, the Scottish mathematician who was taken on as a sort
of financial consultant by the Regent of France following the death
of King Louis XIV in 1715.

The king on his death had left his court saddled with enormous
debts for various projects (see palace at Versailles) and the country was in need of money. Law's theory, though, was that money
objects were just inert 'Signs of Transmission' so they didn't have
to be made of precious metal. Printed paper would be just as good.

The Regent wasn't entirely convinced, but allowed Law to set up
the small Banque Générale, on condition that he financed it himself. Its banknotes, which at first were issued against coin deposits,
were so successful that they actually traded at a small premium,
being easier to handle than coins. In 1718 the bank was nation-
alised, becoming the Banque Royale. Which was when Law did
two things: he delinked the banknotes from reserves of precious
metals, turning the money into a fiat currency. And he established
the Mississippi Company, whose stocks could be bought using the
notes, and which had exclusive trading rights over the enormous
Mississippi river area.

The combination of fiat currency and stock market speculation
turned out to be a potent one. Interest in the Mississippi Company
was fuelled by rumours of huge deposits of gold, and its share price
soared in concert with the money supply. In a sense, the money
was backed by gold again, but it was imaginary gold. Law, suddenly
the richest man in the world, arranged for the company to buy the
national debt and take over the collection of taxes – but by then
his System, as he called it, was already starting to unravel, as inflation picked up and people began to lose faith in the Mississippi
Company. The result was a run on the bank, a crash in the shares,

and a general economic disaster. Law was exiled to Venice, and French banks avoided the word *banque* until the late nineteenth century, preferring names such as *caisse* or *société*.[2]

As Adam Smith summed it up in *The Wealth of Nations* in 1776: 'The idea of the possibility of multiplying paper to almost any extent was the real foundation of what is called the Mississippi scheme, the most extravagant project both of banking and stock-jobbing that, perhaps, the world ever saw.' He might have been surprised to find out that Law's System would turn out to be the blueprint for our modern financial system – complete with dramatic booms and busts, and the idea that money objects are just inert 'Signs of Transmission'. (Today of course it is bitcoin that is called 'the mother of all bubbles' and 'not unlike the Mississippi land bubble', so maybe in a couple of centuries we will all be using cryptocurrencies.[3])

Law's System, version II

While Law's work had the effect of inoculating the French against financial innovation for some time, it was more warmly received across the ocean in the United States, where the new colonial governments were struggling with a similar shortage of cash. One enthusiast was a young Pennsylvania printer called Benjamin Franklin, who in 1729 at the age of 23 wrote (and printed) a pamphlet entitled 'A Modest Enquiry into the Nature and Necessity of a Paper-Currency'. Following Law, whose work he had read, Franklin pointed out that the money supply needs to be able to expand along with the economy.[4] This couldn't be done with precious metal – especially when its quantity was tightly controlled by colonial masters – but it was no problem if the money were made of paper.

Experiments with paper money in Pennsylvania and elsewhere were quite successful, but were soon stamped out by the

British parliament, who insisted on gold or silver for the payment of taxes. Franklin blamed the resulting economic contraction for the American Revolutionary War of 1775. After the war, the government tried to set up a central bank along the lines of the Bank of England, but the project met more resistance than in England and lasted only twenty years. In the meantime, private banks were proliferating: the 1859 edition of *Hodges' Genuine Bank Notes of America* listed 9,916 notes issued by 1,365 banks.[5] It was only in 1913 – following a number of financial crises such as the 'Panic of 1907' – that the government finally managed to establish a central bank with the cooperation of financiers. It was called the Federal Reserve.

While the Fed, as it is sometimes called, sounds as if it is part of the federal government, it is actually an independent not-for-profit corporation consisting of twelve regional Federal Reserve banks, each of which in turn is owned by a consortium of commercial banks. If you ask 'Who owns the Federal Reserve?' then, as in quantum physics, there is no fixed answer, since it is part of an entangled system. As the Fed's own website acknowledges, 'The Federal Reserve System is not "owned" by anyone.'[6] At the same time, though, it is clear that the real power lies with the consortium of commercial banks, given that they get to vote on and participate in the Fed's banking operations.

The Fed is now a bit over a century old. For about half that time, it operated under the gold standard system, so the paper money was backed by gold which was held in its vaults under Manhattan or in the Fort Knox depository. At the Bretton Woods conference in July 1944, the US dollar was set as a reference currency which could be redeemed for gold bars at a rate of $35 per ounce. In the early 1960s, though, the system came under strain, in part because the gold supply couldn't keep pace with economic expansion, but also because the US government was printing money to fund its military programmes, including the Vietnam War and the Cold War. On 15 August 1971, President Richard Nixon unilaterally imposed wage and price controls, an import surcharge, and – like Law before him – halted direct convertibility to gold. By November of that year, the price of gold had reached $100. Soon after, the Bretton Woods currency system ended, and exchange rates between major currencies were allowed to float freely.

Nixon's sudden abandonment of the system became known as the 'Nixon shock'. In a way, though, the gold standard had already been on the way out for a while. Gold bullion reserves were important for things like stabilising exchange rates between countries, but gold coins had largely disappeared from use after the First World War; and at least on a national level finance was largely dominated by private banks, which had the ability to create their own money through the magic of fractional reserve banking, thus fractionally diluting its relationship to metal. This may explain why in 1963 the words 'PAYABLE TO THE BEARER ON DEMAND' were replaced with 'IN GOD WE TRUST' on newly issued US dollar notes.

As mentioned above, money has historically switched between its real and virtual phases only once or twice per millennium, and the process is not immediate. Indeed, in many respects our money system still seems to have one foot in the gold standard era, in the sense that institutions such as central banks have changed remarkably little, at least in terms of appearances.

Nothing for something

The difference between John Law's System and our current system, or even the one in force during the later stages of the gold standard, is only one of degree. And the fact that money creation is controlled by private banks continues to create some perverse incentives. One of the first to point out the dangers of fractional reserve banking, even before the general adoption of full fiat currencies, was the English chemist Frederick Soddy. After being awarded a Nobel Prize in 1921 for his work on the basic properties of radiation, he decided to devote his time and intellect to improving the field of economics, which he saw as a pseudoscience. In his 1926 book *Wealth, Virtual Wealth, and Debt*, Soddy defined money as 'the NOTHING you get for SOMETHING before you can get ANYTHING'. Money objects were obtained in exchange for valuable goods and services, so they served as a store of that value, like a battery. Soddy described money wealth as Virtual Wealth, and actual goods and services as Real Wealth.

The problem, as discussed also in Chapter 2, is that virtual wealth is based on number, while real wealth isn't. Or as Soddy put it, 'The Virtual Wealth of a community is not a physical but an imaginary negative wealth quantity. It does not obey the laws of conservation, but is of psychological origin.' In one of his examples, he notes that if a farmer has two pigs, it is twice as good as having one pig. Paper money, in contrast, represents a debt, so it is a negative quantity, which does not exist in the real world: 'It is impossible to see minus two pigs.'[7] Having a house and a job is real wealth, but owning shares in the Mississippi Company is virtual wealth.

Furthermore, under fractional reserve banking, money is created by private banks and lent out at interest – a power grab that Soddy saw as a threat to the state: 'The "money power" which has been able to overshadow ostensibly responsible government, is not the power of the merely ultra-rich, but is nothing more nor less than a new technique designed to create and destroy money by adding and withdrawing figures in bank ledgers, without the slightest concern for the interests of the community or the real rôle that money ought to perform therein ... To allow it to become a source of revenues to private issuers is to create, first, a secret and illicit arm of the government and, last, a rival power strong enough ultimately to overthrow all other forms of government.'[8]

Because interest-bearing debts increase exponentially for ever, while in the real world non-living things generally don't, the Virtual Wealth expands until it dwarfs Real Wealth to such a degree that a crisis occurs: people lose confidence in the system, and they all attempt to cash in their virtual chips at the same time. The result is financial disaster. Soddy was explicitly motivated by what he saw as the banking sector's threat to world peace – a danger which was all the more extreme, given the possibility he foresaw of nuclear weapons.[9]

It is understandable that Soddy would have been one of the first people to warn of the dangers of both uncontrolled nuclear fission and uncontrolled private banking. Both of them involve inherently unstable positive feedback effects, in which a process builds on itself until it ultimately spirals out of control. His warnings were borne out during his lifetime by the Great Depression, the resultant rise in Germany of Nazism, and the use in the Second World War of nuclear weapons.

Going critical

Soddy, along with the New Zealand-born physicist Ernest Rutherford, had earned his Nobel prize for showing, while working at McGill University, that radioactivity is due to the transmutation of elements. During beta decay, for example, a neutron transforms into a proton, and ejects an electron and an anti-neutrino. Because neutrons and protons were considered fundamental particles, this meant that radiation was the result of a kind of alchemy that changed one substance into another. Naturally occurring uranium decays in a series of steps to form substances including lead, polonium, radium, and radon.

As discussed in Chapter 1, radioactive decay is a quantum process which has no classical analogue. According to classical physics, if the nucleus of an atom were stable, there is no reason why it should suddenly become unstable. In quantum physics, though, there is no such immutable bond. Particles, Houdini-like, can escape their constraints, and one element can morph mysteriously into another.

A similar puzzle afflicts mainstream economics. As with Aristotelian physics, mainstream economics is based on the idea of stability, and assumes that free markets drive prices towards their natural resting place (see the box at the end of this chapter). But if that were really the case, then every asset would be perfectly priced and there would be little incentive to trade – which seems incompatible with the fact that trillions are spent every day betting on currencies alone.

When a uranium atom decays it releases both energy (because some of its mass is converted to energy) and neutrons. If these neutrons strike other uranium atoms nearby, then those atoms will also decay – releasing still more energy and more neutrons. If a sufficient amount of the material, known as the critical mass, is compressed together, then the reaction becomes self-sustaining and grows exponentially. In its controlled form, this effect is exploited in nuclear reactors to create heat and generate electrical power. Or alternatively it can be allowed to run free, in which case the result is a nuclear bomb.

Money has a similarly transformatory nature. It might not be able to turn neutrons into protons, or uranium into lead, but as we have seen, it can change its host from wood tallies to gold coins to banknotes. It also contains a great deal of stored energy, because creating money requires work. In ancient Greece, the work was supplied by slaves working in mines. With tallies, the work was supplied by the sovereign, exerting his power to impose debts on his subjects. This is why money has long been associated with the state and particularly the military. Cybercurrencies rely instead on constant network surveillance, which is work of another form (for one thing, it uses a lot of electricity).

With money objects, this power exerts itself – not by physically blowing up the world – but by transforming the world in its own image, in another kind of alchemy. Just as money objects have both a virtual and a real side, but lean always towards the virtual – their point, after all, is to put a number on things, a value on value – so the economy tends to split into two distinct components: the real economy where things are made and services supplied, and the virtual economy in financial centres such as Wall Street where symbols are manipulated. The creation of money through bank credit is therefore free to grow exponentially until, as Soddy warned, the gap between the virtual and the real reaches breaking point.

Perhaps the biggest problem with fractional reserve banking, though, is that it turns out not to be a true description of the financial system. The reality is even more unstable – as central banks admitted only in the last few years.

Fairy dust

As described theoretically in textbooks such as Mankiw's, fractional reserve banking apportions most of the job of creating money from the sovereign to the private banking system, but the central bank is still firmly in control. However, Soddy's warnings take on a new dimension when we consider that the practice today is rather different. In reality, private banks are free to create as much money as they like by issuing loans, subject only to things like regulatory or self-imposed capital requirements. The vast majority of money (in the UK, for example, about 97 per cent) is created by private banks lending money for things like mortgages on houses.[10]

One person to point out the role of banks in money creation was the Austrian economist Joseph Schumpeter. In his 1934 *Theory of Economic Development*, he defined entrepreneurs as innovators who come up with ideas and realise them in high-growth companies; a process which usually involves upfront expenses and the need to borrow money. He argued that the primary funding mechanism was money creation by banks: 'It is always a question, not of transforming purchasing power which already exists in someone's possession, but of the creation of new purchasing power out of nothing.'[11] In his final work, published after his death in 1950, he complained that 'It proved extraordinarily difficult for economists to recognize that bank loans and bank investments do create deposits.'[12]

Other commentators have made similar remarks over the years. Bizarrely, though, this fact was only formally acknowledged by central banks quite recently. Indeed, as economist Richard Werner remarks, 'The topic of bank credit creation has been a virtual taboo for the thousands of researchers of the world's central banks during the past half century.'[13] In 2014 the Bank of England created a considerable stir in the financial press when it broke this taboo by noting that 'The reality of how money is created today differs from the description found in some economics textbooks ... the central bank does not fix the amount of money in circulation, nor is central bank money "multiplied up" into more loans and deposits.'[14] Adair Turner similarly observed in 2014 that 'Economic textbooks and academic papers typically describe how banks take deposits from savers and lend the money on to borrowers. But as a description of what banks actually do this is severely inadequate. In fact they create credit money and purchasing power.'[15] Or as Werner drily concluded the same year, 'The money supply is created as "fairy dust" produced by the banks individually, "out of thin air"'.[16] (See also the Bank of Norway quote from 2017 at the start of this chapter.)

The loan creation process helps explain why this freshly-created money tends to go into things like real estate – where loans are apparently backed by assets – rather than funding Schumpeter's risky entrepreneurs, or new technologies where the 'asset' might seem to have little proven value.* It also explains why money seems to dry up in a recession. Since money is created by private banks when they issue debts, a flip side is that when the debts are repaid, the money just disappears back into the void, like a particle annihilating with its anti-particle. As noted by the Bank of England, 'Just as taking out a new loan creates money, the repayment of bank loans destroys money ... Banks making loans and consumers repaying them are the most significant ways in which bank deposits are created and destroyed in the modern economy.'[17] So unless new loans are constantly created to replace these funds, the money supply will shrink, further exacerbating a downturn.

Of course one might ask why it took quite so long to clear up the misconceptions promoted by what the Bank of England called 'some economics textbooks' (for 'some' read 'major') on the topic of money, or why the ability to create what Turner calls 'potentially infinite' funds in this way was largely 'written out of the script of modern macro-economics'.[18] As Werner notes, the fact that 'such important insights as bank credit creation could be made to disappear from the agenda and even knowledge of the majority of economists over the course of a century delivers a devastating verdict on the state of economics and finance today. As a result, the

---

* In the UK, for example, about a half of bank lending typically goes to mortgages, and only a sixth goes to non-financial corporates (aka the productive economy), with the rest going to other financial corporations and things like credit card debt and overdrafts. Data from the Bank of England: https://www.bankofengland.co.uk/statistics/visual-summaries/money-and-credit-statistics

public understanding of money has deteriorated as well. Today, the vast majority of the public is not aware that the money supply is created by banks, that banks do not lend money, and that each bank creates new money when it extends a loan.' This is true even of policy-makers: according to one 2017 poll of UK Members of Parliament, 'Only 15% of MPs were aware that new money is created when banks make loans, and existing money is destroyed when members of the public repay loans.'[19]

One reason, suggested by Werner, is 'the predominance of the hypothetico-deductive research methodology in economics, which begins by posing axioms and assumptions'.[20] In other words, economists are not letting empirical facts get in the way of a good theory. Another explanation is that the mechanistic worldview is fundamentally hierarchical, because it views systems as being built up in an ordered fashion from individual parts. With this analogy, it makes sense to see the central bank as a central control unit for the financial system, from which power radiates out to the parts, just as a general submits orders to the troops. From a quantum viewpoint, however, the parts are better viewed as making up a coherent whole, whose function is characterised by feedback loops, so there is no single central node.

The most obvious reason for omitting the pivotal role of banks, though, was because economists *wanted* to keep money out of the equation. Only by doing so could they maintain the pretence that the economy is some kind of barter system based on rational exchange. Just as subjectivity is considered taboo in sociology, so the emotion-laden topic of money creation is taboo in economics. More troubling, perhaps, are 'indications that attempts were made to obfuscate, as if authors were at times wilfully trying to confuse their audience and lead them away from the important insight that each individual bank creates new money when it extends credit.'[21] We return to this later.

The levitation trick

To see how this magical money creation works in practice, let's return again to the example of purchasing a house – an entity which in many ways exemplifies the real/virtual split, since it combines the psychological properties of owning a 'real' home with the financial properties of an estate (hence real estate). We'll suppose that the market is hot so you are willing to pay a high price on the expectation that prices will soon rise further still. In fact, we'll suppose you are in Toronto in March 2017, when house prices – which at least in the detached market mostly reflect the price of land – have surged by 33 per cent in the past year alone. The only thing holding you back is that in order to qualify for the best mortgage, you have to make a significant down-payment of 20 per cent, which you can't possibly afford. Fortunately a secondary lender has agreed to loan you that amount, though at a somewhat punishing interest rate.

Your realtor informs you that the house is going to auction, so you have to show up on the appointed day with the best offer you can make – with a certified cheque for the suitably impressive deposit stapled to it. You therefore call up your bank to arrange a slightly higher loan, which they agree to. In a rising market, the question *how much* often seems to be less about *how much is it worth*, than *how much can you borrow*.

To your delight, you win the auction against seven other would-be buyers! Of course that means you paid well over the average of what a good sample of potential buyers thought the house was worth, but that doesn't matter because everyone knows houses will be at least 20 per cent higher next year anyway. Your bank sends the vendor the funds, and you are the proud owner of a new house/asset.

So what actually happened in monetary terms? When the bank sends the vendor the money, it doesn't scrape together the amount by borrowing it from its clients' savings accounts – it just makes it up by entering it in their computer system. It is like creating a brand-new tally stick. You get the foil – the short end of the stick – meaning you have to pay up over time. Meanwhile the stock – in return for title over the house – is transferred to the vendor, who is now free to go out and spend it. So when you analyse it in these terms, you see that the purchase is far more than some tit-for-tat exchange. An entirely new money object, equal in value to the price of the loan, has been created by the bank. This money then goes out into the economy, and much of it is used for bidding up the prices of homes. The higher prices go, the more money is created, and so on in a positive feedback loop. Eventually the loan is repaid, but that might take 25 years or more, by which time many more new loans will have been created.

According to the quantity theory of money, if too much money is in circulation, the result is inflation. However, because the virtual economy is largely decoupled from the real economy, inflation can occur in the former but not the latter. And because traditional inflation metrics focus only on the real economy, it appears that inflation remains low. This is illustrated by the figure below, which compares the Teranet house price index with a broad measure of money supply in Canada from 1999 (when the index began) until 2017. During this time period, both the house price index and the money supply tripled, while inflation remained negligible and gross domestic product was also relatively stagnant. The most strik-ing – but least remarked – empirical fact about the housing boom is that it was matched by a money boom.* The story was similar in a number of other countries, but Canada's build-up was

* I for one only learned about it while plotting the data myself for *The Evolution of Money*.

unusually smooth and extended in that it was almost unaffected by the financial crisis of 2007–08.

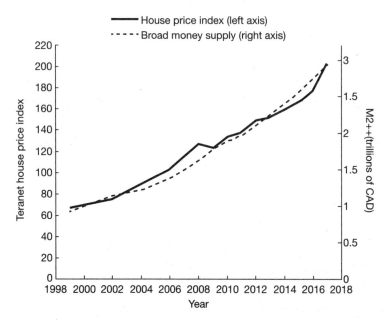

Figure 3. House prices and money supply in Canada both triple in less than twenty years (Statistics Canada).

The point here is not that there is in general a perfect match between money supply growth and house price growth, only that the house price inflation seen in places like Canada can be largely attributed to the feedbacks between money supply and property prices. Real estate is acting like a kind of breeder reactor for money. To understand the dynamics of the process, computations based on the idea that supply and demand of houses drive the system to an optimal equilibrium won't get you very far. And to understand its fragility, you need to appreciate that it is based on a foundation of debt, rather than something more solid like bricks and mortar.

It is often said that some aspects of quantum physics seem magical, for example in the ability of particles to appear out of the void or disappear back into it. Quantum money has similarly magical properties which banks have learned to exploit, as they make houses levitate while convincing their audience that the effect they see is real. An important part of any magic trick is the magician's patter, his ability to distract the audience from what is going on by creating a different narrative. With house prices, the narrative is supplied by people like realtors, banks, and economists, many of whom are employed by banks. For example, according to a 2017 report from the Toronto Real Estate Board, 'Key drivers of record home sales included population growth, low mortgage rates, low unemployment, and above-inflation economic growth'.[22] The head wizard of the central bank, Stephen Poloz, agreed that the rise in house prices is due to 'fundamentals ... The greater Toronto economy is creating five per cent per year more jobs. Population growth is continuing to be strong. The same thing with Vancouver. That automatically generates more demand for housing at a time when there are constraints around supply'.[23] In other words, it all comes down to supply and demand, like in the textbooks. Yet census figures in 2017 showed Toronto growing at its slowest rate in 40 years, while wages were increasing at the slowest rate in twenty years. Mortgage rates were very low, but total consumer debt was also at an all-time high which more than compensated.

Another article in the *Globe and Mail* noted that: 'Mortgage rates are low. Ontario's economy is superheated ... and, to make matters worse, land is in short supply.' In addition, Toronto is becoming a 'world class' city, 'owning a house is now the investment of choice for most of the middle class', and of course, 'Dark words are muttered about how foreign money is to blame'.[24] (That was actually from a 1988 article on a previous housing boom, but not much has changed.) Of course, the boom cycle eventually turns to bust. For any of a number of reasons – government action, buyer fatigue, a rise in interest rates, the collapse of a lending institution, all of which happened in mid-2017 – sentiment can change on a dime. And just as rising house prices lead to more money creation in a self-reinforcing feedback loop, so falling house prices lead to less money creation (though the correlation will be less neat as disruptions work through the system and the central bank tries to compensate).

The dynamics are therefore much the same as with John Law's System. One could argue that the loans are backed by 'real' houses, as opposed to the fictional gold of the Mississippi Company. Indeed, one reason why people prefer to invest in houses rather than assets such as stocks is because they are something physical that they can see and touch, and either live in themselves or rent out to others. But house prices in Toronto and other cities can easily levitate to a point where they far exceed any sensible valuation in terms of things like the ratio of house price to rent. Instead they are better viewed as a financial asset that is hoarded not because of its productive value, but in the hope that it will go up in price. Their value is more virtual than real.

Inflation

As with most forms of inflation, the causes of house price inflation therefore have more to do with the basic mechanics of money creation than any of the reasons typically given. It is a simple banking trick: banks create new money that is used to bid up the price of assets which are then used as the collateral for new loans. It is one example of the credit cycle, whose dynamics are not particularly mysterious and have been clearly explained by a variety of people including, perhaps most famously, the American economist Hyman Minsky.

According to Minsky's Financial Instability Hypothesis, which dates to 1972, the desire for credit tends to increase during an expansion.[25] More money is therefore created through loans, and invested in financial assets, which today usually refers to real estate rather than companies. This investment has the knock-on effect of raising asset prices, which in turn provides collateral for further loans, and so on. Confidence builds on itself as 'Success breeds a disregard of the possibility of failure'. More people are drawn in, with the last being what Minsky called the Ponzi borrower, who can't afford to service interest payments but relies for their financial survival on the borrowed asset increasing in value.

On the surface, everything seems to be going well, but only if you ignore the mounting and destabilising levels of debt. However, at some point – now known as the Minsky moment – people lose faith and stop playing the game. Asset prices stop rising, so speculative borrowers who can't make payments try to cash out. The inflating bubble suddenly collapses.

The role of the central bank is to control this process before it gets out of hand, but its power is limited by a number of factors. One is the fact that since most of the money supply is created by private institutions, it only has indirect control over events. Another is that central banks are eager to step in during an emergency, but are understandably reluctant to spoil what seems like a good thing. The biggest problem, though, is that mainstream economics has left them unable to correctly diagnose the problem, for the simple reason that it ignores the power of money. As a result, rather than improve the situation, their actions can even make it worse.

Because their mandate to control inflation does not usually include asset prices, central banks focus instead on inflation in the real economy, a small amount of which they see as a good thing, if only to avoid its opposite – deflation – which encourages people to hoard money and slows economic activity. Since the 2007–08 crisis, a number of countries have therefore tried to boost inflation by reducing interest rates to near-zero levels, with little success. In 2014, for example, the Governor of the Bank of Japan forecast that inflation should 'reach around the price stability target of 2 per cent toward the end of fiscal 2014 through fiscal 2015' but it apparently didn't get the memo, preferring to remain well under 1 per cent.[26] Similar policies in other countries have helped fuel, not the expected inflation, but only inequality-boosting asset bubbles and a destabilising global explosion in private sector debt.

Central bankers are increasingly admitting that they have no satisfactory model of inflation – as former Fed Governor Daniel Tarullo said in 2017, 'We do not, at present, have a theory of inflation dynamics that works sufficiently well to be of use for the business of real-time monetary policymaking' – but again that is obvious, because they have no satisfactory model of money.[27] Economists look at the circulation of money in aggregate – for example, the quantity theory of money states that the average price level is proportional to the average amount of money in circulation, and assumes that the average velocity of money (the rate at which it changes hands) is stable. However, this is like a meteorologist presenting the average wind speed for a country instead of a chart showing the speed at each location. And because money is treated as little more than a convenient medium of exchange, the main impact of inflation is to introduce some 'friction' into their models, since firms have to constantly update their prices, which leads to loss of efficiency.[28] Models also tend to endow the economy as a whole with perfect rationality and essentially infinite foresight, so they assume that agents take a long view of inflation rather than reacting over more reasonable timescales.

Such drawbacks may explain why central bankers have struggled with too much inflation in things like houses, and not enough in things like wages (and why, when faced with such puzzles, they can only come up with Victorian-sounding platitudes like 'What we do know is the laws of demand and supply have not been repealed').[29] Inflation is better seen as the emergent property of a complex system, whose exact course is as hard to predict as that of something like climate change. The idea that central banks can fine-tune it seems a good example of what behavioural scientists call the 'illusion of control' – but a first step to understanding it is to adequately model the flow of money, including into things like real estate.

Dissidents such as Soddy and Minsky who have drawn attention to the dynamics of money have long been dismissed as 'monetary cranks' or 'banking mystics'.[30] It is no surprise then that most central bankers have long seemed remarkably complacent about the risks in things like real estate, even when, as Dirk Bezemer and Michael Hudson note, 'real estate assets have grown into the largest asset market in all western economies, and the one with the most widespread participation'.[31] An exception is the former Deputy Governor of the Bank of Canada, William White, who noted in 2014: 'We've got the potential to do so much harm by not getting the creation of fiat credit and money right. We've got the capacity to do so much harm that we should be focusing much more on making sure that doesn't happen.'[32] Central banks like to make sage announcements about 'risks to the economy' but one of the biggest risks is their own models.

Given that the actual mechanics of money creation and the credit cycle are rather obvious, it seems strange that they don't get more critical attention. It is like a magic trick which has been explained over and over with slow-motion demonstrations on YouTube videos, but which people are still willing to pay with their life savings to take part in. So how do we bring the money bomb back under control? Can we learn to predict or even prevent its explosions, before metaphorical mushroom clouds appear once again over the financial system?

Stable versus unstable

One approach to modelling complex systems, known as systems dynamics or nonlinear dynamics, uses traditional equations similar to Newton's equations of motion, but allows those equations to incorporate nonlinear effects, which greatly complicates their behaviour. A property of organic systems, from a cell to the human body to the Earth's atmosphere, is that they are characterised by complicated networks of opposing nonlinear feedback loops, which act to amplify or dampen out signals. The same is true of the economy, where the credit cycle, for instance, is a highly nonlinear phenomenon with unstable boom-bust dynamics. An example of this systems dynamics approach is the 'Minsky' model developed by a team led by Steve Keen. His 2017 book *Can We Avoid Another Financial Crisis?* described how this model, which featured only three variables and nine parameters to model key macroeconomic variables, picked out escalating levels of private debt as a risk factor for financial crises. An important feature of the model is that it pays attention to basic accounting principles, such as the flow of money and credit, and explicitly includes the financial sector.

Such a diminutive model might sound like little more than a toy description of the system, but its design reflects a basic reality, which is that as with any mathematical model, the parameters, and the form of the equations, often cannot be pinned down from the data. As the writer of a declassified CIA document – who was charged with an evaluation of systems dynamics – put it in 1975, 'Depending on the functional forms and the parameters we assume, a systems dynamics model can yield vastly different predictions'.[33] It is therefore necessary to use a minimal set of equations that extracts the features of interest.* Sometimes less is more – after all, it doesn't require a complicated model incorporating the intricacies of quantum behaviour to estimate the yield of a nuclear device, and similarly one can build a model of the money creation process without writing out wave equations.

Another technique (discussed also in the previous chapter) is agent-based modelling. One study from a team led by Jean-Philippe Bouchaud found that simulations of a toy economy showed a surprisingly high variation of possible inflation scenarios, depending on factors such as inflation anticipations.[34] In other words, if people expect inflation, then they are likely to get it, in another feedback loop. One can imagine such models being used as a kind of flight-simulator for central bankers. Again their predictive ability is limited by sensitivity to the exact choice of parameters that govern the behaviour of individual agents – 'micro-rules do matter, as they can lead to very different macro-states' – but this just reflects the inherent uncertainty in the system, which itself is useful information for policy-makers. Agent-based models can also be used to motivate simpler models which capture their basic properties.[35]

Finally, as discussed also in Chapter 8, complexity models emphasise data over abstract theory. A starting point in economics, as many heterodox economists have pointed out, is the flow of money and credit.[36] In recent years, mainstream economists have prided themselves on what is sometimes called the 'data revolution'

* Paul Wilmott relates a story about coming across a book called something like 'The Treasury's Model of the UK Economy' which contained 770 equations. As Wilmott notes: 'What you want to do is throw away all but the half dozen most important equations and then accept the inevitable, that the results won't be perfect.' Wilmott, P., and Orrell, D. (2017), *The Money Formula: Dodgy Finance, Pseudo Science, and How Mathematicians Took Over the Markets* (Chichester: Wiley).

as they make more effort to test their theoretical constructs against real data.[37] But a real data revolution occurs when the data is used to falsify key assumptions, such as the related ideas that money is an inert medium of exchange; the financial sector is just an inter-mediary; and the economy is drawn to a stable equilibrium. It is time for more economists to turn their telescopes towards the workings of finance, because those crystalline spheres holding the economy aloft are not made of ether, they are made of money (see box below).

To summarise the main findings of the book so far:

- Like quantum entities, money objects have dual real/virtual properties, which explains their confounding effects on both minds and markets.

- The creation of money is symmetrical in the sense that – like matter and anti-matter – it has two entangled and entangling aspects, representing positive credit and negative debt.

- Market prices are not determined by fixed laws, but are the emergent result of a kind of quantum measurement process.

- The money creation process is highly dynamic and often unstable.

Money can therefore be seen as a quantum system in its own right, with its own versions of duality, measurement, entangle-ment, and so on (interference effects will make their presence felt in Chapter 7). In the second half of the book, we draw on areas such as quantum finance and quantum social science to show how these quantum properties of money feed into the economy as a whole, to often perplexing – but at the same time very familiar – effect.

The crystalline spheres

While neoclassical economics was based on Newtonian mechanics, it also has much in common with an earlier system of thought – that of Aristotle. When Aristotle's work, stored away in the library in Alexandria, was rediscovered by medieval scholars, it offered what appeared to be a complete model of the universe. His ideas formed the basis of the curriculum at the new universities established in cities such as Bologna, Paris and Oxford. He became known simply as The Philosopher, his word taken as gospel truth.

In Aristotle's system, everything this side of the Moon was composed of earth, water, fire, and air, each of which had their own natural level. Earth tended to sink down towards the centre, with water floating on top, air above that, and fire pushing upwards. The celestial bodies rotated around the Earth in crystalline spheres that were made of the fifth element, ether. The tendency of heavy objects to fall downwards reflected their desire to reach their correct level. The speed of fall depended on weight and the density of the medium, and so would be infinite in a vacuum (one reason a vacuum couldn't exist). Things moved horizontally only when externally pushed. The heavens were static apart from the circular rotations of the spheres.

The Aristotelian model began to show cracks during the Renaissance as empirical evidence against it mounted. The sixteenth-century astronomer Tycho Brahe, for example, tracked a comet and showed that it would have smashed through those crystalline spheres, had they existed. Galileo showed that objects of different weight fall at the same speed, apart from frictional effects due to air resistance. He also pointed his telescope at Jupiter and found four moons, which hadn't been mentioned by the Greeks. He called them the Medician Stars after the Medici children he was tutoring.

Like Aristotelian dynamics, neoclassical economics presents an essentially static view of the economy, in which things move only when they are pushed by external forces, such as news or technological developments. According to efficient market theory (Chapter 6), prices don't just seek their natural state, they snap there instantaneously, as if they existed in an Aristotelian vacuum. Instead of crystalline spheres, mainstream economics has made-up lines of supply and demand, which are said to reflect an unobserved quantity called utility. And as discussed in Chapter 2, its theory of money is copied straight from The Philosopher himself.

The theory is also equally resistant to change. One reason that the Aristotelian model persisted so long, according to the author James Hannam, was that it offered 'a complete system of reality', so that 'rejecting any significant chunk of it would cause the whole edifice to collapse'.[38] The same can be said of neoclassical economics, with its interlocked and self-reinforcing ideas of rationality, efficiency, and stability. But as with Aristotelian physics, the theory only holds up so long as you ignore the empirical evidence – and the cracks are looking pretty wide.

PART 2

THE QUANTUM ECONOMY

CHAPTER 6

THE UNCERTAINTY PRINCIPLE

It is in this middle field that economics lies, unaffected
whether by the ultimate philosophy of the electron or
of the soul, and concerned rather with the interaction
with the middle world of life of these two end worlds of
physics and mind in their commonest everyday aspects.
Frederick Soddy, *Cartesian Economics* (1921)

The most fundamental attribute of financial
markets is uncertainty. *Just when you think you*
know what is sure to happen, the financial markets
are about to prove that you are wrong.
Jason Zweig, *The Devil's Financial Dictionary* (2015)

In quantum mechanics, the uncertainty principle states that there is a strict limit on how accurately we can measure a particle's position and momentum – the better we know one, the less we know about the other. In finance, there is a more extreme version, sometimes expressed as 'nobody knows anything'. This chapter shows how the tools used in quantitative finance to measure and analyse risk have their roots in quantum physics, and specifically the methods developed for the nuclear bomb programme after the war (which may explain their tendency to blow up). Today some 'quants', as quantitative analysts are known, are reviving this connection, by showing that market behaviour can be expressed in terms of quantum dynamics. But is this just a computational

convenience, or does it say something important about the markets themselves?

In the year 1905 – in what is sometimes called Albert Einstein's *annus mirabilis*, or miraculous year – the physicist produced five papers for the journal *Annalen der Physik* which together rewrote the rules of physics. The papers covered topics including quantum physics, relativity, and also a way to answer the question, *how much does an atom weigh?*

Einstein approached that problem by considering the random motion of a very small particle as it is buffeted by atoms in a gas or fluid. This phenomenon was known as Brownian motion after the nineteenth-century Scottish botanist Robert Brown, who observed it while viewing pollen grains suspended in water under a microscope. If you could simulate the motion of the particle, then it should be possible to work out the mass of the unseen atoms.

When the atoms collide with the particle, they impart momentum in a random direction. The particle therefore experiences what the statistician Karl Pearson called a random walk. Pearson illustrated the problem using an example of a drunken man walking randomly in an open field. The man takes a step in one direction, then another step in some different direction, and so on, gradually getting further and further away from his starting point. The expected distance travelled is seen to grow with the square root of time. But if you need to find him, 'the most probable place to find a drunken man who is at all capable of keeping on his feet is somewhere near his starting point!'[1]

When Einstein did the calculations for Brownian motion, and compared them with experimental results, he was able to quite accurately estimate how much an atom weighed (the answer was, not much). However, some three decades later, it was discovered that, despite their diminutive stature, atoms could do more than bounce pollen around – they could potentially blow up the world.

Monte Carlo

In 1938, the German scientists Otto Hahn and Fritz Strassman carried out a series of experiments in which they bombarded atoms of uranium-235 with slow-moving neutrons. They had assumed that the extra neutrons would merge with the atoms to form a heavier isotope – but instead, they found that the products were *lighter* than uranium. What happened to the missing atomic mass? It turned out that the neutron had broken the uranium nucleus into two roughly equal portions, but that some of the mass – about a fifth of a proton's worth – was converted via $E=mc^2$ into energy.

The reaction also released two or three free neutrons, which would travel through the material in a random walk, colliding with uranium atoms as they went, and seeding more divisions. As noted earlier, if the quantity of material present was above a certain critical mass of around a few kilograms, the result would be a self-sustaining chain reaction that grew at an exponential rate. Word quickly spread of the momentous discovery – and within days, J. Robert Oppenheimer at the University of California, Berkeley, had sketched out the basic plan for a bomb. He went on to run the Manhattan Project which developed the first nuclear devices, including those detonated in Hiroshima and Nagasaki in 1945. Quantum physics had been weaponised.

After the bombs were dropped, an appalled Einstein reputedly said, 'If I knew they were going to do this, I would have become a shoemaker'.[2] However, the reality is that very few physicists decided to leave the field (an exception was Joseph Rotblat, who left the Manhattan Project and went on to found, with Bertrand Russell, the Pugwash Conferences on Science and World Affairs). Instead, the weapons programme soon led to vast increases in recruitment for nuclear and high-energy physicists, and a focus on developing new techniques for analysing probabilistic systems. The methods of quantum mechanics could be used to compute the decay rate of a radioactive material like uranium or plutonium, while random walk theory was used to predict the motion of neutrons in fissile material, and thus determine the critical mass needed for a nuclear device.

Another key technique was the Monte Carlo method, invented in the late 1940s by Stanislaw Ulam while working on weapons projects at the Los Alamos National Laboratory. Ulam was trying to compute the details of a nuclear chain reaction, but the complexity of the system meant that it was impossible to solve using conventional equations. He therefore hit on the idea of simply simulating the random path of an individual neutron as it bounced around, which was a much more tractable problem, and repeating this many times over.

As an example from another context, suppose you wish to calculate the probability of rolling two sixes in a row. If you studied probability theory, then you know the answer is 1/6 multiplied by itself, or 1/36. But if you were bad at maths and had a lot of time on your hands, you could just repeat the dice-throwing experiment hundreds of times over, and estimate the odds directly by dividing the number of times you roll two sixes, by the total number of trials.

For this problem, it would have been easier to look up the answer if you didn't know it yourself. But for a more complicated probabilistic system – such as a random walk through a nuclear core – it may be impossible to find a neat equation that gives the answer, and the only alternative is to divide it up into a sequence of random operations. In 1946, Ulam explained the idea to the mathematician John von Neumann, who immediately began setting it up on the world's first high-speed computer, a 25-ton punch card machine known as the ENIAC, which was capable of executing 5,000 instructions per second (high-speed is relative; for comparison, an iPhone can carry out tens of billions of instructions per second).

The secret project acquired the code name Monte Carlo, because of the city's association with gambling. But it didn't stay secret for long (perhaps Vegas would have been a better town, since we all know what happens in Vegas stays in Vegas). The method was key to the development of nuclear weapons at Los Alamos and elsewhere, but soon found applications in many other fields, including finance. Warren Buffett later quipped that 'derivatives are financial weapons of mass destruction'. He was referring to the tendency of these financial instruments to blow up – as they did rather spectacularly in the crisis of 2007–08 – but they also have their intellectual roots in real weapons of mass destruction.

Atomic stocks

When Einstein worked out the equations for a random walk, he was probably unaware that the same technique had already been used some years earlier, by a young student at the Sorbonne – whose interest was not in the random motion of pollen particles, or drunks, but in the equally random motions of the Bourse in Paris.

In his 1900 dissertation *Théorie de la Spéculation*, Louis Bachelier argued that the price of assets such as stocks represents a balance between buyers and sellers.[3] No one ever has a clear idea what is going on, and opinions about the market 'are so divided that at the same instant buyers believe the market is rising and sellers that it is falling', but their effects cancel out so the market could be viewed as being in an essentially 'static state'. At the same time, though, the market is constantly being perturbed from its equilibrium by things like news. The resulting motion of a stock's price was therefore effectively a random walk. As with drunks, or grains of pollen, even if you couldn't figure out exactly where stocks were going to go, you could still estimate the distance travelled in a certain time, and also know the best place to look for them, which was where they started. In other words, the expectation for profit or loss was zero.

Bachelier used this formula to compute the price of options, which are financial instruments that give the owner the right to buy or sell a security for a certain price on a future date – thus singlehandedly creating the field of quantitative finance. However, his thesis was awarded only a mediocre grade – 'too much on finance' was the verdict from France's leading probability theorist, Paul Lévy – and was all but forgotten until 60 years later, when the economist Paul Samuelson happened upon a copy 'rotting in the library of the University of Paris'.[4]

As financial instruments go, options are not exactly new. In *Politics*, Aristotle described how the philosopher Thales had predicted, on the basis of astrology, that the coming olive-harvest would be much larger than usual. He therefore arranged an option with local olive pressers to guarantee the use of their presses at the usual rate, and 'made a lot of money' – thus proving that 'it is easy for philosophers to become rich, if they want to; but that is not their object in life.' (Though I'm not sure he was speaking for the products of philosophy programmes in elite universities, a surprising number of whom have gone on to careers in finance.) The problem Bachelier had set himself was how to figure out the mathematically correct cost of the option. To illustrate the basic idea, a simple example might be useful.

Suppose that you are playing a game with a friend where you toss a coin three times in a row and each time you get heads, your friend pays you a dollar, and each time you get tails, you pay them a dollar. The expected value of each bet – defined as the average gain over a large number of tosses – is zero for either of you because the coin is fair and has an equal chance of producing heads or tails. But suppose now that your friend adds a new twist. They will sell you – for one dollar – the option to *only win* at this game. You play as usual, and if you end up with more money at the end, you get to keep it – but if you end up with less, you get it returned. In other words, your friend is offering you insurance on the game, for only the price of the stake. If you get three heads in a row, you can win three dollars, and the worst you can do is break even. Is purchasing the option – which is a derivative on the coin toss – a good deal?

If there were only one coin toss, it would be easy to calculate the price of the option. The only possible outcomes are that you win a dollar (if you toss heads) or win zero (if you toss tails) since the option protects against loss. Because the probability of either event is the same, the expected value of the option – i.e. the amount that you would expect to win on average, assuming you bought it – is the average, or 50 cents. So that would also be the fair value, and a dollar would be too expensive. But here it is more complicated because there are three tosses of the coin, so you potentially stand to lose more money, and maybe purchasing the option is worth it.

The usual way to solve this problem is to work backwards in time from the different possible end points, as shown in the Appendix. The answer is that the fair value of the option is $0.75. Therefore your friend's offer to sell you the option for a dollar is too expensive, and you should turn it down (unless you are risk-averse, but then you could always decline to play at all).

This example might not seem to have much to do with finance. For one thing, stock prices can't be negative. Indeed, one of the problems with Bachelier's random walk theory was that stock prices could random walk all the way down to zero and keep on going, which fortunately doesn't happen in the real world. After Samuelson rediscovered his work, economists modified it by noting that what we care about is not so much the change in price, but the proportional change in price – e.g. how much it moves in percentage terms. In mathematical terms, this can be handled by using the logarithm of the price, which *can* go negative.

Another difference is that real financial markets move in continuous time rather than in discrete steps, and prices can go up or down by amounts other than plus or minus one dollar, as in the coin toss game. Economists usually assume as Bachelier did that price changes follow a normal distribution (the so-called bell curve), with a typical range characterised by the standard deviation. Bachelier referred to this quantity as the 'nervousness' of the stock. In 1970 Eugene Fama's efficient market hypothesis lent academic credibility to this idea that price changes can be viewed as random perturbations to a stable equilibrium, despite objections that there was no stable equilibrium or well-defined standard deviation (see box below).

The trickiest problem, though, was how to incorporate the possibility of *not* playing the game. Suppose that instead of buying an option you had the possibility of putting that money into a risk-free savings account and making a guaranteed return, which might seem an attractive choice especially during times of high inflation. How would that affect the price of the option? The answer was a formula which is frequently described as the most influential equation in finance – the Black-Scholes formula (see below, page 162).

Efficient markets

One of the most persistent ideas in mainstream economics is that markets have a stable equilibrium, enforced by Adam Smith's invisible hand, so price changes can be viewed as random perturbations. It therefore follows that, as with Pearson's randomly walking drunk, the best forecast for an asset's future location is somewhere near where it was last spotted. This idea is applied in everything from macroeconomic models, which generally assume a stable equilibrium, to quantitative finance.

According to Bachelier, price fluctuations were caused in large part by irrational factors, which cancelled out symmetrically in the aggregate, so the expectation for profit or loss was zero. In another doctoral thesis, published this time by the University of Chicago in 1965, Eugene Fama said effectively the same thing – but this time attributed the randomness to 'efficient markets' in which 'competition among the many intelligent participants leads to a situation where, at any point in time, actual prices of individual securities already reflect the effects of information based both on events that have already occurred and on events which as of now the market expects to take place in the future. In other words, in an efficient market at any point in time the actual price of a security will be a good estimate of its intrinsic value.'[5] He later noted that one can't actually test the 'intrinsic value', for example by summing up the present value of expected future returns, since those are affected also by things like the discount rate, but these details didn't detract much from the central message that the current price was the best estimate of that value.[6]

Fama's version therefore made no difference to Bachelier's random walk result, but it did give a more compelling story. Markets were impossible to predict, not because they were irrational, but because they incorporated all available information. Economist Michael Jensen claimed in 1978 that 'the efficient market hypothesis is the best established fact in all social sciences'.[7] But does the hypothesis itself reflect all information about how markets behave?

Early critics of the theory were economists Andrew Lo and A. Craig MacKinlay, who in the 1980s produced data which showed that price changes were not completely random. At the time, as they wrote in their book *A Non-Random Walk Down Wall Street*, it was not warmly received: 'One of the most common reactions to our early research was surprise and disbelief. Indeed, when we first presented our rejection of the Random Walk Hypothesis at an academic conference in 1986, our discussant – a distinguished economist and senior member of the profession – asserted with great confidence that we had made a programming error, for if our results were correct, this would imply tremendous profit opportunities in the stock market.'[8] (The programming was fine.)

As Lo wrote, the efficient market theory's 'compelling motivation for randomness is unique among the social sciences and is reminiscent of the role that uncertainty plays in quantum mechanics'.[9] However, the random walk model assumes that the standard deviation of the price changes is stable and known, when in fact it varies depending on the historical time period considered, and will be different again in the future (its 'nervousness' is not constant). As many have pointed out, the assumption that markets have a stable equilibrium also seems a little counterintuitive, especially given the highly nonlinear behaviour of money (we return to this in Chapter 8). The theory's brand of randomness is therefore a neutered and distorted version of the indeterminacy seen in the economy.

Despite such arguments, the efficient market theory didn't go away – instead it cemented its place at the centre of financial modelling, including the macroeconomic Dynamic Stochastic General Equilibrium models discussed later.[10] In 2011 the economist John Cochrane echoed Jensen when he described it as 'probably the best-tested proposition in all the social sciences'.[11] In a research note the same year, economist Martin

Sewell agreed that even if the demand that markets reflect *all* available information is too exacting to be literally true, its accuracy still puts it 'in contention for one of the strongest hypotheses in the whole of the social sciences'. Furthermore, 'science concerns seeking the best hypothesis, and until a flawed hypothesis is replaced by a better hypothesis, criticism is of limited value'.[12] Or as Myron Scholes put it in 2009: 'To say something has failed, you have to have something to replace it, and so far we don't have a new paradigm to replace efficient markets.'[13]

Indeed, science traditionally evolves when a theory is replaced by one that makes better predictions. But the efficient market theory only predicts that we can't predict. That is no better than the explanation that markets are dictated by unpredictable gods. And in other fields – say, public transportation – the fact that a system is unpredictable isn't usually considered evidence of its efficiency, or of its ability to magically synthesise all available information.

The main reason that the efficient market hypothesis persists, I believe, is that it tells a story which those who work in the finance industry want to hear, while also giving a convenient explanation for missed forecasts like the financial crisis. The story that comes out of quantum economics might not be quite as flattering – there is less emphasis on efficiency, stability, and rationality – but as argued in this book, it is more informative about real human behaviour. And as a bonus, it also provides forecasters with an even better excuse than the efficient market hypothesis for forecast error – namely that predicting the economy is harder than quantum physics.

The quantum coin toss

The Black-Scholes formula (sometimes called Black-Scholes-Merton) originally received little attention when it was published by Fischer Black, Myron Scholes, and Robert C. Merton in 1973, but it later won Scholes and Merton the economics version of the Nobel Prize (Black died before the award was made). The equation itself was not particularly original – indeed it was a version of a heat equation which had been in use for well over a century. The hedge fund manager Ed Thorpe had also worked out the formula independently, though without publishing a detailed proof. Its main insight was that, given numerous idealised assumptions, one could construct a zero-risk portfolio by constantly trading stocks and options in such a way that one balanced the other – a process known as dynamic hedging. The option price could therefore be deduced by equating the hedged returns with what could be earned in a risk-free account.

Although options had been around for a long time, they had long been viewed as a disreputable way of gambling on stock price movements. In the United States, they came close to being banned after the crash of 1929, and even in the 1960s were only traded in a small New York market.[14] Black-Scholes changed all that by doing three things: it provided an apparently consistent technique for pricing options; it suggested that risk could be magically hedged away; and most importantly, it changed the story around options.

As discussed in the box above, Fama's efficient market hypothesis was basically an updated version of Adam Smith's invisible hand, applied to finance. But the Black-Scholes equation took this assumption and ran with it. If markets automatically assigned assets their correct value, then the formula went further and gave people a way of correctly evaluating and even protecting against risk. For example, if you wanted to purchase an asset but insure against loss, you could hedge the purchase by taking out an option. The paper came out with perfect timing, just as the Chicago Board Options Exchange opened for business in the spring of 1973. As its council later noted, it was the Black-Scholes formula that 'gave a lot of legitimacy to the whole notions of hedging and efficient pricing' and thus 'enabled the exchange to thrive'. Rather than 'speculation or gambling, it was efficient pricing'.[15] Risk had been reduced to an equation; and just as transactions affect markets, so do mathematical models.

Not content with simple derivatives such as options, traders and 'quants' working in quantitative finance soon began to develop increasingly elaborate derivatives, as discussed further in Chapter 8. Many were so complicated that they could only be solved by performing Monte Carlo simulations on fast computers. Most of the people working in the area were unaware that they were building a financial bomb that would eventually blow up the world economy in the crisis of 2007–08. But the connection with quantum physics may go much deeper than that.

Returning for a moment to the coin-tossing game: it is clear that the outcome of a coin toss is random, in the sense that it has an equal chance of being heads or tails; but the actual process is deterministic. In principle it should be possible to calculate the coin's trajectory from the moment it leaves our hand, and determine which side will come out on top. A coin toss is a fully mechanistic process, so uncertainty is a result of our computational shortcomings, and is not inherent to the process itself.

Or is it? Some scientists have argued that when you roll a die or even toss a coin, tiny quantum uncertainties during the collisions with a surface or the air are amplified up so that they affect the outcome. Something like a coin toss is similar to performing a quantum experiment: the outcome is undetermined until it is actually measured.[16]

But whether or not we think the coin toss is the genuine result of quantum uncertainty, we can certainly treat it as if it is, and see where that takes us. For example, we could imagine that instead of tossing a coin, we are measuring the spin of a random photon by seeing if it passes through a horizontally polarised filter: yes it is heads, no it is tails. Either way, the odds are the same. Using quantum mechanics, we could therefore write out an equation for the photon spin, which is characterised by numbers known as eigenvalues whose squared magnitudes represent the probability of different possible outcomes for a measurement.* The word 'eigenvalue' comes from the German *eigen* for 'own' or 'inherent' so therefore means something similar to the oft-recited 'intrinsic value' or 'fundamental value' from mainstream economics, with the difference that there can be more than one such value (indeed there may be infinitely many). In the figure on page 41 for the case with polarisation, there were two eigenvalues whose magnitude is given by the projections onto the vertical and horizontal axes. In this unpolarised case the two eigenvalues each have squared magnitude 0.5, corresponding to the 50 per cent chances that the photon does or doesn't pass through the filter.

To simulate a series of coin tosses, we would simply combine the equations for each step to produce a composite model. This can then be used to compute the probabilities of the various different payoffs from the option, and therefore the fair price of the option. If we carried out the required computations – which are much more complicated than the simple method shown in the Appendix – we would find that the correct price for the option is: $0.75. More interestingly, if we consider the case where prices

* The numbers may be complex, meaning that they involve the square root of −1.

change continuously rather than at fixed time intervals, it turns out
that the Black-Scholes equation is the result of a financial version
of Schrödinger's wave equation, for the special case where markets
are assumed to be highly liquid and efficient.[17] Markets even get
their own version of the uncertainty principle, expressed this time
for a financial asset in terms of a lower bound on the uncertainty
in price multiplied by the uncertainty in momentum.[18]

In other words, not only was much of traditional quantitative
finance inspired by quantum mechanics, it actually *is* quantum
mechanics, though of a rather contrived sort, given the restrictive
nature of the assumptions. Paul Samuelson may have described it
as 'pathetic' when an economist tries to 'force analogies between
the concepts of physics and the concepts of economics' or 'makes
reference to a Heisenberg Principle of [quantum] indeterminacy in
the social world', but economists did much the same thing anyway
while being careful not to use the trigger word 'quantum'.

Now, this certainly seems to be a rather elaborate way of solving the problem, just to get the same answer, which is one reason
quantum finance has so far not been widely adopted by practi-
tioners; but advocates claim there are a number of advantages to
using the quantum approach.[19] For one thing, the formalism can
be generalised quite easily for more complex derivatives, of the
sort that would otherwise have to be solved numerically with the
Monte Carlo approach. By reframing the problem, it also makes it
natural to explore departures from efficiency. While the efficient
market approach treats price-influencing factors as being truly
random and uncorrelated, a characteristic of quantum variables
is that they can be entangled. Since in the real world investors are
not truly independent, news is not completely random or uncorrelated, and so on, this is a useful feature, as discussed further below.
And because the quantum approach treats the bid-ask spread as a
fundamental limit on our knowledge of the asset's price – unlike

the traditional model which assumes that prices can be known accurately so long as they are measured sufficiently often – it is especially useful for cases and timescales where the price fluctuations are small relative to this limit. For example, quantum models are used by some trading firms (e.g. Algostox Trading, based in New York) to capture how volatility as measured over a period of seconds behaves differently from volatility measured over hours or days, or how illiquid securities respond while trying to liquidate or accumulate a large position.[20]

Perhaps the main advantage of these quantum methods, from a purely computational perspective, is that for some problems they can be faster to run than conventional models – and in the world of finance, where trading algorithms operate on micro-second timescales, speed is of the essence. This speed advantage will be even greater if the models are run on machines which are perfectly suited to take advantage of their unique features: quantum computers.

Straight versus crooked

If the Copenhagen interpretation has one overriding weakness, it is the idea of observer-caused wave function 'collapse' – as shown by the fact that the term often appears in quotation marks. What mechanism causes this mysterious collapse? Why is the evolution of the wave function deterministic, but the outcome of a measurement random? What counts as an observer? The concept seems intuitively obvious with money, where value collapses down to a single price, but is puzzling when it comes to the fabric of reality.

In 1957, the American physicist Hugh Everett came up with an astonishing answer.[21] It was that the wave function never collapses. Instead, each event that we interpret as a 'collapse' actually represents a branching point, in which the universe divides into two or more versions. In one copy of the universe, Schrödinger's cat lives; in the other, it dies. Because such branching events are happening all the time, an implication is that there are a large and growing number of universes all playing out in parallel with one another. In one, shares in Tesla are trading at $170 and a dozen eggs cost $3.73; in another those numbers are reversed. Somewhere there exists a universe where economists' predictions always come true (as discussed in Chapter 8, this isn't it).

Of course, this theory had problems of its own, since for example it meant that copies of the same person would live in multiple universes – which was perhaps why Everett in his work only referred to 'reality' in quotation marks. But in doing away with the notion of collapse it had the advantage of a kind of internal logic and aesthetic purity. According to one of its advocates, the Oxford physicist David Deutsch, 'It is not some troublesome, optional interpretation emerging from arcane theoretical considerations. It is the explanation – the only one that is tenable – of a remarkable and counter-intuitive reality.'[22]

Imagine now that we could build a computer which had access to all of these universes. High-speed supercomputers divide computational tasks among tens or hundreds of independent processors running in parallel. A 'many worlds' computer could do the same thing, carrying out calculations on different versions of itself in other universes, then bringing the answers back together at the end in a final observation. It would make any normal computer look like the ENIAC from the 1940s.

While access to other worlds has so far been denied us – we have yet to find the magic portal to the other side, or sides – we can do something rather similar using a quantum computer. The field of quantum computing was founded in a 1985 paper by Deutsch. In classical computers, the processors store information as strings of bits, which – like binary yes/no Aristotelian logic – can only take on the value 0 or 1. Quantum computers, in contrast, are based on entities known as qubits, which are in an indeterminate quantum state that can be viewed as a superposition of 0 and 1. A candidate storage device for a qubit would be a single photon, but there are many other options such as charged atoms held in place by an electromagnetic field.

The advantage of qubits over bits is that they can take on many more values. In the coin-tossing game, one classical bit would represent one outcome (heads or tails) of a single coin toss. Four bits would therefore represent one possible sequence of heads (H) and tails (T) for a game involving four tosses in a row, such as H T T H. Four qubits, on the other hand, could represent *all* possible sequences at the same time, of which there are 16:

HHHH	HTHH	THHH	TTHH
HHHT	HTHT	THHT	TTHT
HHTH	HTTH	THTH	TTTH
HHTT	HTTT	THTT	TTTT

This difference scales up rather quickly. A game with 50 coin tosses would require 1,125,899,906,842,624 bits, but only 50 qubits, to represent all the possible sequences. A larger version could easily take on as many different states as there are atoms in the known universe.

Because the qubits form an entangled system, operations such as changing the states of particular qubits, or adjusting the coupling between them, are equivalent to performing calculations with the overall wave function, but based on quantum rather than classical logic. In classical logic probabilities add together in a linear fashion, so for example if there is a 10 per cent chance that a system is in state A, and a 20 per cent chance that it is in state B, then the chance that it is in state A or B is the sum of these, which is 30 per cent. With quantum logic, which was first elucidated by John von Neumann in the 1930s, A and B are in superposition and may interfere with one another, as in the double-slit experiment where probability waves cancel or add to form an interference pattern, so they no longer sum in a linear fashion.[23]

The nature of quantum interference can be summarised as shown in the figure below. The right-angled triangle at the top has sides whose squared lengths equal A and B. According to the Pythagorean theorem, the square of the hypotenuse – which represents the probability of A and B – is equal to A+B. In a quantum version, the triangle is no longer a right-angled triangle, and the length of the diagonal may be more or less than the sum of the parts, depending on the configuration.[24] Instead of adding in a linear

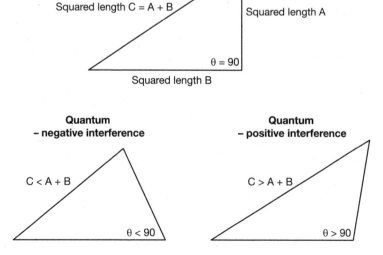

Figure 4. In classical logic (top case) probabilities A and B add linearly. In quantum logic, probabilities can interfere to produce a smaller (bottom left) or a larger (bottom right) total result.

manner, there is now also an extra term that involves the angle and can make the total larger or smaller. (In the next chapter, we show how similar interference terms appear in models of cognition.)

In a quantum computer, the outcome of a particular simulation is determined by performing an observation, which collapses the state of each qubit down to a single value. This represents only one of the possible outcomes, but as in a Monte Carlo simulation, one can perform many simulations and thus determine the probability of different outcomes. As Richard Feynman pointed out in 1982, before quantum computers were invented, such machines would be the ideal way to model quantum systems.[25] So if the financial system is quantum in nature, then quantum computers will have a huge advantage over conventional approaches.

Intrinsic value

Of course, there are a few problems with the idea that quantum computing and quantum finance are going to join forces and take over the field of computational finance. One is that, at the time of writing, quantum computing is more of an exciting challenge than a practical reality. Physicists and engineers are getting better at isolating and controlling individual qubits such as trapped ions or photons, but the hard part is keeping the delicate system isolated so that – like a particularly unstable mathematician – it can carry out its computations without prematurely collapsing. However, thousands of researchers are now working in the area, and big firms such as IBM, Hewlett-Packard, Google and so on have their own projects. Microsoft has developed a specialised programming language known as Q# and is experimenting with a machine based on an exotic particle known as a Majorana fermion. There are also many state-led consortia and start-up companies working in the space. The laboratory at Los Alamos has its own program, which was quickly dubbed the 'Manhattan Project of quantum computing'.[26] Finance companies such as Royal Bank of Scotland and Goldman Sachs are also investing in the area. Extending the bomb-making analogy, RBS's director of innovation Kevin Hanley told Bloomberg that 'We think financial services is kind of in the cross hairs'.[27]

Even if these technical problems are solved, the problems with quantitative finance – as quant Paul Wilmott and I argued in *The Money Formula* – have less to do with a lack of clever mathematical algorithms, than with basic ethics, a shortage of common sense, and flawed assumptions about how markets work.[28] The main aim of quantum finance, in its current form, seems to be less about changing its methods, than making them run more efficiently – which is not necessarily a good thing when it comes to promoting financial stability.[29] However, there are signs that quantum finance may be able to supply a genuine alternative to the current approach.

The conventional random walk model, as first championed by Bachelier, takes for granted the existence of an underlying equilibrium, and also assumes that perturbations have a stable standard deviation and are independent and linear in the sense that they accumulate in a straight-line fashion (for example, two pieces of news which move the market in the same way, have twice the effect of just one). One consequence of this inherent stability and linearity is that extreme changes are effectively impossible. The model does not just fail to predict the timing of crashes, it predicts that they cannot happen in the first place. Quantum models make it easier to relax some of these assumptions, and explore effects such as departures from efficiency.

It is frequently said (at least by non-economists) that markets are driven by psychology. A study by the CFA Institute found that the most common investor bias was 'herding – being influenced by peers to follow trends'.[30] Indeed, simple models have been produced which mimic the statistical behaviour of real markets based on the assumption that agents react in an unpredictable way to news (Bachelier) but also have a tendency to follow the group (herding).[31] One approach is based on the tendency of atoms in a disordered magnetic material known as a spin glass to align their spin directions under the influence of a varying magnetic field, which here plays the role of external news. Because atoms are affected also by the alignment of their neighbours, there is a tendency to produce a nonlinear, all-or-nothing response, in which they all line up in unison.[32] In other words, financial markets can still be usefully modelled using the atomic theory, but now the atoms are quantum and talk to one another.

Another oddity of traditional quantitative finance is that, as always in economics, the actual finance part doesn't play a very big role. For example, the Black-Scholes model assumed that stocks were correctly priced, and that 'speculators would try to profit by borrowing large amounts of money' to exploit any small anomaly that might appear.[33] However, agents are entangled through the financial system, meaning that any market downturn may be accentuated by a sudden drying up of credit – as happened to the investment firm Long-Term Capital Management, whose partners included both Scholes and Merton, when it blew up in 1998 and had to be rescued at a cost of $3.6 billion in order to prevent an even greater crisis. As discussed further in Chapter 8, credit and debt were also at the heart of the 2007–08 crisis. Such effects are an obvious and natural extension to quantum finance.

Perhaps the most useful contribution of quantum finance will be to change the way we think about the financial system. Instead of seeing stock prices as particles that are randomly jostled from their stable resting place by interactions with many independent investors, we begin to see them as fundamentally indeterminate quantities. In quantum physics, particles can never be perfectly still because that would violate the uncertainty principle. In the same way, markets can only be still when they are turned off – and even then, investors can still find ways to bet on related derivatives in some other market. When Brown first saw the motion of pollen particles, he assumed it was because they were alive; with markets, that would be the right interpretation.

Theories such as the efficient market hypothesis talk about the unique 'intrinsic value' of an asset – one standard definition says that 'the price of an asset reflects all relevant information that is available about the intrinsic value of the asset' – but in fact there is no such thing.[34] The quantum version would state that the price corresponds to an *eigenvalue* of the system, in the sense of a possible value. In a quantum system, the number of eigenvalues is the same as the number of possible states, which may be infinite.

Of course some of these states have a higher probability than others; but for an entangled system the behaviour does not generally conform to a neat or mathematically well-behaved statistical distribution. In practical terms, one consequence of this quantum uncertainty as applied to finance is that many of the complex derivatives which are sold by quants, with risk profiles neatly described using standard statistical methods, may in fact be too complicated to properly price (an example is the collateralised debt obligations discussed in Chapter 8). Rather than expanding the market for such instruments, the quantum approach would suggest that we limit it. And while quantum finance running on a quantum computer could in principle help make high-frequency trading even faster, the theory – by stripping unpredictable markets of their automatic association with efficiency – could also be used to justify a financial transactions tax which would severely curtail such activity, on the basis that it serves no useful social purpose.[35] Markets are human institutions, and they should be designed for humans, not machines.

In quantum economics, the only kind of object which always has a single eigenvalue – and where the wave function has been stamped down so there is no possibility of further collapse – is a money object. The price of an asset, in contrast, is interpreted as an emergent feature that is both revealed, and constructed, through the exchange of money objects – just as the position of a particle is indeterminate until measured. However, as revealed in the next chapter, the quantum quality of money only really comes into its own when it interacts with another delicate quantum system – the one which designed it. Our brains.

CHAPTER 7

Quantum games

Symbolism is the art of the missing link, as the word implies:
sym-ballein, to throw together. It is the art of syncopation.
It is the basis of electricity and quantum mechanics,
as Lewis Carroll understood via Lobachevski, and
non-Euclidean geometries. The chemical bond, as understood
by Heisenberg and Linus Pauling, is RESONANCE.
Echoland. The world of acoustic space whose center is
everywhere and whose margin is nowhere, like the pun.
Marshall McLuhan and Wilfred Watson,
From Cliché to Archetype (1970)

Classical theory has bounded rationality,
quantum is unbounded rationality.
Alexander Wendt, *Quantum Mind and Social Science* (2015)

Mainstream or neoclassical economics was initially based on the idea of *Homo economicus*, or rational economic man. In recent years, and especially since the crisis of 2007–08, this creation has come under increased criticism. Behavioural economists have shown that, when it comes to making financial decisions, we often show what they politely describe as 'bounded rationality' or what psychologists call 'complete insanity'. But is our behaviour really illogical – or is it just that economists have been using the wrong kind of logic? This chapter explores the fields of quantum cognition and quantum game theory, and shows that our behaviour has much in common with the rules followed by subatomic particles.

When neoclassical economics was first developed in the late nineteenth century, the idea was to literally translate concepts from Newtonian physics into economics, to produce what the French philosopher – and founder of sociology – Auguste Comte had called a 'social physics'. A property of Newtonian dynamics is that it can be expressed mathematically as a kind of optimisation problem: objects moving in a field take the path of least action, where 'action' represents a form of energy expenditure. For example, the diffraction of light through a glass prism can be viewed as light waves (or individual photons) taking the most efficient path. Newton's contemporary, Gottfried Wilhelm Leibniz, explained the idea by comparing God to an architect who 'utilizes his location and the funds destined for the building in the most advantageous manner'.[1] Following the same script, neoclassical economists assumed that in the economy, individuals act to optimise their own utility by spending their limited resources. Economists could then make Newtonian calculations about how prices would be set in a market economy, to arrive at what William Stanley Jevons called a 'mechanics of self-interest and utility'.[2]

The equating of mechanics with economics was illustrated in the 1892 book *Mathematical Investigations in the Theory of Value and Prices* by Irving Fisher, which was based on his Yale thesis (he was awarded that university's first PhD in economics).[3] The table below, from his text, shows how concepts from one field mapped onto concepts from the other.

Mechanics	Economics
Particle	Individual
Space	Commodity
Force	Marginal utility/disutility
Work	Disutility
Energy	Utility

Economic agents were viewed as particles, while the marginal utility or disutility for a particular commodity (defined as the satisfaction gained from consuming one more unit of it) was viewed as a force acting in a kind of commodity space. For a simplified case with only three commodities, this space had three dimensions with one axis for each commodity; while the general case with N commodities was represented by an N-dimensional abstract mathematical space. Since in the real world there are thousands of commodities, rational economic man lived in a very complicated space indeed.

If a person consumed an amount x of a certain commodity, that would be represented by a gain in utility as the agent moved a distance x along the axis representing that commodity. The amount of utility gained would depend on their preference for that commodity. If on the other hand they produced the commodity, they would gain disutility by moving in the negative direction. So, for example, as you consume (read) these words you are gaining some kind of psychic energy, the amount of which depends on your preference for this sort of explication of neoclassical thought, while as I produced (wrote) them I was gaining disutility, which was precisely compensated for when you bought the book. The point zero on the axis represents the place where the utility and disutility cancel, because nothing is being done. 'This corresponds', wrote Fisher, 'to the mechanical equilibrium of a particle the condition of which is that the component forces along all perpendicular axes should be equal and opposite.'

There were of course a few complicating issues. One was that while the basic constituents of matter are identical – one electron is like another – people aren't. Economists argued instead that what counts is the behaviour of the 'average man'. This concept was first introduced by the French sociologist Adolphe Quetelet, who wrote in 1831 that 'If the *average* man were ascertained for one nation, he could represent the type of that nation. If he could be ascertained according to the mass of men, he would represent the type of human species altogether.'[4]

Another complication was that axes in the high-dimensional space correspond to different commodities. When there is only one commodity, say orange juice, and one person with a known degree of fondness for that beverage, then it might seem reasonable to postulate a 'law of demand' for that person where demand varies with price. But suppose now that one axis represents 'exciting job' while another axis represents 'horrible commute'. This is a difficult trade-off – for example, one can imagine a situation where a person values the exciting job highly during an interview and forgets about the commute, with the converse happening later while stuck in traffic on the way to work. Economists, however, simply assumed that preferences could be expressed as fixed numerical quantities which would remain stable over time, so it was possible to measure along each axis and compare the numbers.

Finally, while particles (it was believed) obeyed mechanistic laws, people didn't. Light might choose the most efficient line, but people often seem to take a more circuitous route to their destination – or wander off the path altogether. Again, though, economists argued that most people could make rational decisions to optimise their own utility – or as economist Francis Edgeworth put it, 'the first principle of Economics is that every agent is actuated only by self-interest'.[5] They might not get it right every time, but it could be safely assumed that these wrinkles would iron themselves out on average. Thus was born *Homo economicus*, or rational economic man – the atom of the economy, whose actions would drive prices to a stable equilibrium, via Adam Smith's invisible hand.

Light versus dark

Obviously *Homo economicus* was something of a caricature, and no sooner was he born than economists began to distance themselves from their creation, claiming that their approach was actually much more sophisticated. As Lionel Robbins put it in 1932, 'if it were generally realised that Economic Man is only an expository device – a first approximation used very cautiously at one stage in the development of arguments which, in their full development, neither employ any such assumption nor demand it in any way for a justification of their procedure – it is improbable that he would be such a universal bogey'.[6] (Today, economists prefer to use the term 'straw man'.) Yet despite such protestations, the importance of rational economic man in economics only grew – and not just in introductory classes.

One area where he played an outsized role was the field of game theory, founded by the brilliant and prolific mathematician John von Neumann (who also appeared in the previous chapter) in the late 1920s. This studied the interactions in artificial games between rational actors who are trying to optimise their own 'expected utility' – i.e. utility of an outcome, multiplied by the probability of that outcome. As he wrote with Oskar Morgenstern in their 1944 *Theory of Games and Economic Behavior*, 'It does not seem to us that these notions are qualitatively inferior to certain well established and indispensable notions in physics, like force, mass, charge, etc. ... we wish to find the mathematically complete principles which define "rational behavior" for the participants in a social economy, and to derive from them the general characteristics of that behavior.'[7]

A key technique in game theory was something known as Brouwer's fixed-point theorem, which is a method for demonstrating that a system of equations – in this case representing the possible outcomes of a game – has a stable and optimal solution.

Game theory was initially developed for economics but came into its own during the Cold War, when Von Neumann, working together with military strategists at the RAND Corporation, developed the doctrine of Mutually Assured Destruction (MAD). According to this theory, rational actors can achieve a stable equilibrium if both know that starting a war will lead to instant annihilation of both sides. Of course, it only works when a number of other assumptions also hold, e.g. perfect information (so each side knows where attacks come from), symmetry (comparable powers), belief that the other side is willing to destroy the world, and so on. Indeed, as Von Neumann's biographer Steve Heims notes, game theory 'portrays a world of people relentlessly and ruthlessly but with intelligence and calculation pursuing what each perceives to be his own interest'.[8] Entanglement is right out; sociopaths might do well.

Rational economic man also found another role in the Cold War, which was to help win the ideological battle with the Soviet Union. During this period, the US Department of Defense was pumping funds into all kinds of scientific programmes in an attempt to gain technological supremacy over its Soviet rival. Two recipients of its largesse were the economists Kenneth Arrow and Gérard Debreu, who had worked with RAND and were funded in part by grants from the Office of Naval Research.[9] In a proof that again involved Brouwer's fixed-point theorem, they showed, based on a highly idealised version of a market economy, that free markets lead to an optimal 'fixed point', in which prices are set at their correct levels, and nothing can be changed without making at least one person worse off – a condition known as Pareto optimality.[10] But to accomplish this feat, the powers of rational economic man had to be extended to a ridiculous degree so that they included things like infinite computational power and the ability to devise plans for every future eventuality. Note also that the definition of

Pareto optimality is very narrow, because rather than claiming that the outcome is in some sense fair or good, it just says that it can't be changed without hurting someone.

The Arrow-Debreu model was sometimes called the 'invisible hand theorem' because it seemed to provide mathematical proof of Smith's theory that free markets – at least in principle – are inherently self-stabilising and set prices to their optimal levels. During the Cold War, it also had useful propaganda value in showing that capitalism, rather than communism, was the best guide to organising society.[11] It soon came to be viewed as the crown jewel of neoclassical economics, and inspired the development of General Equilibrium models and later Dynamic Stochastic General Equilibrium (DSGE) models which are still relied on by policy-makers today. Pareto optimality, according to behavioural economists George Akerlof and Robert Shiller, who make use of this 'remarkable result' in their 2015 book *Phishing for Phools*, means that once a competitive free-market economy is in equilibrium, 'it is impossible to improve the economic welfare of everyone. Any interference will make *someone* worse off. For graduate students, this conclusion is presented as a mathematical theorem of some elegance – elevating the notion of free-market optimality into a high scientific achievement.'[12]

The rational gene

Far from being a 'universal bogey' as Robbins called him, rational economic man had morphed into the Cold War economics version of a universal soldier. As discussed in the previous chapter, he soon switched into the more lucrative field of finance, playing a key role in efficient market theory and quantitative finance. He also received a degree of validation from the idea of 'the selfish gene', a controversial hypothesis popularised by zoologist Richard Dawkins in his 1976 book of the same name. According to this theory, we might think we are living, conscious, independent people, but actually we are just the puppets of our genes, which are bent only on propagation. As physicist David Deutsch wrote: 'An organism is the sort of thing – such as an animal, plant or microbe – which in everyday terms we usually think of as being alive. But ... "alive" is at best a courtesy title when applied to the parts of an organism other than its DNA.'[13] Life therefore reduces to genes – and even if people sometimes *appear* irrational, our genes are experts at hyper-rational game theory, since the only reason they are here is because they have been ruthlessly maximising their own chances of survival for millennia. All change, including even the emergence of life in the first place, is due to random mutations, or what biologist Jacques Monod called in his 1970 book *Chance and Necessity* a 'Monte Carlo game'.[14]

Economics could therefore apply to much more than the economy – it could serve as a blueprint for all the social sciences. As Gary Becker wrote in his book *The Economic Approach to Human Behavior*, written like Dawkins' book in 1976, 'the combined assumptions of maximizing behavior, market equilibrium, and stable preferences, used relentlessly and consistently form the heart of the economic approach ... I have come to the position that the economic approach is a comprehensive one that is applicable to all human behavior.'[15] His University of Chicago colleague Robert Lucas pushed the idea of rational economic man to its limits with his theory of rational expectations, which says that people are not just rational, but also have a perfect mental model of the economy, in the sense that they don't make systematic errors. Markets *must* be at equilibrium, because disequilibrium can be caused only by irrational behaviour.

Faith in the powers of our own rationality provided intellectual justification for the rollback of financial sector regulations that gathered steam in the early 2000s. After all, if the market was rational, and risk could be hedged away through the use of complex derivatives, how could regulation help? As Chairman of the Federal Reserve Ben Bernanke told Congress in 2006, 'the best way to make sure the hedge funds are not taking excessive risk or excessive leverage is through market discipline'.[16] It also led to an incredible degree of complacency in economics, captured by Lucas when he announced in his 2003 talk, cited in the first chapter, that 'the central problem of depression prevention has been solved, for all practical purposes, and has in fact been solved for many decades'.[17]

Not everyone agreed with this rosy picture, even within the mainstream. The economist Robert Solow wrote the same year: 'The preferred model has a single representative consumer optimizing over infinite time with perfect foresight or rational expectations, in an environment that realizes the resulting plans more or less flawlessly through perfectly competitive forward-looking markets for goods and labor, and perfectly flexible prices and wages. How could anyone expect a sensible short-to-medium-run macroeconomics to come out of that set-up?' He noted that if we want to understand the economy, 'A model that rules out pathologies by definition is unlikely to help'.[18] And a range of heterodox economists had long argued, to little avail, that assumptions such as equilibrium and rationality were unrealistic.

The crisis of 2007–08 confirmed these concerns about the models – but perhaps surprisingly, did little (as we'll see) to dislodge rational economic man from his position at the centre of both economic models and economic education.[19] One reason for his ongoing appeal is that we have unconsciously internalised him to the extent that he has become a model of how we *should* behave, were we just a little more rational – what economic historian Mary Morgan called 'a normative model of behaviour for real economic actors to follow'.[20] This is especially true of economists

themselves, since numerous experiments have shown that exposure
to an education in economics makes people behave in a less altru-
istic manner.* As economist Kate Raworth wrote in 2017, rational
economic man 'is the protagonist in every mainstream economics
textbook; he informs policy decision-making worldwide; he shapes
the way we talk about ourselves; and he wordlessly tells us how to
behave.'[21] For something that is supposedly made of straw, he has
proved to have remarkable staying power.

Behavioural economics

The main challenge to rational economic man, at least to date, has
come from the field of behavioural economics. This was founded in
the 1970s by psychologists Daniel Kahneman and Amos Tversky,
who carried out a long series of experiments in which they probed
the various cognitive shortcomings of their subjects. The most
basic lesson of behavioural economics seems to be that making
decisions is hard, so we look for shortcuts. And we are easily influenced when someone – the state, an advertiser, our social group, or
even our own habits – supplies that shortcut. For example, we prefer to stick with what we know and dislike change, which explains
why investors often cling on to shares which do nothing but go
downhill. Recency bias means that we put too much weight on
new information (like last year's investment returns) than older
information (such as historical returns). If a workplace cafeteria
reduces the distance between the beverage station and the snack
station, their employees may gain weight because they eat more

---

* For example, students at Cornell University were asked at the start and
end of a term whether they would return a lost envelope containing cash.
If they studied economics, they became less honest, while if they studied
astronomy, they became more honest. Frank, R.H., Gilovich, T., and Regan,
D.T. (1993), 'Does Studying Economics Inhibit Cooperation?', *Journal of
Economic Perspectives*, 7 (2), pp. 159–71.

snacks. And in general our decisions are shaped by things like history and context, which makes them open to manipulation.

Their findings were later supplemented by those of neuroscientists, who tested which parts of the brain lit up on a scanner when people were asked financial questions (they weren't always the rational part). As behavioural economist Richard Thaler, whose 2008 book *Nudge* (co-authored with Harvard Law School professor Cass R. Sunstein) was influential on governments including those of the US and UK, summarised for *The New York Times* in 2015: 'Economists discount any factors that would not influence the thinking of a rational person. These things are supposedly irrelevant. But unfortunately for the theory, many supposedly irrelevant factors do matter. Economists create this problem with their insistence on studying mythical creatures often known as *Homo economicus*.'[22] He also notes that: 'To defenders of economics orthodoxy, markets are thought to have magic powers.' The idea that markets might have irrationality at their core therefore strikes such ideologues as a 'heresy'.[23]

Indeed, behavioural economics was initially very controversial. Kahneman related meeting a well-known American philosopher at a party: after Kahneman started to explain his ideas, the philosopher turned his back, saying, 'I am not really interested in the psychology of stupidity'.[24] However, it went on to be highly influential on economics and the social sciences in general, especially after the crisis (that anecdote comes from Kahneman's biography for his 2002 economics Nobel, and Thaler was awarded the 2017 prize). A number of governments have set up groups like the UK's Behavioural Insights Team (or 'Nudge Unit' as it is known) to investigate how behavioural science can improve policy, for example by nudging (hassling?) people to pay their taxes. Businesses regularly tap techniques from behavioural economics – such as the importance of framing issues – to exploit our cognitive biases. One trick, for example, is to supply default options in online menus to prompt us to make certain choices. Perhaps the area where behavioural economics has had the greatest impact is in the world of finance, where cognitive effects such as herding behaviour and recency bias are regularly cited, as discussed further below.

Behavioural economists have provided a rich literature of empirical findings which has certainly enhanced our understanding of how people make economic decisions. At the same time, for a field which dares to commit 'heresy' and dabble in what Thaler describes as 'treacherous, inflammatory territory' it has hardly threatened to upend the mainstream.[25] The neoclassical economist John Cochrane notes that, after being around for over three decades, it has produced a host of new phenomena but very little in the way of testable predictions (as opposed to explanations), while many of the more concrete proposals sound like something marketers could have told them.[26] For example, the idea of nudging people into making decisions is hardly revolutionary; it is the basis of advertising, marketing, and government propaganda – the UK's Nudge Unit has nothing on Russia's influence on up to 126 million American Facebook users around the time of the 2016 presidential election, or for that matter Facebook's ability to manipulate its users by itself.[27] And as Eugene Fama told Thaler in a 2016 debate, 'I still think there is no full-blown testable behavioral asset-pricing model' to rival efficient market theory.[28]

One problem is that the field presents a taxonomy of individual effects, rather than a coherent model. The 'list of cognitive biases' on Wikipedia provides over 180 different types, including the 'Google effect' which is defined as the 'tendency to forget information that can be found readily online by using internet search engines' (I'm sure there is a Wikipedia effect too, but maybe they forgot it).[29] The idea of 'rationality' is also a little hard to pin down, since what looks rational for one person might not for another.

Thaler, for example, relates how the lawyer and economist Richard Posner objected that what appeared to be 'cognitive quirks' could in fact have been the products of evolutionary biology. If something enhances our chance of survival – or that of our selfish genes – then it is rational, even if it appears irrational. Even the manic behaviour of investors during financial bubbles can, it seems, be reframed as rational, if you try hard enough.[30]

Another issue is that, even if some behaviours are accepted as irrational, mainstream economists tend to frame these as pathological exceptions that should be treated as isolated cases (as Fama put it, 'There's a difference between anecdotes and evidence, right?'). As Akerlof and Shiller note, this attitude has been reinforced by the tendency of behavioural economists themselves to treat deviations from rationality on a 'case-by-case basis – but just as rare exceptions. This message is not intended, but the presentation of behavioral economics, perhaps unconsciously, yields this implication.'[31] (Not mentioned is the fact that such an approach obviously makes the field more amenable to the mainstream.)

I would argue, though, that the problem with behavioural economics is not that it adds little to conventional theory, but that it doesn't go far enough. As I pointed out in *Economyths*, economists have proved adept at adding epicycles to their models to adjust for certain effects; and the emphasis in behavioural economics on ideas such as 'bounded rationality' shows that it is less a threat to mainstream economics than a relatively minor tweak that is used too often as a fig leaf for rational economic man. It doesn't seriously question the premise that the economy consists of atomistic individuals, or the goal of Pareto optimality, but only suggests that the path towards equilibrium may be complicated by our cognitive biases. The fact that it only partially challenges the basic tenets of mainstream economics has won it both mainstream acceptance and tremendous influence over many areas of social science, but also limited its impact. And the fact that its acknowledgement of irrational behaviour – which would come as little surprise to most non-economists – could be described as the academic version of 'treacherous, inflammatory territory' says more about the ingrained attitudes of the economics mainstream (i.e. its 'loss avoidance' and 'illusion of validity' as behavioural economists call it), or perhaps the desire for a theatrical display of tolerance, than anything else.

While it may have made sense in Victorian times to model the economy as a mechanistic system, if its founders were alive today they would probably be wondering why modern economists weren't drawing their inspiration from more recent areas of physics. An alternative picture is now being developed by the new areas of quantum cognition and quantum social science, which argue that the problem is less to do with what counts as logical behaviour in humans, than with what kind of logic is being used: classical, or quantum.

Quantum logic

As already noted, it is something of a cliché to say that quantum physics is so weird that it is beyond human understanding. Money too often appears to be an impenetrable mystery which defies conventional logic. But perhaps the problem is actually less to do with these realities than with classical logic; and perhaps quantum physics has more to do with human nature than we have supposed. For there is plenty of evidence to suggest that, like particles, we use a different kind of logic, based on quantum principles.

As discussed in the previous chapter, the basic difference between classical and quantum logic is that the first allows only for Aristotelian, binary, yes/no distinctions, while quantum logic sees a system as being in a superposition of multiple states, which snap down to a single answer only at the time of measurement. The measurement process is therefore an active process which can influence the outcome. For example, a basic property of classical logic is that measurements should be commutative, meaning that their sequence has no effect on the answers. If we measure the width, and then the height, of a box, we get the same result if we reverse the order. With quantum logic, that is no longer necessarily true, because the first measurement changes the state of the system.

Also, while it may make sense in classical logic to speak about the fixed preferences of rational economic man, this concept has no meaning in quantum logic. Preferences are described by a time-varying probabilistic function which is sensitive to both measurement and context. We might usually prefer to drink red wine with a meal, but it's not a hard and fast rule, it changes with time, and we might choose white or rosé depending on the exact situation – such as a subtle nudge from a companion or a waiter.

Like Schrödinger's cat, we can therefore be in more than one state at the same time, at least until we need to make a choice. This idea of potential beings is acknowledged also in behavioural economics. As one paper by Karla Hoff and Joseph Stiglitz puts it: 'We can imagine that people are born with many different kinds of actors inside them. Consider an individual, Fred, and call two of the potential actors inside him A and B. Let A be a scrupulously honest person and B be a less scrupulously honest person. An insight of modern behavioral economics is that Fred can be induced to act more or less scrupulously by changing the cues to which he is exposed. We say that Fred is primed to be A or B. At any given moment, it may be easier to prime Fred to be A than B. But now having gone to work for an international bank in a period when social norms against dishonesty towards clients are lax, the set of stimuli that elicit Fred to behave dishonestly expands. This changes who Fred is. In general, after being embedded in a new context for a long time, an individual can become more B than A.'[32]

Of course, we are not limited to just a couple of 'actors' or sets of preferences; and more generally, as Amos Tversky and Itamar Simonson noted in a 1993 paper, 'There is a growing body of evidence that supports an alternative conception according to which preferences are often constructed – not merely revealed – in the elicitation process. These constructions are contingent on the framing of the problem, the method of elicitation, and the context of the choice.'[33] We therefore behave rather like participants in a quantum system. When Bohr's colleague Pascual Jordan wrote that 'observations not only disturb what has to be measured, they produce it', he sounded as much like a psychologist as a physicist.[34]

The order effect

In fact, the correspondence with quantum physics had already been noted back in 1978, before behavioural economics even existed as a field. In a paper that year, the Pakistani mathematical physicist Asghar Qadir argued that the quantum formalism is ideally suited for handling situations where 'consumer behavior depends on infinitely many factors and that the consumer is not aware of any preference until the matter is brought up.'[35] Instead of modelling people as mechanistic particles, pushed and pulled by forces of utility and disutility, it made more sense to model them as quantum entities, with a state described by a social version of a probabilistic wave function, and decisions represented by wave function collapse.

Qadir didn't develop his ideas further, or extend them to the topic of money, and his paper fell on deaf ears. (At the time of writing, it has two citations on Google Scholar. For comparison, Kahneman and Tversky's seminal paper 'Prospect Theory: An Analysis of Decision under Risk', which came out the following year, has 47,191.) However, the idea re-emerged separately in the 1990s in the field known as quantum cognition, and in recent years there has been growing interest among psychologists and others in the quantum approach, which has proved useful not just at explaining our numerous departures from perfect rationality, but also the nature of thought processes in general. According to cognitive scientists Jerome Busemeyer and Peter Bruza, 'the wave nature of an indefinite state captures the psychological experience of conflict, ambiguity, confusion, and uncertainty; the particle nature of a definite state captures the psychological experience of conflict resolution, decision, and certainty.'[36] While many questions will have a straightforward answer, others evoke a more complex response that needs to be constructed at the time, and so depends on the particular context. And just as a particle's behaviour is affected by measurement, so our own behaviour is affected by being asked questions.

Consider for example one of the staples of behavioural psychology, alluded to by Qadir in his paper, which is the order effect. As Qadir wrote, a consumer's choice 'will depend, among other things, on the order in which his requirements for various commodities are found out'. Similarly, pollsters and survey writers have long known that the answers they receive depend on the exact wording of the questions, but also on their order. The response to the first question changes the context for the second question, where here the context includes the responder's own state of mind. The phenomenon is so common that in psychology 'non-commutivity should be the ubiquitous rule', according to psychologists Harald Atmanspacher and Hartmann Römer.[37] The situation is therefore similar to that encountered in quantum physics, where a measurement of position affects a particle's momentum and vice versa.

In a 2014 paper, researchers analysed the results of 70 US surveys, and found that the way the answers changed showed an underlying symmetry.[38] One example they used was a Gallup survey from 1997 which asked in consecutive questions whether respondents thought Bill Clinton and Al Gore were trustworthy. The number of people who described them both as trustworthy was 49 per cent if Clinton was named first, but rose to 56 per cent if Gore was named first, a difference of 7 per cent. Conversely, the number who described them both as untrustworthy was 28 per cent if Clinton was named first, but fell to 21 per cent if Gore was named first, again a difference of 7 per cent. So the increase in joint trustworthiness was balanced by a decrease in joint untrustworthiness. This result makes no sense from a classical perspective, but was exactly what was expected using quantum theory. In essence, the first question acts as a measurement event which changes the context for the second question. The quantum model predicts the yes–yes versus no–no symmetry will always hold, because it is a structural feature of the model (see Appendix).

As the study's lead author Zheng Wang from Ohio State University notes, 'Whenever something comes up that isn't consistent with classical theories, we often label it as "irrational". But from the perspective of quantum cognition, some findings aren't irrational anymore. They're consistent with quantum theory – and with how people really behave.'[39] Or as the *Economist* reported, 'what is clear is that the kind of judgments we make when responding to a survey are not simply read out of our memory, but are dependent on our cognitive state (which may be highly uncertain) and the context in which it is operating (which can be influenced by question ordering, among other factors). In other words, the cognitive equivalent of those puzzling phenomena that led physicists to develop quantum theory in the first place more than a century ago.'[40]

Do you want to play again?

While the order effect is a nice illustration of the quantum approach, it shows only the effect of context, which could also be addressed using some other ad hoc model. A clearer illustration of quantum cognition involves interference when making decisions under uncertainty. An example of such effects was a well-known experiment from 1992, where psychologists offered subjects a game in which they had an even chance of either winning $200 or losing $100.[41] After playing once, they were offered the chance to play again. If they were told that they won the first game, 69 per cent decided to gamble their winnings, perhaps because they thought they had a hot hand, or were playing with free money. If they knew they lost, then 59 per cent played another round. But if they were not told the result, then only 36 per cent opted to repeat. According to expected utility theory, which again is based on classical logic, the answer should be the average of the first two possibilities, which is 64 per cent – a huge difference from the observed number.

This so-called disjunction effect applies to many other situations where one is trying to choose between a number of options with uncertain outcomes (e.g. the economy). It can be explained using behavioural psychology by saying that winning or losing the first round provides a reason for playing again – having a hot hand, the desire to win back losses – while if the result is not known then no such reason is supplied. But a more elegant solution is to model the response as a quantum process. The decision to play a second time is again entangled with the result of the first game; and when this is unknown, the uncertainty between a positive reason (having a hot hand) and a negative reason (desire to win back losses) creates a kind of mental interference pattern which affects the decision-making process, rather like the fruit/vegetable conflict discussed in the box in Chapter 1.[42] As one paper notes, the situation is 'analogous to wave interference where two waves meet with one wave rising while the other wave is falling so they cancel out'.[43]

As one more example (there are many), another key result from behavioural psychology is the phenomenon known as preference reversal. Consider the following two games, from a 1990 paper by Tversky and Thaler, each of which offers a chance to win a monetary prize.[44] Game A gives an 8/9 chance of winning $4, while game B has a 1/9 chance of winning $40. Which is better?

The expected payoff from A is $3.56 ($4 multiplied by 8/9) while for B it is $4.44 ($40 multiplied by 1/9). So according to expected utility theory, game B is higher value. But in the experiment, the ranking of the two games depended on the situation. If the person was playing the game themselves, then 71 per cent preferred to go with game A. The payoff may be lower, but it is also lower risk, and most people dislike uncertainty. On the other hand, if their job was to price the game for someone else, they suddenly put on their accounting hats, with 67 per cent correctly saying that game B was more valuable.

Physicists Vyacheslav Yukalov and Didier Sornette applied quantum decision theory to such problems, and found that it was possible to explain the result by complementing the utility function with another 'attraction' function which describes subconscious preferences, such as risk aversion, and their quantum interference with the uncertain prospects. The outcomes then depend on the specific context, i.e. playing or pricing. As the authors note: 'It is the appearance of interference terms that makes the structure of quantum expressions richer than the related classical ones and that allows one to explain those psychological phenomena that, otherwise, are inexplicable in classical decision making.'[45]

Such preference reversal can also be seen in action in the game known as 'stopping smoking'. People who are trying to quit will rank the utility of not smoking in the future higher than that of smoking (which is why they are trying to quit). However, if asked to rank the utility of *actually stopping smoking right now* they often prefer to reverse their preferences and pull out a cigarette, in defiance of classical logic and their doctor. Smokers can now blame their inability to quit on quantum interference. (Actually, the author Jonathan Franzen already did that in a piece where he wrote of his younger self: 'My state of mind was like a quantum wave function in which I could be totally a smoker but also totally not a smoker, so long as I never took measure of myself.'[46]) The same 'planning paradox', as it is sometimes known, extends also to societal attitudes towards the prevention of climate change; or to something like a loan, where the decision to default offers short-term relief at the expense of uncertain future consequences, as discussed below.

The prisoner's entanglement

The connection of such cognitive effects to the principles of economics becomes more apparent still when we consider that many of the findings of neoclassical economics are based on fixed preferences, independent agents, expected utility, and game theory. Consider for example one of the most famous problems from game theory: the prisoner's dilemma. This game was first invented at RAND in 1950 as a way to show why rational people might choose to not cooperate, even if it would be better for both of them if they did. The game involves two imaginary members of a criminal gang, who have been arrested for a crime and held in separate cells. The prosecutor can give each a reduced charge with a penalty of one year, unless he can make one testify against the other, in which case he can obtain a three-year sentence. He therefore offers each prisoner a choice: testify that the other person committed the crime, or remain silent. Their penalties, he tells them, will then be as follows:

> If both prisoners remain silent, they both get one year on the lesser charge.

If both prisoners betray the other, they both get two years.

If only one prisoner betrays the other, he gets off and the other gets the full three years.

So how would rational economic man respond? According to standard theory, he would maximise his expected utility, or equivalently minimise his expected disutility, which in this case would be the sentence. If he chooses to betray the other person, then his sentence is either zero years at best, or two years at worst. If he assigns equal probability to either outcome, his expected disutility is the average of these, which is 1. If however he chooses to not betray, then the sentence is either one or three years, with an average disutility of 2. He will therefore choose to betray.

Clearly this is a highly stylised game, since in real life prisoners might be asking themselves what happens to snitches after they are released (though it was exactly this type of abstract theorising which led to the 'first strike' doctrine, and later the doctrine of Mutually Assured Destruction, during the game known as the Cold War, when what happened after the game may have seemed irrelevant). But it also turns out to not work in an experimental setting either. When the game is actually played by subjects in a psychology lab, people cooperate about half the time – which implies either that they don't understand logic, or again that they are playing with quantum rules.[47]

In the classical version of the prisoner's dilemma game, each player's strategy can be represented by a single bit – for example, 0 for cooperate, or 1 for defect. In the quantum version, players are represented instead by qubits, which can be entangled to a degree. This means that rather than having a single fixed strategy, it is more accurate to say that – like a spin-up or spin-down photon – each player has a superposition of strategies, with an actual state only being selected by a measurement event. Furthermore, because the states are entangled, it means that their decisions are linked. As with entangled photons, the point is not that the two players are in communication, but that they are part of the same system.

In the classical framework, such entanglement would be impossible because of the way the game is defined. But the quantum version essentially gives another dimension to the game, which represents the degree of entanglement. The fact that participants choose to betray only about half the time (when played as a single game with no follow-up) rather than always, implies a rather high degree of entanglement. This is not surprising, since most experimental subjects (and presumably even hardcore criminals) are tied together by things like a shared culture and language, some version of an ethical framework, and a general feeling of empathy and connection with other people – a mental activity which is rooted in the brain's right orbitofrontal cortex. An exception, notes Iain McGilchrist, is 'highly unempathic people, such as psychopaths, in whom this part of the brain is defective'.[48] If classical game theory is for psychopaths, quantum game theory is for normal people.

The phenomenon of entanglement is shown even more clearly by another classic experiment known as the ultimatum game. Two subjects are offered an award of, say, ten dollars, but are given an ultimatum: one person must decide how to split the money, and the other has to decide whether to accept the offer. If the offer is rejected, all the money is returned, so they both lose. Classical theory would imply that any offer would be accepted, no matter how low, because it is better than nothing. However, the game has been performed in many countries around the world, and the results consistently show that people reject an offer that is overly cheap, just to stop the offerer making an unfair profit. The amounts vary, but most offers are near to five dollars, and the typical minimum acceptable offer is around two or three dollars. As in the auction process described in Chapter 1, there is a certain minimum amount – a quantum of kindness – before a deal takes place.

Neuroscientists who tested subjects while they were having their brains scanned showed that when someone was given a cheap offer, say two dollars, the part of their brain responsible for reasoning lit up, but so did the bilateral anterior insula, which is associated with anger and disgust – emotions they were willing to pay to express. Again, it can be argued that this represents some counterintuitive version of rational behaviour, or is a clever ruse by our selfish genes, perhaps because they think there is just a tiny, tiny chance of procreating after the game. But if the game is replayed using quantum logic rather than classical logic, any degree of entanglement between the two players means that the offerer can no longer 'maximise his utility' by offering the other person zero.[49] People have a sense of fair play which in fact is not unique to humans but is shared by animals: in tests where dogs or wolves were rewarded for performing tasks, 'if one animal was given a more substantial reward when performing a task, the other one downed tools completely'.[50]

The default option

In order for this entanglement to be 'truly' quantum, we would need to show that people, or for that matter animals, are in quantum states, appropriately defined (though note again that the interpretation is up for debate).[51] Alexander Wendt argues in his 2015 book *Quantum Mind and Social Science* that we are indeed what he calls 'walking wave functions' so that 'a normal human mind will be in a superposition rather than well-defined state'.[52] Furthermore, 'by virtue of our entanglement from birth in social structures, human minds are not fully separable'.[53] We return to this later; but from an economic perspective, the main test is whether the quantum model of decision-making is more realistic and useful than the classical model – and as seen already, there is plenty of empirical evidence to suggest that it is.

As an illustration of how these cognitive effects come together with the quantum theory of money and value in an economic context, suppose that a person has taken a loan out from a pawnbroker, using for collateral a treasured possession such as a wedding ring, but comes under financial stress and has to decide whether to pay the next instalment or default on the loan. We can model the debtor as being in a superposed quantum state in which he is simultaneously entertaining both options at the same time, as shown in the figure below (note I am re-using the photon polarisation figure from Chapter 1, with axes relabelled, which draws out the quantum connection). A decision is represented by collapsing this state to the corresponding axis. Here the probability of default is given by the square of the projection onto the horizontal axis (i.e. the square of the eigenvalue, 0.35), which is about 0.12 (12 per cent).

Where this gets more complicated than the simple photonic version is that the likelihood of default at a particular time, as expressed by the angle of the grey line, will be affected by external events such as job loss, but will also involve complex behavioural factors which resonate and interfere with one another like waves in a turbulent sea. The debtor's estimate of the value of the collateral will be sensitive to context, and his desire to honour the contract is related to issues of trust, of the sort treated in quantum game theory, both with the creditor and with himself. People often choose to pawn objects with sentimental value exactly because they don't trust themselves to repay, so they want to raise the stakes.[54] Another factor is the planning paradox, applied this time to saved payments rather than cigarettes: the debtor begins with the intention of repaying the loan (stopping smoking), but changes his mind under stress, effectively deciding to sell the collateral and accept future consequences, in return for the saved payments (cigarettes).

The pawnbroker's modelled state concerning this loan is opposite to that of the debtor, in the sense that a default means that the debtor saves the money for payments while the creditor loses that money. Of course it will take time for the lender to actually learn of the default, and there may be a negotiation or legal procedure before the situation is resolved (it also takes time to mechanically perform and communicate measurements on photons, during which other effects may come into play), but that doesn't change the fact that the state of the loan (as opposed to its formal legal status) changes the moment the debtor decides to default.

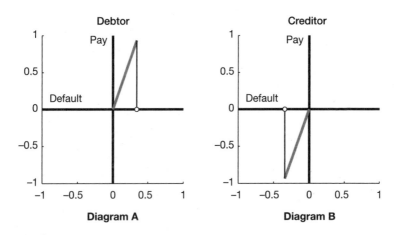

Figure 5. The status of a loan from the point of view of the debtor (diagram A) and the creditor (diagram B). A decision occurs when the state vector (grey line) is collapsed to one of the axes, representing pay or default (here the latter). This decision affects the status of the loan agreement, which is viewed as a single system. The state of the creditor is opposite that of the debtor in the sense that if the debtor decides to default, the creditor will not receive payment.

A loan agreement in all its rich complexity is therefore a paradigmatic example of a quantum economic phenomenon, involving entanglement, indeterminacy, and the sort of overlapping cognitive effects that, as already seen, elude explanation in classical terms.[55] As always in economics, these effects ultimately arise from the dual real/virtual nature of its money, and the tension between numerical price and subjective value, the quantifiable and the unquantifiable, the abstract debt and the concrete consequences of default.

A model of this process, while obviously more difficult to calibrate against data than the simpler models considered above, could be embedded, for example, in the quantum version of an agent-based model, where each individual is represented as a quantum entity. Like a more general version of the spin glass models discussed in the previous chapter, this leads to clustering of beliefs into groups, alignment with shared norms and values, and feedback between the state of the economy and that of the individual agents. Prototype versions of such quantum agent-based models have been developed by computer scientists, and while to my knowledge they have yet to be tried in economics, it is easy to imagine how they could be used in a targeted manner to explore, say, the role of social norms and psychological factors in large-scale mortgage default, of the sort that occurred during the 2007–08 financial crisis.[56]

What perhaps counts even more from a mathematical modelling perspective than the details of the technique, though, is that the quantum approach draws attention to things like loans in the first place. As systems thinker John Sterman wrote: 'The most important assumptions of a model are not in the equations, but what's not in them; not in the documentation, but unstated; not in the variables on the computer screen, but in the blank spaces around them.'[57] As seen in the next chapter, mainstream models have traditionally excluded events such as mass defaults because loans are treated, like other financial transactions, as just a neutral tit-for-tat exchange. Models affect the way we see reality, and also the way we don't see it.

As another example of how these conflicting forces play out on a national scale during an economic crisis, at the time of writing Venezuelan bonds are sometimes known as 'hunger bonds' because the government can only pay its creditors by restricting imports of vital things like food and medicines. The choice to pay or default therefore involves a trade-off that can be measured in human lives. Meanwhile on the street, desperate people are pawning even things like old photographs – 'Sometimes, the stuff doesn't have any kind of value', as one pawnbroker told a reporter – in order to pay debts or buy food.[58]

Why quantum?

In summary, it appears that many cognitive phenomena of the sort studied (or not) by behavioural economists, and that play such a critical role in the economy, can be readily explained by adopting a quantum formalism. As Alexander Wendt wrote: 'the situation in cognitive science today seems similar to physics in the early 1900s. In both domains rigorous testing of classical theories had produced a string of anomalies; efforts to explain them with new classical models were ad hoc and partial; and then a quantum theory emerged that predicted them all with great precision.'[59] So will rational economic man be replaced by his quantum version?

To play devil's advocate, one criticism of quantum cognition, as with – let's face it – most findings in social science, is that rather than *really* making testable predictions, it is actually just explaining something that is already known. This is an important distinction. For example, supporters of string theory in physics sometimes claim that it 'predicts gravity' – as if gravity had never been noticed before it came along to predict its arrival – while in fact what the theory does is offer one possible explanation for gravity. John Cochrane's criticism of behavioural economics is that it has provided many explanations, but fewer important predictions.

A mathematical model based on quantum cognition will obviously be better at fitting experimental data than its classical counterpart, just because it has extra knobs to twiddle, for instance in the degree of entanglement. And while predictions are the traditional test for a scientific theory, these are hard to properly validate in the social sciences, because data for things like survey results are notoriously variable and noisy.[60] But it certainly seems that (unlike in string theory, where there are countless parameters) the additional features of quantum cognition are very well suited to the problem at hand, as illustrated by the natural way in which it incorporates effects such as interference and order dependence. Relative to models used in behavioural psychology, comparative studies have shown that the quantum model is actually quite robust and parsimonious in terms of parameters, and it has the appealing advantage of supplying a consistent approach rather than just a taxonomy of different effects.[61] The structural properties of quantum models therefore appear to match the structure of our cognitive processes, which itself is a kind of prediction in the sense that it can be tested empirically.[62]

A criticism of cognitive science in general is that its experiments usually involve tests or games with well-defined rules conducted under carefully controlled conditions. The real world isn't like that – instead we often make decisions under near-total uncertainty about the possible outcomes. Also, the emphasis on individual decision-making seems misplaced given that many of our decisions are shaped by social influences along with institutions such as employers, advertisers, the state, and so on. It might therefore seem that there is little practical use in theories claiming that we follow a kind of quantum logic under laboratory settings. However, while such factors certainly limit the usefulness of economic modelling in general, they are really a validation of the quantum approach, which assumes indeterminacy rather than clairvoyance about the future, entanglement rather than independence, and the importance of context in general in shaping our perceptions and decisions. The job of marketers and advertisers, for example, is to rotate our mental frame in such a way that we are more likely to decide positively on a purchase.

Another point is that, just as behavioural economics has only managed to tweak the results of mainstream economics, so it might seem that most of the quirks of quantum cognition will come out in the wash. As William Hubbard from the Coase-Sandor Institute for Law and Economics notes: 'In the realm of physics, the Correspondence Principle tells us that Newtonian mechanics is basically wrong, but it's a pretty good approximation at the scale of human society, most but not all of the time. The analogous principle in behavioral economics is that neoclassical economics is basically wrong, but it's a pretty good approximation at the scale of human society, most but not all of the time.'[63] According to Gregory Mankiw's textbook, while a 'hotly debated issue is whether deviations from rationality are important for understanding economic phenomena', even if the rationality assumption is not *exactly* true 'it be may be true enough that it yields reasonably accurate models of behavior.'[64] Or as Cochrane puts it: 'People do a lot of nutty things. But when you raise the price of tomatoes, they buy fewer tomatoes, just as if utility maximizers had walked into the grocery store.'[65] But one area where this averaging out doesn't work is money, which, as we have seen, has quantum properties of its own.

While discussions of rational economic man, and his role in economics, inevitably get bogged down in questions of what is rational, irrational, genetic, etc., one thing that is much easier to assess is the field's neglect of the topic of money. Again, this will probably seem remarkable to most non-economists, but it

makes more sense when you realise that economics has traditionally approached the subject from the vantage point of rational
economic man – and the only way to save the appearances is to
leave money out. Money is the most emotionally volatile substance we have invented, and it doesn't mix well with the notion
of the economy as a self-stabilising, rational, mechanistic system.
One thing that tends not to come across in dry academic studies of behavioural psychology is the powerful effects of money on
the human mind, combining as it does the conflicting effects of
abstract number and concrete ownership. As Stanford University
neuroscientist Brian Knutson observed of his controlled experiments on human behaviour: 'Nothing had an effect on people like
money – not naked bodies, not corpses. It got people riled up. Like
food provides motivation for dogs, money provides it for people.'[66]
It seems we really, really like our keepable numbers.

Forced to choose between the precision of rational economic
man and the vagaries of money, economists chose the former (at
least in their models). This is one reason why the basic question
of money creation was turned into a taboo topic; why financial
events such as loan defaults don't trouble macroeconomic models;
and why, as Akerlof and Shiller note, people's money worries 'are
central concerns of the financial advice books, but you will have
to search hard to find such a word, relating, as it does, people's
finances and their emotions, in any economics textbook'.[67] In fact,
money is so invisible that it is rarely mentioned even in books on
quantum cognition, other than in its role as a reward in games.[68]
The reason behavioural economics (or its quantum cousin) has had
little effect on mainstream economics, then, is because its main
channel of action – money – has been removed from the models.
Conversely, it is the focus on the quantum properties of money
which promises to forge from the different branches of quantum
social science the basis for a new economics.

Finally, a sceptic might point out that there is no causal explanation for why humans should use quantum logic. After all, we're not electrons – and most supporters of quantum cognition tend to steer clear of any kind of claim that mind is actually based, like subatomic matter, on quantum processes, preferring to see quantum probability as just the simplest extension of classical probability (we return to this question of whether nature is 'quantum all the way down', as Alexander Wendt suggests, in Chapter 9). Perhaps the best answer is that, like quantum finance (which so far has mainly been used to duplicate the findings of quantitative finance with small variations), so quantum cognition is important because it changes the way we think about the economy. Instead of rational economic man optimising his utility in an efficient economy, we have quantum economic person engaged in a kind of collective dance with other quantum economic people. We may not be able to describe a mechanistic link in the brain between quantum processes and cognition, but nor is there a mechanistic link showing that we behave mechanistically – and there is plenty of empirical evidence to suggest that we don't. And if rational economic man has influenced our behaviour, so quantum economic person may do the same by supplying a more humanistic role model. One distinction between the social and physical sciences is that social predictions influence the outcome and can turn into self-fulfilling prophesies – meaning that, as predicted in the final chapter, quantum economics can change the economy.

Behavioural economics, with its 'bounded rationality', is a perturbation to rational economic man, an epicycle that can be added when conditions or appearances demand; but quantum cognition, with its indeterminacy and entanglement, calls into question the most basic precepts of economic modelling. In particular, it draws attention to our relationship with that most potent and persistent of nudgers, money.

Creative leaps

As we have already seen, money acts as both a measurement device and an entanglement device. A purchase transaction is a way of collapsing the internal, fuzzy notion of value for either party down to a single number; a loan agreement between a debtor and a creditor is like an entangled system where the debtor is in a superposition of two states, pay or default, and a decision immediately affects the state of the loan for both parties. It is no coincidence that many of the experiments used by psychologists involve rewards or gambles of money, exactly because it is an efficient way of provoking a decision and making comparisons of different effects. The money system, with its dualistic real/virtual nature, acts like a kind of massive quantum computer, exhibiting a full panoply of quantum effects such as entanglement, indeterminacy, interference, and so on, none of which fit with the classical picture of atomistic behaviour. A quantum framework therefore offers many advantages in understanding how money affects our decisions, not just about things like investments but also on broader economic issues such as financial stability, inequality, climate change, and innovation.

On the former, behavioural economics has already provided a wealth of examples of things like herd behaviour and recency bias that tend to accentuate the rise and fall of financial bubbles. The quantum approach allows economists to also consider other forms of entanglement. For example, a 2010 study of the financial crisis used a simple, schematic quantum game theory model to conclude that a major contributor to the crisis was aggressive utility-maximising behaviour on the part of traders, of the sort modelled by rational economic man, which had the unfortunate effect of destabilising the economy rather than making it more efficient (see also the box below). One way to interpret this is to say that traders were entangled through money, rather than through social factors. Recommended measures included 'the provision of a value basis that prevents aggressive behaviour through educational measures, the strengthening of disapproval regarding aggressive behaviour in an economic context through the general public and the change of the legal basis for the provision of variable payment systems' (e.g. multi-million-dollar bonuses).[69]

On inequality, a basic point is that the neoclassical notion of Pareto optimality is not fit for purpose when it comes to running the economy; and here we see a clear distinction between the behavioural and quantum approaches. While Akerlof and Shiller see the goal of Pareto optimality as consistent with their behavioural approach – their modification is to include things like deception in the equilibrium – from a quantum perspective the aim of economics is not to find an imagined equilibrium state which cannot be changed without making one person worse off. When people are entangled, that doesn't even make sense. Far from 'elevating the notion of free-market optimality into a high scientific achievement', this concept has done much to distort the ideas and priorities of economists. More in Chapter 9.

Another kind of quantum entanglement is our relationship with the planet – and here money has played a definite role in rotating the axes of our belief system in a rather odd direction. As the ever-trustworthy Al Gore told *The Guardian* in 2017, 'Our democracy has been hacked … I mean that those with access to large amounts of money and raw power have been able to subvert all reason and fact in collective decision making. The Koch brothers are the largest funders of climate change denial. And ExxonMobil claims it has stopped, but it really hasn't. It has given a quarter of a billion dollars in donations to climate denial groups. It's clear they are trying to cripple our ability to respond to this existential threat.'[70] Of course neoclassical economists say they 'take climate science very seriously' as one put it, but in fact the two fields aren't very compatible, as discussed further in Chapter 9.[71] Financial instability, inequality, and environmental damage are not 'market failures' as they are commonly portrayed. They are just money expressing itself.

Finally, an enduring mystery from the standpoint of neoclassical economics, with its emphasis on static equilibrium, is how an economy generates new ideas and technologies. Such developments are usually modelled as a form of external shock to the economy, as if they come out of nowhere, like freak but unusually productive weather. Or they can be handled as the mechanistic result of a Darwinian selection process, so new ideas are akin to random genetic variations which only take root if they aid survival. Mainstream economics therefore perceives creativity as essentially alien and/or machine-like, while still vicariously taking credit for innovation by describing it as the outcome of properly designed markets. The quantum viewpoint in contrast tends to emphasise what Alexander Wendt describes as 'the creativity and freedom of individuals to resist and overcome structural constraints', like an electron tunnelling through a barrier.[72] Creativity is not external to the economy, or the result of some blind mechanical process; it is part of what makes the economy alive. The creative leap, where a complex idea springs unbidden into our minds as a complete whole, as if it has been there all along and we are only remembering it, may be the closest the human mind comes to a direct, visceral experience of a quantum phenomenon. One thinks of the songwriter who woke up one morning in 1963 with an almost-complete melody stuck in his mind, which he thought he must have picked up from somewhere else, but the only thing he had for lyrics was the repeated phrase 'scrambled eggs'. That part required some further deliberation, and the songwriter (Paul McCartney) later changed it to the words to 'Yesterday'.[73]

Quantum cognition therefore has profound implications for the way we see the economy – and ourselves. In her 2017 book

Doughnut Economics, Kate Raworth calls for economists to replace rational economic man with a more complex portrait of human behaviour: 'First, rather than narrowly self-interested, we are social and reciprocating. Second, in place of fixed preferences, we have fluid values. Third, instead of isolated, we are interdependent. Fourth, rather than calculate, we usually approximate. And fifth, far from having dominion over nature, we are deeply embedded in the web of life.'[74] The most natural and appropriate framework for sketching this portrait in mathematical terms, as Asghar Qadir posited in 1978, is the quantum formalism.

This is not to say that quantum economists should launch their own version of a Manhattan Project and build a giant quantum model of the global economy up from the scale of people's brains to compete with the neoclassical approach.* But perhaps if economists had been more receptive to ideas from quantum physics such as indeterminacy, entanglement and interference – economists are often accused of physics envy, but really it is Victorian physics envy – we wouldn't all still be calling for the demise of rational economic man (or *The Twilight of Homo Economicus*, as Tomáš Sedláček, Roman Chlupatý and I once called it in a book).[75] We

---

* Though some neuroscientists and economists have suggested something rather similar. As the Harvard economist David Laibson told *The New Yorker* in 2006: 'Natural science has moved ahead by studying progressively smaller units. Physicists started out studying the stars, then they looked at objects, molecules, atoms, subatomic particles, and so on. My sense is that economics is going to follow the same path. Forty years ago, it was mainly about large-scale phenomena, like inflation and unemployment. More recently, there has been a lot of focus on individual decision-making. I think the time has now come to go beyond the individual and look at the inputs to individual decision-making. That is what we do in neuroeconomics.' Cassidy, J. (18 September 2006), 'Mind Games: What neuroeconomics tells us about money and the brain', *The New Yorker*.

discuss this further in the next chapter, which looks at how the complex entanglements which characterise the economy also make its behaviour exceedingly difficult to predict.

Corporate man

While *Homo economicus* is a fictional character – really, what kind of person is completely rational and objective and acts only to maximise his utility? – the legal entity known as a corporation (from the Latin *corporatio* for 'to combine in one body') has been designed to approach him quite closely in its behaviour. Corporations have a legal status whose defining features are limited liability and profit maximisation. The first means that an investor is not responsible for the debts or obligations of the corporation, while the second means that the corporation is legally bound to make as much money for that investor as possible.

In the early 1800s, when the first corporations were formed, limited liability was intended as an incentive for people to invest in risky enterprises. If a corporation such as the British East India Company failed in its colonialist ventures, then the investors would not be liable to pay creditors. In the US, the first corporations were special public ventures such as insurance or canal building. Incorporation was viewed as a special status, and had a limited lifespan of typically twenty to fifty years. As corporations flourished, this was relaxed, and their lifespan became indefinite.

In 1886, the Michigan Supreme Court ruled that a corporation was entitled to a legal status of 'corporate personhood' which is similar to that of a real person, with rights including freedom of speech. (Interestingly, this was the same year tomatoes were granted the legal status of vegetables – see box at end of Chapter 1.) In 1916, when Henry Ford tried to prioritise business investment over dividends, his stockholders successfully sued, the court ruling that the main purpose of a corporation is to maximise the shareholders' profits. As Milton Friedman wrote in 1962: 'Few trends could so thoroughly undermine the very foundations of our free society as the acceptance by corporate officials of a social responsibility other than to make as much money for their stockholders as possible.'[76]

This approach is epitomised by large pharmaceutical companies, which, according to a 2017 study by the Institute for New Economic Thinking, 'allocate the profits generated from high drug prices to massive repurchases, or buybacks, of their own corporate stock for the sole purpose of giving manipulative boosts to their stock prices. Incentivizing these buybacks is stock-based compensation that rewards senior executives for stock-price "performance." Like no other sector, the pharmaceutical industry puts a spotlight on how the political economy of science is a matter of life and death.'[77] Corporate persons, in other words, take priority over the living and breathing type.

Today, many 'investors' in corporations are also highly 'rational' and goal-focused because they are not human, they are emotionless computer algorithms of the sort that now dominate much trading in financial securities. Unfortunately the net effect of having many such algorithms operating at the same time does not seem to be one of overall sober rationality, as evidenced by the fact that most just shut down or dump their holdings when they don't understand what is going on, which seems to be rather often judging by the flash crashes which periodically afflict markets.

As quantum cognition shows, there is more to both mind and markets than classical logic would imply. According to a 2018 study by the Global Strategy Group, 81 per cent of Americans 'believe that corporations should take action to address important issues facing society'.[78] Has the time come for the quantum corporation, which combines in one body (or one social wave function) the entangled needs and desires of its shareholders, employees, customers, society, the environment, and so on?

CHAPTER 8

ENTANGLED CLOUDS

*'The forecast,' said Mr. Oliver, turning the pages till he
found it, 'says: Variable winds; fair average temperature;
rain at times.' ... There was a fecklessness, a lack of
symmetry and order in the clouds, as they thinned and
thickened. Was it their own law, or no law, they obeyed?*
Virginia Woolf, *Between the Acts* (1941)

*Orthodoxy means not thinking – not needing
to think. Orthodoxy is unconsciousness.*
George Orwell, *Nineteen Eighty-four* (1949)

A long-standing tenet of mainstream economics has been that
people act as individual atoms – they don't interact, communicate, collude, or look after one another. Today it is increasingly
acknowledged that people do not behave this way – which
should not be a surprise, given that atoms don't either. Indeed,
particles can become entangled in such a way that making a
measurement on one instantaneously gives you information
about the other, even if it is on the other side of the universe.
Einstein's speed limit – that nothing, including information, can
travel faster than the speed of light – apparently doesn't apply. A
similar effect occurs in the economy, where people are entangled
by things like money and contracts. Changing the view of the
economy from a collection of inert atoms, to a complex system
where even the observer is entangled, has profound implications

for how we model it – and explains why it is even harder to predict than the weather.

Perhaps the most basic of physical laws are the so-called conservation laws, which state that some measurable quantity remains constant during interactions. An example is conservation of mass: in his *Principia*, Newton assumed that, while one substance might possibly transmute into another, the total amount of mass in a closed system is constant (Einstein later extended this rule by showing that energy was another form of mass). Newton also showed that conservation of momentum (mass times velocity) was a consequence of his laws of motion. Another quantity that tended to be conserved in certain experiments was what Leibniz called the *vis viva* (living force), later renamed kinetic energy, which corresponds, for example, to the mechanical energy of a ball rolling down a ramp. To lift the ball back up requires another kind of energy, called work.

One of the more mysterious forms of energy was the thermal energy stored in heat. According to the kinetic theory of heat, developed in the early nineteenth century, this was associated with the average kinetic energy of atoms as they randomly jostle around. When warmed, the atoms move more quickly and push against one another as they collide, which is why substances tend to expand as they warm. In his 1824 book *Reflections on the Motive Power of Fire*, the French military engineer Sadi Carnot – sometimes known as the 'father of thermodynamics' – derived a formula which computed how efficiently steam engines can convert heat into work (a relevant question for the military, which relied heavily on steam engines). He found that, for a perfect engine where no energy is wasted, its efficiency depends only on the difference in temperature between the input (or heat source) and output (or heat sink), which for a steam engine were the fire and the outside air.

Finally, in 1847, the German physician and physicist Hermann Helmholtz proposed that mechanics, heat, electricity, magnetism and light were all different aspects of a single type of energy that was at all times conserved.[1] It was this principle which later led Max Planck to deduce that energy came in quanta. Helmholtz was motivated by his studies of human muscles, which converted food into work. So when neoclassical economists decided to base their theory of human behaviour on the physics of the time, it seemed natural to equate utility with a form of energy. The economy was a giant thermodynamic system, which converted work into utility.

Maxwell's demon

One slightly puzzling aspect of thermodynamics, which has long been a source of dispute, is the second law of thermodynamics, which says that entropy always increases, where entropy is a measure of disorder or randomness. Suppose for example that you leave a cup of hot coffee in a room. At the beginning, the room/coffee system has a high degree of order, in the sense that the heat is concentrated in the cup; but as time goes on, the heat dissipates out until the coffee is the same temperature as the rest of the room. Unlike other laws of physics, which are generally agnostic as to whether you run them forwards or in reverse, this rule seems to put a kind of direction on time, because it never goes the other way: the coffee doesn't spontaneously heat up by extracting heat from the room.

The law is puzzling, at least from a reductionist perspective, because it is a statistical result which holds only for an ensemble of atoms, rather than individual atoms. The idea of order also seems to be slightly subjective, since it is not a basic quantity like length. This ambiguity was illustrated in 1867 by James Clerk Maxwell, when he came up with a paradox that became known as Maxwell's demon. Imagine a container with two compartments, each containing the same gas at the same temperature; and suppose that some imaginary demon sits at the intersection between the two containers. When he sees a fast-moving atom in the left compartment, he opens a small window that allows it to pass to the right. Conversely, slow-moving atoms in the right compartment are selectively allowed to pass to the left. After a while, the left (slow team) compartment will be cool, and the right (fast team) compartment will be hot. It would then be possible to extract energy from this heat difference, which would appear to violate energy conservation.

One explanation, first proposed in 1929 by physicist Leó Szilárd – who went on to conceive of the nuclear chain reaction four years later – was that the demon was actually doing a kind of work, by manipulating information. In 1982, the physicist Charles Bennett made this more explicit by pointing out that the demon, like all information workers, will eventually run out of memory storage, so he will have to physically erase memory – a process which consumes energy (estimated to be at least 2.9 zeptojoules per bit). As a result, the demon creates more entropy just by thinking than he removes. This result suggests that information and thermodynamics are somehow fundamentally linked.

The connection between the two areas has recently been made even stronger by the advent of a new field of physics, known as quantum thermodynamics.[2] In classical thermodynamics, of the sort imitated by economists, particles are viewed as inert atoms that interact only by bouncing off one another. Its quantum version, however, acknowledges that particles are quantum entities which become entangled as they interact. For example, when two electrons 'collide', rather than just careening off in different directions, their wave functions effectively merge into a larger version which describes them both. One way to see this is as an exchange of information: the electrons are storing a kind of knowledge about each other.

Over time, as interactions continue and the particles become increasingly entangled, information accumulates throughout the system, which has an equilibrating effect. According to quantum thermodynamics, this is the real reason why entropy always increases with time. The coffee cup cools, according to physicist Sandu Popescu, because the information it contains 'leaks out and becomes smeared over the entire environment' through the process of entanglement.[3] However, while entanglement can bring a system to equilibrium, that is not the only possibility. A property of living systems is that they have found ways to lower entropy internally, and – like Maxwell's demon – create order out of chaos. And rather than exist in a state of stable equilibrium, they are better described as being far from equilibrium.

The role of quantum entanglement in biological systems is not clear. It has been implicated in a number of otherwise mysterious phenomena including photosynthesis, avian navigation, and even the chemistry of DNA, including adaptive mutations.[4] But one example of a living system where entanglement (at least of the monetary sort) plays an obvious role is the economy.

A leap too far

Just as classical thermodynamics assumes that matter is made up of inert, lifeless atoms, so neoclassical economics is based on the idea that the economy is made up of selfish rational utility-maximisers who interact only by bouncing off one another in the marketplace. Of course there is a degree of variation between individuals, but it is generally assumed that these differences come out in the wash when a large number of people are considered. It therefore makes sense to focus on average quantities. For example, macroeconomic models typically model countries or sectors by the use of one or a few representative consumers and producers, in the same way that thermodynamic concepts such as temperature or entropy only make sense for an ensemble of atoms. The assumption that the system is linear, so one can simply average over all the people in the population, allows economists to claim that the models are built on secure microfoundations.[5]

An early example of this approach was provided in 1817 by the British economist David Ricardo, who used it to demonstrate that it made sense for a country to concentrate on areas where it had a comparative advantage over other countries. If a country was skilled at producing a particular good, then it should focus on that, because there would always be demand for any excess product from other countries, as long as the price was right. Ricardo illustrated his theory with a simple example: two countries, Portugal and England, trading two products, wine and cloth. He demonstrated that each country would benefit if it concentrated only on manufacturing whichever good it could produce more cheaply (cloth for England, wine for Portugal), and importing the other. The result would be a net improvement in 'the sum of enjoyments'.

While Ricardo's simplified analysis ignored many complicating factors – Joseph Schumpeter later defined the 'Ricardian Vice' as the practice of choosing assumptions that give the desired result – it set new standards for deductive logic in economics, and inspired future thinkers from Karl Marx to Paul Samuelson, who called it the only proposition in social science that 'is both true and non-trivial'.[6] As economist Reinhard Schumacher notes, it serves as an 'intellectual cornerstone' for the programme of trade liberalisation long promoted by institutions such as the World Trade Organization, and its influence on economists is also felt in the fact that polls consistently show 'an overwhelming academic support for free trade among the profession'.[7] But as is often pointed out, there are a couple of obvious problems with it.

One is that Ricardo assumed straightforward barter of goods, so there would be no movement of labour or capital between countries: 'the fancied or real insecurity of capital, when not under the immediate control of its owner, together with the natural disinclination which every man has to quit the country of his birth and connexions, and intrust himself with all his habits fixed, to a strange government and new laws, check the emigration of capital.'[8] Also, any trade deficit would be corrected by an adjustment in local prices – if Britain drank too much Portuguese wine, then gold would flow to Portugal, which according to the quantity theory of money would raise prices there, making its products less competitive. On the other hand, Ricardo assumed that labour and capital were *internally* mobile, so workers and factories could switch from making cloth to producing wine at will.

In fact, as with most macroeconomic models, the analysis contains another mental leap, or sleight of hand, which can be viewed as a form of premature wave function collapse. While money is not present as an active substance, it *is* present as a metric; and the model assumes that the value of a cloth or wine industry can be collapsed down at any moment to a certain value of gold, which can then slosh around and find its own equilibrium. So really the comparison is about two roundabout ways of obtaining gold – either by making wine and exchanging it for gold, or by making cloth and exchanging that for gold. However, while retooling a factory to change the medium of choice from cloth to wine might sound OK in principle, it could run into a few snags in the real world, because context matters.

Indeed, there is plenty of empirical evidence to show that things don't turn out like the Ricardian picture in practice. When American factory workers saw their jobs decimated by overseas competition, they didn't retrain as fintech consultants, they just voted for Donald Trump. Capitalists are quite happy to invest in other countries, especially if labour is cheaper and regulations less restrictive than at home. Trade deficits are not magically balanced out by adjustments in price, but can persist indefinitely (an example is the UK). And specialisation in a handful of industries is characteristic of poor or unstable countries such as Ghana – where fuels, precious metals, and cocoa comprise 81 per cent of exports – or Venezuela, where oil alone makes up 73 per cent of exports, rather than rich and stable countries like Germany or Japan.

In fact, it turns out that the theory of comparative advantage has it the wrong way round. In a 2014 paper called *The Atlas of Economic Complexity: Mapping Paths to Prosperity*, which is based on actual international trade data for 128 countries, a team of data scientists at Harvard University led by Ricardo Hausmann concluded that prosperity depends not so much on specialisation, but 'on the diversity of knowledge across individuals and on their ability to combine this knowledge, and make use of it, through complex webs of interaction'.[9] In particular, innovation requires exposure to a variety of ideas, not doing exactly the same thing you have always done. As with any living system, what counts is the structure's ability to process energy and information.

Unfortunately, such effects cannot be captured by conventional models exactly because these deal in aggregates, ignore complexity, see the economy as an equilibrium system, and flatten the intricate structure of an economy down to a single uniform dimension. The archetypal example of this approach is that workhorse of macroeconomics, the Dynamic Stochastic General Equilibrium (DSGE) model. The name is misleading, because in Orwellian newspeak fashion the words are used in a special way which has little to do with their normal interpretation.[10] 'Dynamic' refers only to changes to a model equilibrium over time as it adjusts to external shocks – not to any internal dynamism. 'Stochastic' (meaning randomly determined) refers to random perturbations such as oil price shocks or technological developments which are treated as external effects; however, these are usually assumed to be ergodic, which means that they come from a stable distribution and so can be estimated from past experience, and linear in the sense that small shocks have small effects and a shock twice as big as another has double the effect.[11] The word 'General' means that the model is supposed to include all markets, but this omits things like derivatives or other forms of financial entanglement (exceptions are discussed below).[12]

The models assume that supply and demand drive prices to an equilibrium point where consumers are maximising their utility, firms are maximising their profits, and all markets clear. Consumers and firms are usually modelled using one or at most a few representatives, such as high- and low-income individuals, as are the goods available for consumption. Where monetary variables do occur, they are reactive rather than active, so for example a central monetary authority sets interest rates in response to inflation, which is linked to output. The models can then be used to assist policy decisions, say by comparing the results with and without a particular policy change. The overall picture is the same as that of the efficient-market models used in quantitative finance, where a stable equilibrium is perturbed by independent, random fluctuations.

Such models are obviously far more elaborate than Ricardo's first-draft version, and some versions also take a degree of heterogeneity, bounded rationality, or other mechanistic 'frictions' into account – though as discussed further below, these refinements come at the expense of extra parameters and complications, without changing the overall behaviour too much. From the quantum economics viewpoint, however, these models need far more than a tweak or a few added epicycles, because the basic assumptions are completely wrong. In particular, it is not possible to aggregate or average over people as if they are inert, independent atoms, because they are entangled with themselves (i.e. their own ideas, habits, and emotions), with other people they meet, with social norms, with legal contracts, and so on. People and corporations are not separate, disembodied things, but are part of a connected whole. It is informative to compare Adam Smith's hierarchical, robotic description of workers in a pin factory to feminist scholar Karen Barad's comment on a sociological study of a Kolkata jute mill: 'Workers, machines, managers are entangled phenomena, relational beings, that share more than the air around them; they help constitute one another.'[13] But perhaps the most effective entanglement device, whose complex properties have been excluded from the analysis since at least the time of classical economists such as Smith and Ricardo, is money.

Limited versus unlimited

As discussed in Chapter 3, money is created in a process which involves the entanglement of two parties, the issuer and the holder. An ancient coin was made of gold owned and stamped by the king, and its use thus entangled the holder with the crown (which is why the coin could be demanded back as payment for tax). A medieval tally stick consisted of two parts of equal but opposite value, which entangled the holder of the stock with that of the foil. Modern fiat money produced through a bank loan entangles a mortgage holder with the bank. Use of the euro currency entangles a country like modern Portugal with the rest of the eurozone. And in general, money always has a debt aspect to it, which links the debtor and creditor.

While debt is as old as money, it has never been quite as big as it is today. Global debt in 2017 was estimated at $217 trillion, up $50 trillion over the previous decade.[14] Just as credit card debt allows individual consumers to live above their means, for a while, so this debt gives the global economy the appearance of robust economic growth, boosting GDP in the short term while putting off the day of reckoning. Afraid to spoil the party, central banks use tools such as quantitative easing (purchasing assets with made-up money) and ultra-low interest rates to prolong the problem and pass it on to future generations. As in quantum physics, entanglements can go forwards and backwards in time.

Because mainstream economists see money as an inert chip, the traditional view, as summarised by Ben Bernanke in his *Essays on the Great Depression*, was that debt is 'no more than a redistribution from one group (debtors) to another (creditors)'.[15] Or as Paul Krugman explained in 2012: 'Think of it this way: when debt is rising, it's not the economy as a whole borrowing more money. It is, rather, a case of less patient people – people who for whatever reason want to spend sooner rather than later – borrowing from more patient people.'[16] In this linear view of money, debts and credits conveniently cancel out in the aggregate, and so can be ignored.[17] But even if the debts seem to erase in a numerical fashion, the entanglements remain. In the case of Portugal, its debt became such an issue during the eurozone crisis that, along with Greece, it risked being ejected from the European Union's single currency.[18]

Just as global debt levels have ballooned in recent decades, so the financial system's degree of self-entanglement has increasingly transcended boundaries. In 1980, global trade and global finance were each around equal; but since then, the former has remained fairly stable, while the latter has increased by about a factor of nine. As the Bank of England's Andrew Haldane noted in a 2014 speech: 'Today, cross-border stocks of capital are almost certainly larger than at any time in human history. We have hit a new high-water mark.'[19] As far as finance is concerned, we are all Ricardian free-traders.

The evolution of global finance, and its increasing degree of entanglement, has in some areas led to a form of convergence. For example, bond yields and equity prices have become highly correlated across different countries, because investment managers increasingly look at the world economy as a single system.[20] However, a common feature of networks is that increased integration also makes them more susceptible to effects such as contagion. Instead of shocks dissipating, their effects are amplified as they spread through the network.[21] This was illustrated by the role of complex derivatives such as collateralised debt obligations (CDOs) and credit default swaps (CDSs) in the 2007–08 financial crisis.

CDOs were used to combine loans such as mortgages into products with calibrated levels of risk that could be sold on to investors, while CDSs offered insurance against default. Regulators at the time saw these instruments as a way to pool risk and smooth it away, the equivalent of strapping a spanking new Ricardian radiator onto the world economy to dissipate the heat. As the International Monetary Fund noted in January 2006: 'The dispersion of credit risk by banks to a broader and more diverse group of investors, rather than warehousing such risks on their balance sheets, has helped to make the banking and overall financial system more resilient.'[22] Ben Bernanke echoed the IMF in May the same year when he said that 'because of the dispersion of financial risks to those more willing and able to bear them, the economy and financial system are more resilient.'[23] This changed abruptly during the crisis when institutions suddenly discovered that, through a complex system of linkages, they had exposure to a company default on the other side of the world. The UK's biggest export to Portugal at the time turned out to be, not a commodity like cloth, but something far more toxic – financial contagion.

The notional value of all the financial derivatives in existence was estimated in 2010 by quant Paul Wilmott at $1.2 quadrillion (so $1,200,000,000,000,000). Among the most popular are interest rate swaps, which typically involve the exchange of a fixed rate income stream with a variable rate stream, and these are often used as a highly leveraged way to bet on changes in interest rates. Notional value here means the value of the underlying asset (e.g. the source of an income stream), so the amount at stake isn't that large except in the worst case, such as default; but the sheer size defies any kind of logic, since it is almost twenty times world GDP.[24] It is a bit like all your neighbours taking out fire insurance against your house from the same company, which is great news for that company unless your house actually burns down. Furthermore, unlike insurance companies, derivatives are lightly regulated, are often traded over the counter, and don't always appear on balance sheets, so it is hard for regulators to track systemic risk.[25]

Derivatives therefore form a cloud of entanglements which sits above the usual financial network like a charged atmospheric storm system and adds another level of complexity. Instead of limiting damage, they make it potentially unlimited. As early as 2000 Wilmott warned that the models used to calculate their value, and estimate risk, were flawed: 'It is clear that a major rethink is desperately required if the world is to avoid a mathematician-led market meltdown ... The underlying assumptions in the models, such as the importance of the normal distribution, the elimination of risk, measurable correlations, etc., are incorrect.'[26] Conventional macroeconomic models go a step further and ignore these derivatives altogether, even if in terms of number they are the largest feature of the economy.[27] So how can these models be used to predict or understand financial storms? For the remainder of this chapter, we answer this question by comparing the models used in economics with those used in another field which is based even more directly on thermodynamics: meteorology.

The storm

Economics is often compared to meteorology, and even sometimes models itself after that field. William Stanley Jevons wrote in 1871 that economics would become 'a science as exact as many of the physical sciences; as exact, for instance, as Meteorology is likely to be for a very long time to come'.[28] Weather models work by dividing the atmosphere up into a 3D grid, and applying the laws of motion and thermodynamics to track its flow. The first computerised weather forecast was carried out in 1950 by a team led by the ubiquitous John von Neumann, who realised that the same mathematical techniques he was using to simulate nuclear weapons could also be used to forecast the weather – and possibly even turn it into a weapon (instead of dropping bombs, one could somehow initiate a drought).

Their first forecast was for 24 hours only, and took 24 hours of processing time on the ENIAC machine to compute. Run times soon improved, as did forecast accuracy; but the goal of perfect forecasts, let alone the ability to control the weather, remained elusive. In the 1960s, the mathematician and chaos theory pioneer Ed Lorenz suggested that the weather system was highly sensitive to any small perturbation – the so-called butterfly effect – which rendered exact prediction impossible. While his theory at first had little impact, it became popular in the 1990s when forecasting centres adopted the Monte Carlo technique to run many simulations from randomly perturbed starting points, in so-called ensemble forecasts. The motivation for this approach could again be 'traced back to the Manhattan Project and ultimately to quantum mechanics', as one study notes.[29]

In theory, ensemble forecasting provides both a central forecast, and an idea of the uncertainty. However, as I found while researching my DPhil on the predictability of nonlinear systems in the late 1990s, this approach neglects a more obvious but less computationally tractable contributor to forecast error, which is the fact that the weather is hard to model. In particular, features such as the formation and dissipation of clouds are complex emergent phenomena that can only be approximated by equations. The fact that clouds, and water vapour in general, are one of the most important features of the weather is the main reason weather prediction is so difficult.[30] Alternative techniques such as machine learning, which can be used to look for patterns in weather data, have had little impact.[31]

Economic models take the same mechanistic approach as weather models, with the difference that they assume the economy has a stable equilibrium perturbed by random external shocks – not from butterflies, but from things like new technologies, labour productivity, risk perception, or monetary policy. Economists even use similar language to meteorologists, with their liquidity, currency, capital streams, and depressions. And part of their mandate is also to make forecasts – a term introduced by Robert FitzRoy when he set up the first UK meteorological office in 1854 – and give adequate warning of storms. As Vítor Constâncio of the European Central Bank noted, a useful economic model 'must fit the data reasonably well and should be able to produce effective economic forecasts'.[32] According to the Bank of England, 'Forecasting at the Bank, and at central banks more widely, makes a core contribution to policymaking'.[33] And as Bloomberg noted, 'Forecasting is a critical concern for central-bank credibility as it provides the basis for monetary-policy decisions that affect the companies and households of the real economy'.[34]

To be sure – as many economists have pointed out since the crisis (see box below) – forecasting plays a less central role in economics than in something like meteorology (at least in terms of focus, as opposed to impact). And no one would expect economists to predict the exact timing of a crash, any more than we would ask a doctor to predict the exact date of a patient's heart attack. But even if most economists are not involved in forecasting (neither are most meteorologists), prediction is relied on by the scientific method as a way to distinguish between competing theories, and major misses deserve extra attention because they offer a rare opportunity to tell whether an approach or set of assumptions is fundamentally flawed. As John Maynard Keynes noted in 1923, it isn't enough for economists to ignore short-term crises: 'Economists set themselves too easy, too useless a task, if in tempestuous seasons they can only tell us, that when the storm is long past, the ocean is flat again.'[35] And economists do make predictions all the time which have real consequences. When Ben Bernanke told Congress that 'the economy and financial system are more resilient' because of instruments such as complex derivatives – rather than at risk of Paul Wilmott's 'mathematician-led market meltdown' – he was making a kind of prediction based on his picture of how markets worked, and that prediction had an effect on how law-makers treated those markets. Same for his apparently sincere statement in June 2006 that 'the troubles in the subprime sector seem unlikely to seriously spill over to the broader economy or the financial system' (after Michael Hudson had already supplied an 'Illustrated Guide to the Coming Real Estate Collapse').[36] More generally, the neoclassical belief that markets are self-stabilising is a prediction, because it rules out the kind of cascading event where a disturbance in one area propagates through the system and grows out of control until it turns into a global crisis. And economists regularly publish specific forecasts on variables such as inflation or growth which send signals to individuals, businesses, and governments on the economic climate.

Of course, as the quantum physicist Niels Bohr is supposed to have said, 'prediction is hard, especially about the future'. An example was the financial crash of 2007–08, which the Bank of England's Andrew Haldane described in 2017 as a 'Michael Fish moment' (in reference to the BBC weatherman's forecast, just prior to the Great Storm of 1987, that there was no 'hurricane on the way').[37] According to Haldane, that forecasting error kickstarted a technological revolution at the UK Met Office which economists can copy. But weather forecasting relies on data collection systems and models that are developed globally, not just in the UK, and improvements in forecasting had less to do with any particular storm than they did with things like faster computers (our phones are more advanced too). One reason meteorologists suddenly embraced chaos theory in the early 1990s was because, like the efficient market hypothesis, it gave a perfect excuse for forecast errors like the one in 1987. However, weather forecasters are amateurs when it comes to explaining their forecast misses – and if there is one area where they can learn from economists, it is this.

Let the confabulation begin

On a visit to the London School of Economics in November 2008, Queen Elizabeth famously asked her hosts: 'Why did no one see it coming?' (Economists are tired of hearing this story brought up.[38] However, the issue has never been properly settled by something like a public enquiry; it was historic in nature and inspired the call for alternatives to mainstream economics; and as seen below, the answers supplied over the years have proved quite revealing.) The Queen finally received a response from the LSE in July the next year, which concluded that 'the failure to foresee the timing, extent and severity of the crisis and to head it off, while it had many causes, was principally a failure of the collective imagination of many bright people, both in this country and internationally, to understand the risks to the system as a whole'.[39]

A related question, though, was why did no one – see it? Consider for example the discussion at the US Federal Open Market Committee Meeting in December 2007, when it was later determined that the recession had already begun. 'Overall', reads the transcript, 'our forecast could admittedly be read as still painting a pretty benign picture: despite all the financial turmoil, the economy avoids recession and, even with steeply higher prices for food and energy and a lower exchange value of the dollar, we achieve some modest edging-off of inflation. So I tried not to take it personally when I received a notice the other day that the Board had approved more frequent drug-testing for certain members of the senior staff, myself included. [Laughter]'[40]

In fact the prediction wasn't unconventional in the least, it was merely reflecting common opinion. The same month the OECD predicted that the slowdown in US housing 'is unlikely to trigger a recession'.[41] And a study by IMF economists showed the consensus of forecasters in 2008 was that not one of 77 countries considered would be in recession the next year (49 of them were).[42] That isn't a 'Michael Fish moment' – it is a weather forecaster protesting that the storm that has already begun and is blowing down people's houses isn't actually a storm, as he is marched off for his drug test. Rather than helping economists see into the future, their models were preventing them from noticing what was going on outside their windows.

In 2008 testimony, Alan Greenspan told Congress that the forecasting miss happened because 'the data inputted into the risk management models generally covered only the past two decades, a period of euphoria'.[43] That is like a weather forecaster saying they did not see the storm coming because it had been sunny for so long. (Compare Steve Martin's 'wacky weatherman' character Harris K. Telemacher in *L.A. Story*, whose forecasts of fine weather are always the same – 'So I pretape the weather and some sailors lost their boats, big deal!'[44]) Nobel laureate economist Robert Lucas provided an innovative excuse for forecast error when he clarified in a 2009 article for *The Economist* that 'simulations were not presented as assurance that no crisis would occur, but as a forecast of what could be expected conditional on a crisis not occurring.'[45] That is like a weather forecaster saying their forecast was explicitly based on no storms. (A conditional forecast is one of the form 'If X, then Y, *ceteris paribus*' – see discussion of this clause in Chapter 4. The usage here reflects the fact that standard models treat crises as being caused by random external shocks.)

In 2010, during a US House of Representatives hearing on 'the promise and limits of modern macroeconomic theory in light of the current economic crisis', a robust defence of traditional modelling approaches was provided in testimony – which as we'll see, doesn't seem to have dated much – by V.V. Chari from the Federal Reserve Bank of Minneapolis. According to Chari, 'All the interesting policy questions involve understanding how people make decisions over time and how they handle uncertainty. All must deal with the effects on the whole economy. So, any interesting model must be a dynamic stochastic general equilibrium model. From this perspective, there is no other game in town … The only alternatives are models in which the modeler does not clearly spell out how people make decisions. Why should we prefer obfuscation to clarity?'[46] (Indeed, it frequently seems that just by *calling* their models dynamic, stochastic, and general, DSGE modellers have somehow ruled out all other approaches – like a weather forecaster saying that their General Circulation Model which missed the storm is still the only game in town, because any model must be general and involve circulation.[47])

Chari offered three reasons why these models 'failed to predict the recent financial crisis' and more precisely 'failed to emphasize the risks to which the economy was exposed in the period before the crisis'. The first was Greenspan's excuse that the models were calibrated to a period in history when economic fluctuations in the US were relatively small. The second reason was that 'we

deemphasized the insights of the theoretical literature on the perverse effects of government bailouts because understanding these
effects requires that we impute even more rationality and foresight to economic agents than we currently impute'. In other words,
rational economic man was insufficiently rational.

The third reason was lack of funds. As a solution, Chari suggested more of the same: 'After all, when the AIDS crisis hit, we did
not turn over medical research to acupuncturists. In the wake of
the oil spill in the Gulf of Mexico, should we stop using mathematical models of oil pressure? Rather than pursuing elusive chimera
dreamt up in remote corners of the profession, the best way of
using the power in the modeling style of modern macroeconomics
is to devote more resources to it.' (Quantum approaches would
presumably be right out.) He ended with a rousing plea for 'sub-
stantially more resources' to go towards this 'severely underfunded'
research programme – even if such equilibrium models must be
one of the longest running, best funded and least successful international modelling efforts in the history of applied mathematics.[48]

In 2011, John Cochrane wrote that 'It is fun to say that we did
not see the crisis coming, but the central empirical prediction of
the efficient markets hypothesis is precisely that nobody can tell
where markets are going' (again since changes are due to random
shocks). Future laureate Eugene Fama agreed that his theory 'did
quite well in this episode'. (Nobel-prize winning weather forecaster:
'It is fun to say we didn't predict the storm, but at least our prediction that we couldn't predict it was spot-on.') In 2015, at an event
called 'The Genius of Economics', laureate Paul Krugman said the
crisis 'came as a shock to me as to almost everyone'; of the few
people who did predict it, 'they also saw five crises that didn't happen coming so it doesn't quite count', and 'there's always going to
be something out there that you miss'.[49] (Weather genius accusing
other, successful forecasters of *always* predicting a storm.)

In a 2015 Rethinking Economics debate, Dutch economist Pieter Gautier told students that 'we know that it is difficult to predict a crisis. We can say what we can do when a crisis occurs, such as having enough liquidity. Meanwhile, we know how we can try to prevent crises, such as making sure that banks have enough equity. Unfortunately, we don't always listen to economists.'[50] Unfortunately, we did: all the risk models that were used by financial institutions to price those complex derivatives, for example, were based on standard economic theories, including the efficient market hypothesis. That was the problem.

Why we missed the storm: more great forecasting excuses from the crisis

My work as an applied mathematician involves providing forecasts, and I know how hard it is to make accurate predictions (I even wrote a book on the topic).[51] But when predictions do go badly wrong, the experience often offers useful information that can be used to update and improve your forecasting model. This can be a difficult process, especially since it may involve changing your mental model of reality as well; but in economics it seems to be taking an unusually long time, as shown by the range of explanations and excuses supplied over the years.

- Glenn Stevens, Governor of the Reserve Bank of Australia, in 2008: 'I do not know anyone who predicted this course of events. This should give us cause to reflect on how hard a job it is to make genuinely useful forecasts.'[52]
- Ben Bernanke musing in a 2009 commencement address: 'Like weather forecasters, economic forecasters must deal with a system that is extraordinarily complex, that is subject to random shocks [from the weather gods?], and

about which our data and understanding will always be imperfect ... Mathematicians have discussed the so-called butterfly effect, which holds that, in a sufficiently complex system, a small cause – the flapping of a butterfly's wings in Brazil – might conceivably have a disproportionately large effect – a typhoon in the Pacific.'[53]

- Future Nobel laureate Tom Sargent in a 2010 interview: 'It is just wrong to say that this financial crisis caught modern macroeconomists by surprise.'[54] (The non-modern ones were presumably dead, so even less surprised.)

- US Federal Reserve report from 2010: DSGE models 'are very poor in forecasting, but so are all other approaches'.[55] (Funny how this was mentioned less before the crisis.[56])

- The Bank of England's Sujit Kapadia to Queen Elizabeth on her visit in 2012: 'People thought markets were efficient, people thought regulation wasn't necessary ... people didn't realise just how interconnected the system had become.'[57]

- Nick Macpherson (aka The Lord Macpherson of Earl's Court), former head of the UK Treasury, in 2016: 'I see myself as one of a number of people ... who failed to see the crisis coming, who failed to spot the build-up of risk. This was a monumental collective intellectual error.'[58]

- Christopher Auld from the University of Victoria, in a 2017 *Times Higher Education* article: 'Economists don't claim to be able to make unconditional forecasts of future states of a system as complex as the macroeconomy', and criticism which relegates the field to 'failed "weather" forecasting is not just misguided, it is anti-intellectual and dangerous.'[59]

- A 2017 *Prospect* article in which six eminent UK economists respond to 'dangerous' (but more dangerous than flawed economic models?) and 'ill-informed expert bashing' of their profession from 'Writers, students and even

some social scientists from other disciplines' (mathematicians, physicists, quants, etc. are not mentioned): 'Like
most economists, we do not try to forecast the date of the
next financial crisis, or any other such event. We are not
astrologers, nor priests to the market gods. We analyse data.
Gigas and gigas of data.'[60] (Since the crisis, economists have
distanced themselves from the whole business of macroeconomic forecasting and risk analysis, by emphasising that
they apply their theories to many other things as well.*)

- Andrew Haldane, chief economist at the Bank of England,
  in 2017: 'Michael Fish getting up: "Someone's called me,
  there's no hurricane coming but it will be windy in Spain."
  It is very similar to the sort of reports central banks issued
  pre-crisis, that there is no hurricane coming but it might be
  very windy in sub-prime.' (Michael Fish answered that his
  forecast was 'better than the Bank of England's.'[61])

- Paul Krugman, responding directly to 'The Queen's question' – and summing up some of the lines in this chapter –
  as part of the 'Rebuilding Macroeconomic Theory Project'
  in 2018: 'My answer may seem unsatisfying, but I believe it
  to be true: for the most part what happened was a demonstration of the old line that predictions are hard, especially
  about the future. It's a complicated world out there, and
  one's ability to track potential threats is limited … If you
  like, it's as if meteorologists with limited resources concentrated those resources in places that had helped track
  previous storms, leading to the occasional surprise when a

---

* There is even a Twitter hashtag, #whateconomistsreallydo – though
#youhadonejob might be more appropriate. Smith, N. (2018), 'OK, here
is a thread for econ critics'. Retrieved from Twitter: https://twitter.com/
Noahpinion/status/950079662121615361

storm comes from an unusual direction ... My bottom line
is that the failure of nearly all macroeconomists, even of the
saltwater [Krugman's] camp, to predict the 2008 crisis was
similar in type to the Met Office failure in 1987, a failure of
observation rather than a fundamental failure of concept.
Neither the financial crisis nor the Great Recession that
followed required a rethinking of basic ideas.'[62] (What then
would it take?)

The penny drops

While, as shown in the box above, many mainstream economists
have continued to make excuses for their epic forecasting miss, not
all have been so sanguine. George Akerlof and Robert Shiller wrote
in their 2015 *Phishing for Phools*: 'It is truly remarkable that so few
economists foresaw what would happen. There are about 2¼ million article and book listings regarding finance and economics on
Google Scholar. That may not indicate enough economist-monkeys
to randomly type *Hamlet*, but it should have been enough to generate quite a few papers that would tell how Countrywide, WaMu,
IndyMac, Lehman, and many, many others would in short order
flame out and crash. We should have known that their positions in
mortgage-backed securities and credit default swaps were fragile.
At the time we should have also foreseen the future vulnerabili-
ties of the euro.'[63] The authors ascribe this to the 'mental frame' of
economists which sees markets as fundamentally efficient, blames
pathologies on externalities, and ignores the fact that 'competitive
markets by their very nature spawn deception and trickery, as a
result of the same profit motives that give us our prosperity'. (An
exception was Shiller, who himself pointed out in 2005 that the US
housing market was in a bubble.[64]) Indeed, this points to a basic
contradiction in neoclassical models, which assumes on the one

hand that people are rational utility-optimisers, and on the other hand that they will always honour contracts – so no systematic fraud from bankers, or 'jingle mail' from homeowners returning the keys rather than pay their mortgage.

In July 2016, Narayana Kocherlakota – who like Chari was formerly a president of the Federal Reserve Bank of Minneapolis – noted in a report that 'we simply do not have a settled successful theory of the macroeconomy'.[65] A couple of months later Paul Romer, who is now chief economist at the World Bank, released a paper called 'The Trouble With Macroeconomics' in which he described the area as a 'pseudoscience' because the models are packed with implausible assumptions and parameters that are made up to give reasonable-looking answers, and all changes are attributed to external shocks (Chari responded by saying that 'Burning down the edifice, and saying we'll figure out what we'll build on its foundations later, just does not seem like a constructive way to proceed', though it would be a start).[66]

Finally, some ten years after the crisis began, in a May 2017 speech, Portuguese economist Vítor Constâncio of the European Central Bank told his audience: 'In the prevalent macro models, the financial sector was absent, considered to have a remote effect on the real economic activity. In these model frameworks, macroeconomic fluctuations resulted mostly from technological or productivity shocks or from monetary policy unexpected measures. The economy was supposed to be mostly self-correcting and move quickly towards its steady state. No defaults of any agent were possible. Thus, excessive debt could not be a problem. As many wrote, for any debtor there was a creditor and so debt was a non-event at the macro level. This ignored the fact that banks create money by extending credit *ex nihilo* within the limits of their capital ratio.'[67] (Weather forecaster: with the benefit of hindsight, it may have been a mistake to *leave out all the wet stuff*.) One reason perhaps for this omission is that, as discussed in Chapter 5, the ability of private banks to create money out of nothing was only spelled out by the Bank of England in 2014.

Constâncio's comment points to the real issue, which is not that mainstream economists failed to predict 'the timing, extent and severity' (as the London School of Economics put it) of some freak storm – economists have never been held to any such standard of forecasting skill, and no one asked for an exact date. It is that they *could not* have predicted or warned of the crisis, even in principle. Furthermore, the models directly contributed to the crisis both by creating a false sense of security, and by enabling the financial sector to develop increasingly risky and dangerous products. The efficient market hypothesis did not perform well during the crisis, unless you count creating it.

Because the models could not understand the causes of the crisis, they were not useful for suggesting the appropriate policy responses afterwards.[68] And the main reason for this failure is even simpler than leaving out things like deception and trickery (Akerlof and Shiller), or insufficient data/rationality/funding (Chari) – it is because the models left out money (which of course is a main cause of deception and trickery). Only by doing so could economists maintain the illusion that independent rational consumers and producers with set supply and demand curves drive the economy to a stable equilibrium through what amounts to barter. Chari mocked the idea that we should 'stop using mathematical models of oil pressure' in the event of an oil spill, but in economics the problem was that money – what David Hume called the oil of trade, what Jean-Baptiste Say compared to 'oil in a machine' – wasn't there.[69] It was therefore impossible to detect that the housing bubble was feeding the money supply, which was feeding the housing bubble, and so on, with complex derivative schemes helping to hide the risk.

By interpreting crises as random shocks, the models also eliminated any sense of responsibility for failing to prevent them. According to Dean Baker (who presciently warned in a 2005 paper with David Rosnick that for economists to miss the housing bubble would be an 'act of extraordinary negligence'[70]), a rough but conservative estimate would be that it cost each person in the US around $27,000 in lost earnings – to say nothing of the human impact in terms of things like mental health and youth unemployment – so 'how about a little accountability for economists when they mess up?'[71] Many people lost their jobs, but it seems no economists did. Remarkably, in the US their salaries even 'reached a historical high during the recession year of 2009', which as Kocherlakota noted in 2016, 'might help explain the lack of a paradigm shift in macroeconomic research'.[72]

Hush, money

In fact, while the story that no one, apart from a few perma-bears, saw the crisis coming is popular with mainstream economists, the reality is that a good number of people did warn of the crisis – including Baker and Rosnick, William White, Ann Pettifor, Steve Keen, Michael Hudson, Paul Wilmott, Nassim Nicholas Taleb, Nouriel Roubini, Robert Shiller, and traders like those featured in *The Big Short*, to name some of the better-known ones. They did this – not by constantly predicting disaster, as Krugman claimed, or by random chance – but by focusing on the role of debt, finance, and the banking system.[73] Given, then, that these things were effectively absent from the models used by mainstream economists, the question is why experts would not mention this drawback during testimony; why central bankers only felt fit to remark on it during conference speeches several years later; and why, as Joseph Stiglitz noted in 2017, DSGE models and their underlying assumptions are not just still in use, but 'have become a dogma, with little incentive to call them into question especially in a context of peer-reviewed publications'.[74] To find the answer, we need to adopt a quantum approach, look at the context, seek out entanglements, and consider the effect of the observer – or in this case, the economist – on the system being studied.

One clue is provided by Robert Lucas, who wrote that 'The construction of theoretical models is our way to bring order to the way we think about the world, but the process necessarily involves ignoring some evidence or alternative theories – setting them aside. That can be hard to do – facts are facts – and sometimes my unconscious mind carries out the abstraction for me: I simply fail to *see* some of the data or some alternative theory.'[75] Other people, he says, 'will see the blind spot ... keep what is good, and correct what is not'. This seems a reasonable description of the modelling process; but in this case the blind spot was very large, and no one corrected it. Or rather, no insider corrected it. Why?

As mentioned in the previous discussion of quantum cognition, our decisions are shaped by context, including our own mental frames, conscious or unconscious; and as Akerlof and Shiller note, the mental frame of economists was affected by their view of the economy as a rational, efficient system.[76] One way to think of this is in terms of aesthetics, which, as I have argued elsewhere, plays a surprisingly strong role in science.[77] Science in general has long been dominated by a type of machine aesthetic, where a beautiful model is one that exhibits the classical qualities of symmetry, unity, and stability – at least in its ideas, if not the actual execution. An early example was the Greek model of the cosmos, which saw the heavenly bodies as being encased in beautifully symmetric crystalline spheres (even if epicycles had to be added to make the model work). In economics, we have neoclassical economics, with its perfectly rational and symmetric models (again until epicycles are added). Money – with its complex, multi-faceted, nonlinear, and shapeshifting nature – doesn't fit in this neat and tidy picture.

As Paul Krugman put it quite accurately in 2009, 'The economics profession went astray because economists, as a group, mistook beauty, clad in impressive-looking mathematics, for truth'.[78] (For this lapse, John Cochrane responded in a journal article by comparing Krugman to 'an AIDS-HIV disbeliever, a creationist or a stalwart that maybe continents do not move after all'.[79] The Pythagorean good/evil division is very much alive when it comes to the scientific aesthetic – see the box at the end of the next chapter.) But while aesthetics is certainly a powerful influence on the way we see the world, it still doesn't quite explain why it took so long for the truth about these economic models to leak out through official channels. And this points to a more worldly form of entanglement: that between the economics profession and the financial sector, who were happy to keep money – and therefore themselves – out of the picture. After all, if you were a banker, which narrative would you prefer: that the crisis was caused by banks, or – official version – that it was the result of efficiency and rationality?

As economist Barry Eichengreen noted in 2009, in academic economics there is 'a subconscious tendency to embrace the arguments of one's more "successful" colleagues in a discipline where money, in this case earned through speaking engagements and consultancies, is the common denominator of success'.[80] This issue was highlighted in Charles Ferguson's documentary *The Inside Job*, which found that the influence of private money on the profession played a key role in the crisis. As he wrote in 2010, 'These days, if you see a famous economics professor testify in Congress, or write an article, there is a good chance he or she is being paid by someone with a big stake in what's being debated. Most of the time, these professors do not disclose these conflicts of interest, and most of the time their universities look the other way'.[81] A 2012 study in the

Cambridge Journal of Economics concluded that 'economists almost never reveal their financial associations when they make public pronouncements on issues such as financial regulation' and noted that 'Perhaps these connections helped explain why few mainstream economists warned about the oncoming financial crisis'.[82] In 2016, philosopher Alan Jay Levinovitz found while researching this topic that 'Every economist I interviewed agreed that conflicts of interest were highly problematic for the scientific integrity of their field'.[83] That is like a forecaster failing to predict a storm because it would be bad for their show's sponsors. (Economists often either seem to be genuinely unaware that there is an ethical component to their work, including things like forecasts, or take it for granted that they are acting correctly.[84])

It is therefore ironic that V.V. Chari also brought up severe underfunding as being a main culprit for his profession's failure to warn of the crisis. The truth is that DSGE models are a waste of money. That is why quants don't use them to make predictions. And there is a remarkable symmetry in the fact that financial companies are funding economists whose mental frames are rotated in just such a direction that they have a blind spot for those same financial companies. The question is not necessarily one of explicit corruption – the influence may be as much unconscious as conscious – but more the creation of a certain context and set of beliefs. When Stanford's Anat Admati sat down with academics and policy-makers to discuss the role of the financial sector in the crisis, she found that 'many would not engage. It was very disturbing. I realized that we hit a raw nerve in banking … It felt like I encountered a sort of religion, where people want to believe certain things to be true'.[85]

This selective blindness is further cultivated by economics textbooks, which shape the opinions not only of students but of future economists, policy-makers, economic journalists, and the public in general. As we have seen, a basic but also poorly understood feature of money is that most of it is created by private banks when they issue loans. Charging interest on these loans is a highly profitable business, which is the main reason banks dominate stockmarkets around the world and their buildings dominate skylines in major cities. Yet as Norbert Häring observed in 2014, there is a 'complete absence in all major textbooks of any mention of the pecuniary benefit', which as he suggests, 'points to a taboo imposed by the interest of a very powerful group'.[86]

Money is not an externality, it is about as internal as you can get; and omitting money, credit, and a quadrillion dollars'-worth of derivatives from the models is not the same as missing a forecast – it is missing reality. The real reason economists didn't see the crisis coming was because they ignored its entangled, quantum nature. The message for quantum economics is clear: acknowledge the role of money, both in models and in the profession itself. For as always with quantum systems, context matters; and far from being detached observers, economists are very much involved.

A new story

According to Chari's testimony, 'A useful aphorism in macro-economics is: "If you have an interesting and coherent story to tell, you can tell it in a DSGE model. If you cannot, your story is inco-herent"', which is like a weather forecaster saying that, yes they did miss the storm but they did so in an interesting and coherent way. However, Chari was correct in identifying the need to provide such a story in the first place, because stories are how we frame and give context to information.* As a 2017 note from the UK's Economic

---

* As author and story consultant Andy Goodman puts it, 'each of us walks around with a bunch of stories in our heads about the way the world works. And whatever we confront, whatever facts are presented to us, whatever

and Social Research Council remarked, while 'policy makers have been experimenting in an improvised fashion with new kinds of measures', it still seems that 'changes in dominant forms of knowledge have been slow to emerge' (which is why they are bringing in non-economists to take a look).[87] The reason many economists couldn't either face up to their role in the crisis or move forward from it, was that it did not fit with the story that they had been telling themselves and others about how the economy works.[88] So is it possible to come up with another approach – and a story – that incorporates an understanding of 'how people make decisions over time and how they handle uncertainty' and that deals with 'the effects on the whole economy', as Chari put it?

One of the main appeals of DSGE models to economists is that they were built up from microfoundations based on individual behaviour, which gave them an air of Ricardian rigour. As we have seen, though, these foundations incorporated a simplistic, mechanistic view of the world which bears little relation to the complex entanglements of real human behaviour. And by necessity, the models had to exclude money as a force in itself, because money is irrational, entangling, unstable, and so on. The models therefore tried to simulate the economy without ever addressing its most basic feature, which is transactions involving money.

Of course, one can try to modify DSGE models by adding a simplified financial sector; and as Chari also mentioned in his testimony, some models do take a stab at researching the effects

data we run into, we filter through these stories. And if the data agrees with our stories, we'll let it in and if it doesn't, we'll reject it. So, if you're trying to give people new information that they don't have, they've got to have a story in their head that will let that data in.' Goodman, A. (26 September 2016), 'If You're Going to Change the World, You Better Bring Your Stories: An Interview with Andy Goodman'. Retrieved from Frank: http://frank .jou.ufl.edu/2016/09/change-stories/

of what he and other economists call 'financial frictions' which slow the adjustment to equilibrium (odd, since money is usually considered a lubricant).[89] An early attempt was a model by Bernanke, Gertler and Gilchrist, which accounted for the fact that borrowing costs are inversely related to the borrower's net worth.[90] However, while this addressed changes in credit *allocation*, it did not address the issue of credit *creation* by banks, i.e. the new money produced by making loans, and its inclusion had only a 'modest quantitative effect on the way the model economy responds to shocks', as one paper put it.[91] As noted in a 2015 Bank of England article, models which do include money creation run into the problem that 'banks that create purchasing power can technically do so *instantaneously* and *discontinuously*, because the process does not involve physical goods, but rather the creation of money through the simultaneous expansion of both sides of banks' balance sheets'.[92] In other words – as is also the case with events such as credit default or bankruptcy – it is an on/off process, not a smooth mechanical one, and as easy to model using conventional tools as a lightning strike.

DSGE models were designed from the outset to see changes as smooth and continuous rather than abrupt and quantum – nature makes no sudden leaps, as Alfred Marshall's epitaph insisted – and the complexity of financial entanglements means those assumptions of continuity and stability no longer apply. The 'friction' analogy, for example, is a reference to the idea from physics that Newtonian laws of motion, as applied to something like the arc of a projectile, give somewhat different answers when friction is taken into account. Models can therefore be improved in an iterative fashion, first by solving for the frictionless case, and then adding friction if more accuracy is required. But finance acting 'instantaneously and discontinuously' is a completely different thing (unless you count accelerating into a brick wall as friction). Physicists couldn't address quantum effects by adding a few bells and whistles to Newtonian models, and the same is true in economics.

While we therefore need to incorporate money and debt into our model of the economy, it isn't enough to simply bolt a neutered model of the financial sector onto existing models while at the same time assuming the system is stable (economists have long been adept at defusing criticism by going through the motions in this way).[93] Instead the models have to start with the fact that money transactions are at the heart of everything, so assumptions about things like rationality, fixed preferences, utility-maximising behaviour, equilibrium and so on are no longer tenable, even as a first approximation. The most obvious feature of the crisis was that *nothing was fixed* and there *was no equilibrium* – and at times where there is a sense of equilibrium, it often says more about institutional effects, or social or political forces, than it does about markets themselves. It was the government that rescued the markets through a massive bailout (in the US, the Emergency Economic Stabilization Act of 2008), not the other way round.

In recent years modellers have also attempted to make models more fine-grained by doing things like increasing the number of representative agents. However, a problem with reductionist models of any sort, as I noted in my 2007 book *Apollo's Arrow* on the science of prediction, is that as they are made more detailed, the number of unknown parameters whose values cannot be accurately inferred from the data tends to explode.[94] This is one reason why, paradoxically, simple models that are based on sound forecasting principles often outperform complicated models at making predictions.[95] Joseph Stiglitz similarly noted in 2017 the 'Ptolemaic attempt' of modellers to add more and more features until models become 'little more than an exercise in curve fitting'.[96] Adding a financial sector to DSGE models is particularly challenging because of the nonlinearities that it introduces.[97]

Viewed this way, the predictive uncertainty that we confront in economics is not so different from the uncertainty that is taken for granted in other fields where living things are involved, such as medicine or politics. Perhaps the problem is that because money is based on number, we have become used to the idea that the economy is a kind of predictable, mechanical system, rather than something with a life of its own. At his Nobel speech in 1933, the physicist Paul Dirac said that 'There is in my opinion a great similarity between the problems provided by the mysterious behaviour of the atom and those provided by the present economic paradoxes confronting the world. In both cases one is given a great many facts which are expressible with numbers, and one has to find the underlying principles.'[98] But as we've seen, while there are certainly similarities between physics and economics, the numbers themselves only give one side of the story.

Fortunately, there are many mathematical tools available to help with this, and they have been around for a while. But for these tools to succeed, economists first need to stop wasting energy by confabulating excuses and further complicating their models; and instead rotate their mental frames from seeing the economy as a mechanical system, to seeing it as a complex quantum system with a life and an agency of its own.

Negative entropy

In his 1944 book *What is Life?* the quantum physicist Erwin Schrödinger proposed that organisms stay alive by feeding on 'negative entropy'.[99] Like Maxwell's demon, we are information workers, extracting energy from order (low entropy) in our environment by manipulating it. Schrödinger didn't know how this information was coded, or where it was kept, but he believed that any such process would take place on the border between the quantum and the classical world. His thoughts later inspired Francis

Crick and James Watson when they worked out how genetic information was stored in DNA. Instead of allowing information to leak out into our environment, we package it tightly, and pass it on to our descendants. Equilibrium is death.

However, genes are not our only information storage devices – we also have language, social institutions, and of course the financial system. Viewed this way, money takes on the aspect of a kind of active biological molecule, whose quantum interactions are at the heart of the economy. Instead of modelling its flows using linear techniques designed for the analysis of Victorian steam engines, we should use ones that are better adapted for the analysis of living systems, such as network theory, complexity theory, and the nonlinear dynamics discussed in Chapter 6. (Though one of the first applications of the latter, by James Clerk Maxwell, was to Victorian steam engines, which had nonlinear instabilities of their own.)

One of the main findings from the Human Genome Project was that the function of genes and proteins can usually only be understood when they are considered as part of a connected network. The analysis of such networks has therefore become a useful tool for finding which genes and associated proteins are involved in pathologies such as cancer. Similar techniques have been used for analysing the power structure of the economy, as expressed by share ownership, or cross-border flows of the sort discussed above; and for understanding the properties which make a system fragile or robust to perturbations.[100]

The related area of complexity theory concerns systems that are characterised by emergent properties, which even in principle cannot be predicted from a knowledge of the system's parts alone, and therefore resist a reductionist approach. In economics, as discussed in Chapter 4, an active area of complexity research involves agent-based models, which model individuals or firms as separate agents which are then allowed to interact with one another through simulated transactions. These models work in discrete time steps so can easily handle things like instantaneous money creation or loan defaults, and as mentioned in Chapter 7, they can in principle at least be extended to include quantum decision-making.[101]

A first step, though, in predicting a system is to properly see it, and another use for complexity theory is to visualise and understand data. Part of the Harvard *Atlas of Economic Complexity* project was to come up with complexity-based metrics that could be used to quantify the availability of productive knowledge embedded in an economy. The main two metrics were ubiquity and diversity. The former is the number of countries that make a particular product, so is like a measure of entropy (the more ubiquitous a product, the less special and ordered it is), while diversity is the number of products that a country makes. A third metric, proximity, describes the similarity between products. The researchers found that ubiquity and diversity gave insights into an economy's overall complexity, while the proximity of a product to others helped to explain a country's likelihood of developing it. In Ricardo's imagined two-country, two-product example, the diversity would be low, ubiquity would be high, and proximity would be near-zero (a cloth-maker is unlikely to adapt easily to wine-making).

A related approach, from a team led by physicist Matthieu Cristelli, uses a metric they call 'fitness' which sums the value of the exports, weighted for complexity, and serves as a measure of the 'information content' embedded in economic systems.[102] They then plot how fitness and GDP evolve over time for different countries. The study found that 'country dynamics presents strongly heterogeneous patterns of evolution'. Developing countries with a low level of fitness show chaotic dynamics, with little discernible pattern; however, once a country escapes the turbulent low-fitness regime, it enters a smoother regime where its path can be predicted by comparing it with the progress of other countries. For example, if GDP is relatively low for a given fitness, then it can be expected to increase. This type of regime analysis was pioneered in the study of chaotic nonlinear systems. Economists cannot rely on the simplifying tools of traditional analysis, such as looking at aggregate levels of education or investment, but instead 'must face issues which are very close to the problems of predictability for dynamical systems (i.e. atmosphere, climate, wind, ocean dynamics, and weather forecast, etc)'.

The use of such techniques has been accompanied by increasingly sophisticated tools for data analysis. Andrew Haldane of the Bank of England has even called for a 'global financial surveillance system' that would involve real-time tracking of global funds 'in much the same way as happens with global weather systems and global internet traffic. Its centre piece would be a global map of financial flows, charting spill-overs and correlations.'[103] One complication is that money has a propensity to hide. About 10 per cent of the world's wealth is estimated to be held in offshore tax havens, according to the National Bureau of Economic Research, mostly by the ultra-rich.[104] And while foreign direct investment 'is generally assumed to represent long-term investments within the "real" economy', as economic geographers Daniel Haberly and Dariusz Wójcik note, 'approximately 30–50% of global FDI is accounted for by networks of offshore shell companies created by corporations and wealthy individuals for tax and other purposes'.[105]

The crossroads

As mentioned in Chapter 1, the fact that a system is based at some level on quantum principles does not imply that it can or should be modelled using quantum methods – indeed, one of the main lessons of quantum physics is that most properties we observe at larger scales cannot be reduced to quantum principles, because they are emergent phenomena (in which the whole might be more than the sum of its parts). Quantum physics at small scales has yet to be reconciled with relativity theory at large scales, but they each work in their own domain. The main contribution of quantum economics is to draw attention to the role of money – which by its entangled and context-sensitive nature leads inevitably to a quantum approach. By omitting it, and modelling the economy as a stable and self-correcting system, economists helped create an economy that was the exact opposite.

At the same time, the economy differs from something like the weather in that it is not just a complex system, it is a complex quantum system, where some quantum properties do manifest themselves at larger scales. As discussed further in the next chapter, the fact that agents are entangled means that they can show collective dynamics and modes of behaviour that are unique to quantum systems. And while standard complexity models can cope with properties that emerge from agents, in a quantum system the collective behaviour changes the agents in turn. In recent years a number of research centres have been set up to study the emergent dynamics of complex quantum systems in physics – quantum thermodynamics is one example of this approach – and some of those techniques may prove useful in economics.

'Ultimately', according to former chief economist for the Bank for International Settlements Stephen Cecchetti, 'an economic model can only be defeated by an opposing model'.[106] But the mainstream economic model has been defeated by something else – quantum reality. If we take the quantum emergent properties (i.e. those which emerge from quantum transactions, but cannot be reduced to them) of the world economy seriously, there is no reason to think that we should be able to perfectly simulate it using any set of equations. People who predicted the crisis did so by paying attention to what was important, not by building a more elaborate model. So rather than develop a single unified model of 'the effects on the whole economy' as V.V. Chari demanded, it makes more sense to adopt an agile approach where models are seen as patches to fit particular problems.[107] And instead of group-think, with everyone – or more precisely everyone with power and influence – agreeing on the correct model, no matter its flaws, we would be better served by a diversity of techniques. The same is true in physics: as physicists Nigel Goldenfeld and Leo P. Kadanoff wrote in 1999, 'Up to now, physicists looked for fundamental laws true for all times and all places. But each complex system is differ-ent; apparently there are not general laws for complexity. Instead, one must reach for "lessons" that might, with insight and under-standing, be learned in one system and applied to another. Maybe physics studies will become more like human experience.'[108] A quantum macroeconomics approach would incorporate a dash-board of techniques, including complexity-based data mining, machine learning, agent-based simulations (quantum or other-wise), nonlinear dynamics models, and model-free analysis; each a different way of exploring the shapeshifting quantum nature of the economy, and looking for signs of storms. (An analogy would be from my own work in predicting the effects of anti-cancer drugs, where we use a hybrid agent-based/nonlinear-dynamics model of a growing tumour in concert with empirical data-driven approaches and literature research.[109])

One drawback of such a pluralistic approach is that the different tools might not all say the same thing. 'The danger in encourag-ing plurality', explained Oxford economist Simon Wren-Lewis in 2018, 'is that you make it much easier for politicians to select the advice they like, because there is almost certain to be a school of thought that gives the "right" answers from the politicians' point of view. The point is obvious once you make the comparison to medi-cine. Don't like the idea of vaccination? Pick an expert from the anti-vaccination medical school.'[110] This is an interesting (though not unusual – see box in next chapter) choice of analogy, given that mainstream economists were the ones who saw no need to vaccinate the financial system against crisis. Surely a bigger issue than plurality is rebuilding credibility with the public; a 2017 UK survey by YouGov asking which experts could be trusted when talking about their own areas of expertise showed that doctors were trusted by 82 per cent, weather forecasters by 51 per cent, and economists by 25 per cent.[111] But it also points to the fact that mainstream economics, or at least the part of it with influence over policy, remains too much of a monoculture with little real interest in reinventing itself, despite numerous well-publicised initiatives to do just that. It seems that economists' interest in the benefits of competition and new ideas breaks down rather quickly when it comes to their own field.

One 2017 survey of recent progress, written by leading DSGE modellers Lawrence J. Christiano, Martin S. Eichenbaum, and Mathias Trabandt, began by doubling down on Chari's 'only game in town' argument: 'People who don't like dynamic stochastic general equilibrium (DSGE) models are dilettantes. By this we mean they aren't serious about policy analysis.'[112] Explaining that significant progress has been made in 'incorporating financial frictions and heterogeneity into DSGE models', they conclude: 'We do know that DSGE models will remain central to how macroeconomists think about aggregate phenomena and policy. There is simply no credible alternative to policy analysis in a world of competing economic forces.'

In a Bloomberg article called 'Fixing macroeconomics will be really hard', the economist Noah Smith reported on a cutting-edge symposium on rethinking macroeconomics, held by the Peterson Institute for International Economics in October 2017, and featuring luminaries such as Ben Bernanke and Larry Summers. 'In the past few years', writes Smith, 'macroeconomists have been scrambling to shoehorn the financial sector into their standard models. Of course, there's always the danger that the Great Recession prompts macroeconomists to focus *too much* on finance.'[113] However, the 'real sea change' is in the approach to recessions: 'Most modern econ theories posit that recessions arrive randomly, instead of as the result of pressures that build up over time. And they assume that recessions are short-lived affairs that go away of their own accord. If these assumptions are wrong, then most of the theories written down in macroeconomic journals over the past several decades – and most of those being written as we speak – are of questionable usefulness.' According to Smith, 'economists have known for decades that recessions might not be random, short-lived events, but the idea always remained on the fringes. One big reason was mathematical convenience – models where recessions are like rainstorms, arriving and departing on their own, are mathematically a lot easier to work with.' Another complication is that the economy is 'almost certainly a chaotic system. Researchers have known for decades that unstable economies are very hard to work with or predict. In the past, economists have simply ignored this unsettling possibility and chosen to focus on models with only one possible long-term outcome.' On the bright side, better microeconomic data will result in more accurate microfoundations, and therefore 'more realistic models'.

This sounds like weather forecasters announcing at a conference that they have agreed to stop predicting rainstorms that come 'on their own' by tossing a coin. While the emphasis on data, and the recognition of instability, is encouraging, it sounds like we can expect the next DSGE models to be 'complex and difficult' creations with a 'shoehorned' financial sector, 'harder math' (or 'mathiness' as Paul Romer calls it), and extra new chaotic behaviour (which will at least make a good excuse for forecast error).[114]

In other words, a continuation of the same mechanistic weather forecasting approach, though less informed by its sister field's long history of empiricism, honed by daily comparisons of predictions and reality; and less so still by other areas such as biology.

A 2018 paper summarising results from the *Oxford Review of Economic Policy*'s 'Rebuilding Macroeconomic Theory' project admitted that 'The benchmark model ... was not good enough to give any warning of the emergence of crisis in 2008. And it has been of very little help in understanding what to do next. Notwithstanding these failings, there is not yet a new paradigm in sight.' Instead, the basic DSGE model should be updated by: '(i) incorporating financial frictions rather than assuming that financial intermediation is costless; (ii) relaxing the requirement of rational expectations; (iii) introducing heterogeneous agents; and (iv) underpinning the model – and each of these three new additions – with more appropriate microfoundations.'[115] On the last point, the authors add: 'It seems there is an analogy in the natural sciences, chemistry has been "microfounded" through the use of explanations from quantum physics', which will come as news to chemists – so much for emergent properties.[116] (This remark, taken literally, would seem to imply that the only logical way to proceed would be to microfound a model of the global economy based on the behaviour of quantum agents. Unfortunately such faith in the power of reductionism is a hallmark of neoclassical economics, not the quantum version.)

Meanwhile the physicist and hedge fund manager Jean-Philippe Bouchaud, who, as mentioned in the Introduction, called for a 'scientific revolution' for economics back in 2008, told the *Financial Times* a decade on that: 'Following the financial crisis many of us hoped that the economics profession had finally realised that their models were not representative of how the real economy works and that their flawed methods would quickly change. That assumption

was wrong ... no radical change has been made to the workhorse
models used by central bankers, which assume that the economy
can be represented by a single agent with perfect access to information and infinite foresight. This is a wild oversimplification of a
highly complex, interacting system where feedback loops can trigger crises.'[117] He concludes that: 'If we don't embrace new methods
of modelling the economy [such as agent-based models] we will be
as blind to the next crisis as we were to the last one.'

The most obvious difference between the weather and the
economy, from a forecasting perspective, is that we create, and
have some direct control over, the latter. Recessions are not random
storms that come out of nowhere, as economists like to portray
them, but are things that we take part in and can take steps to
actively prevent. Economists are also entangled financially with
the system they are studying. Viewed this way, it is true that it is
not completely fair to compare economics with weather forecasting. Economists' responsibility is far greater, and is more like that
of engineers or doctors – instead of predicting exactly when the
system will crash, they should warn of risks, incorporate design
features to help avoid failure, know how to address problems when
they occur, and be alert for conflicts of interest, ethical violations,
and other forms of professional negligence. Its failings in these
areas, rather than any particular forecast, are the real reason so
many are calling for a genuinely new paradigm in economics, as
opposed to a rehashed version of the old one. And the danger is not
pluralism (doctors don't always agree either), but a monoculture
based on flawed ideas.[118] Macroeconomic forecasting might be a
relatively small part of economics, but its missed predictions and
mis-analysis, with their dramatic real-world consequences, are just
the most visible and concerning symptom of a deeper problem
which starts with the basic assumptions, and affects other branches
of mainstream economics. Instead of finding new applications for

their theories, and confusing this with genuine broadness and diversity, economists should focus on doing the important things right.

The transition in thinking required today in economics, while not technically difficult, seems as much a challenge to orthodoxy as the one a century earlier when classical physics collided with quantum reality. Perhaps I am biased, but Wolfgang Munchau may have been right when he wrote in the *Financial Times* in 2015 that 'The mainstream invested a life's work in developing their DSGE models. They will not let go easily, but continue to tinker with their models ... the successful challenge will come from outside the discipline.'[119] Sometimes, entanglements can hold back progress – but at least these models are no longer the only game in town. In the next chapter, we consider our entanglement with a larger organic system that is of interest to economists and weather forecasters alike – the planet.

CHAPTER 9

MEASURING THE ECONOMY

*Thought processes and quantum systems are analogous
in that they cannot be analyzed too much in terms of
distinct elements, because the 'intrinsic' nature of each
element is not a property existing separately from and
independently of other elements but is, instead, a property
that arises partially from its relation with other elements.*
David Bohm, *Quantum Theory* (1951)

One property of quantum systems, of either the subatomic or
the monetary sort, is that they are affected by measurement.
Another is that context is important, because no measurement
is done in isolation. This chapter applies these principles to
the economy as a whole. The most important metric used to
measure the health of the economy is gross domestic product,
or GDP. Politicians and economists alike put great emphasis
on maximising this number – but doing so then distorts the
economy by encouraging activities that enhance GDP, even if
they are harmful or unnecessary. At the same time, mainstream
economics has a bit of a blind spot for the overall context of
economic activity, such as the environment. In order to bring
the economy back into balance with itself and the world, a
first step is to update our Victorian mechanistic approach to
economics.

In 1967, the author and journalist Arthur Koestler coined the term
'holon' to describe 'self-regulating open systems which display both

the autonomous properties of wholes and the dependent properties of parts'.[1] He saw organisms and societies as being made up of a hierarchical sequence of semi-autonomous holons – cells, organs, bodies, families, tribes, nations – which are in constant interaction through cooperation or competition. At each level of the hierarchy there is a dichotomy between the whole and the part. Every holon has a 'dual tendency to preserve and assert its individuality as a quasi-autonomous whole; and to function as an integrated part of an (existing or evolving) larger whole.' In humans, it is the integrative tendency that results in 'flexible adaptations, improvisations, and creative acts which initiate new forms of behaviour'. A disease such as cancer, in contrast, represents a breakdown in this integrative balance.[2] Koestler referred to the dual atomistic/holistic nature of holons as the Janus phenomenon – after the God whose two faces, probably originally representing the Sun and the Moon, adorned many Roman coins.

The concept of a holon took on a new significance the following year – or to be more precise on Christmas Eve, 1968 – when the Apollo 8 astronauts circumnavigated the Moon. The Moon itself was a little disappointing; crew member Bill Anders said it 'really isn't anywhere near as interesting as I thought it was going to be. It's all beat up.'[3] The star of the show – for the astronauts, as well as the billion people watching on TV – was the Earth. It was the first time that anyone had seen the whole planet – the holon – from the outside. The astronauts, alone in their fragile capsule, seemed especially moved by their privileged view of its royal blue oceans, green and brown continents, and swirling white clouds. Lovell told the viewers back home: 'The vast loneliness is awe-inspiring and it makes you realise just what you have back there on Earth.' Instead of discovering a new world, they discovered our world anew.

The astronomer Fred Hoyle had predicted that 'Once a photograph of the Earth, taken from the outside, is available – once the sheer isolation of the Earth becomes plain – a new idea as powerful as any in history will let loose.'[4] Indeed, the photograph known as Earthrise taken by Anders that showed the Earth, partially lit from one side, rising over the Moon – thus inverting their usual relationship – was described by photographer Galen Rowell as 'the most influential environmental photograph ever taken'.[5] Such images helped to kickstart the nascent environmental movement: James Lovelock's Gaia theory, which argues that the planet regulates its conditions like a living organism, was christened the next year; the first Earth Day was celebrated on 22 April 1970; Greenpeace was created in 1971.

The period also saw the advent of a new approach to science and mathematics. Areas that were suited for the study of living systems such as complexity theory, network theory, and nonlinear dynamics became popular areas of research, their power further boosted by the development of high-speed computers which allowed complex simulations. The mechanistic paradigm that had long dominated science was being challenged by alternative ideas which allowed for the possibility that the whole might be more than the sum of its parts.

As mentioned already, developments in finance have often gone hand in hand with developments in mathematics. The invention of money in ancient Mesopotamia coincided with that of mathematics. During the classical age it was Greek arithmetic and geometry; in the medieval era it was innovations such as the use of negative numbers to describe credit; during the gold standard it was 'rational mechanics'; and in the modern era, beginning in the late 1960s with the collapse of the gold standard and the rise of fiat currencies, we have also seen the adoption (if resisted until recently by the mainstream) of new mathematical techniques such as complexity and chaos theory.

It could, however, be argued that the inspiration for these developments – and even the environmental consciousness-raising that followed the Moon mission – actually goes back further, to the quantum revolution at the start of the twentieth century. In a completely literal sense, the Moon missions – and those planetary selfies – were funded as part of the Cold War battle with the Soviets for dominance in missile technology, which in turn grew out of the nuclear programme. In an era when people were afraid that a nuclear device could at any time be dropped on them from the sky, the symbolism of sending a man to the Moon was a potent force. It wasn't about the Moon, or the Earth, but the atom.

But more generally, the quantum revolution achieved for matter what the Moon mission had done for the Earth – it revealed it as something that looked rather like it had a life, and even perhaps an agency, of its own. And it showed that even apparently isolated particles could only be understood as part of a larger whole. One reason perhaps that quantum ideas, after having been kept on ice for the last hundred years, are now seeing social science applications is that – living in the networked age – we have grown more comfortable with its message that we are part of a connected, entangled, living system.

Thinking electrons

The most basic feature of mechanistic science is that it treats everything as if it were dead. After all, a machine has no will or volition, so it can't make sense of things like time or consciousness. In Newtonian mechanics, time is just a parameter in the equations with no meaning in itself. Consciousness is similarly ignored, or explained away as being the by-product of mechanistic forces. (For one thing, you can't measure it. How big is 'I'? How much does it weigh?)

In 1913, the American psychologist John B. Watson wrote that 'Psychology, as the behaviorist views it, is a purely objective, experimental branch of natural science which needs introspection as little as do the sciences of chemistry and physics ... It can dispense with consciousness in a psychological sense.'[6] When consciousness *is* considered, it is usually viewed as a kind of illusion that has presumably evolved mechanistically because it offers a survival advantage.[7] Many computer scientists today believe that computers will eventually become sophisticated enough that they will produce the illusion themselves, and become conscious. But there seems to be a fundamental difference between something like a computer (at least of the classical sort) that obeys programmed instructions, and a living being. A computer can tell you what the time is to an astonishing degree of accuracy – but will it ever be able to feel the passage of time itself?

One reason the quantum revolution was so unsettling – at least to scientists – was because it seemed to put time and consciousness at the heart of science. The whole point of wave function collapse, after all, is that it is irreversible: once a particle has been measured, it stays measured. You can't therefore just run the process backwards in time and restore the system, as if you were returning a purchase to the store for a refund. And according to the Copenhagen interpretation, the wave function collapses because it is observed. That is why the fate of Schrödinger's cat depended on whether someone was watching (a conclusion which Einstein mocked by pointing out that the Moon does not exist *only* when we look at it).

Most physicists preferred to ignore these issues and concentrate on the mathematics. But as the physicist Freeman Dyson noted in his 1975 book *Disturbing the Universe*, the connection with consciousness may go further, in the sense that the act of thinking could itself be a form of wave function collapse: 'I cannot help thinking that our awareness of our own brains has something to do with the process which we call "observation" in atomic physics. That is to say, I think our consciousness is not just a passive epiphenomenon carried along by the chemical events in our brains, but is an active agent forcing the molecular complexes to make choices between one quantum state and another. In other words, mind is already inherent in every electron, and the processes of human consciousness differ only in degree but not in kind from the processes of choice between quantum states which we call "chance" when they are made by electrons.'[8]

Koestler's friend, the physicist David Bohm, similarly argued that 'The ability of form to be active is the most characteristic feature of mind, and we have something that is mind-like already with the electron'.[9] Of course, the idea that subatomic particles might carry the vestiges of consciousness – a theory known as panpsychism – would be repugnant to most mechanistically-minded scientists. However, as Alexander Wendt notes, given that mind and matter are linked through quantum theory, 'who is to say that when a wave function collapses into a particle, there is nothing like thinking involved'?[10]

Conversely, a number of scientists believe that our own physical act of thinking involves quantum processes. The physicist Roger Penrose, for example, argued that these take place within tiny structures inside brain neurons known as microtubules, which might be small and insulated enough to maintain quantum vibrations in a controlled fashion.[11] Another theory from physicist Matthew Fisher is that a particular configuration of phosphorus nuclei with entangled spins may have the ability to function as the brain's version of a qubit. (In *The Evolution of Money*, Roman Chlupatý and I pointed out the similarity between the energy-storing ATP molecule, which contains a string of phosphate groups, and money.)

Sceptics meanwhile have pointed out that it is difficult enough to maintain quantum decoherence (i.e. prevent premature wave function collapse) under carefully controlled laboratory conditions, let alone in a brain. Neurophilosopher Patricia Churchland said that 'pixie dust in the synapses' would be as useful an explanation for human cognition.[12] But there also seems to be a deeper unease at work. As science writer Phillip Ball observes, 'physicists are often embarrassed to even mention the words "quantum" and "consciousness" in the same sentence'.[13] Even those working in quantum cognition or quantum finance still shy away from the idea, and take great pains to point out that their theories do not rely on quantum consciousness.

This scepticism has eroded somewhat in recent years with the development of quantum biology, which, as already mentioned, has illustrated a number of cases where life forms unembarrassedly exploit quantum physics. Consciousness has also so far eluded any mechanistic explanation; and if processes are quantum at the macro social level, and quantum at the micro level, then in aesthetic terms at least it would make more sense if they were quantum at the intermediate level of the brain as well – i.e. quantum all the way down. According to Wendt, social structures – including the market economy – are best described in physical terms as 'superpositions of shared mental states – social wave functions'.[14] (We might not know what such a social wave function is 'made of', but we don't know what a quantum wave function is 'made of' either.) Viewed this way, money does not just collapse the fuzzy notion of value; it is collapsing a 'real' quantum wave function in our brains, and a 'real' wave function in our society. In which case, the wave function for an electron, or a person, or even a planet are not so different.

Unity versus plurality

Of course, the universe doesn't care about our sense of aesthetics; and from the point of view of economics at least there is no need to try to reduce social phenomena to the result of subatomic quantum processes, as if this would make them more real or physical, because as discussed in Chapter 2, money can be treated as a quantum system in its own right.* Money certainly resonates in an interesting way with the equally dualistic properties of the human mind, especially in the appearance of interference effects, which are psychological in nature and arise from the dissonance between numerical price and subjective value; but to assert that price is the result of an uncertain measurement process, or that one can derive a mathematical model for a particular system using a quantum formalism, does not rely on being able to show that these things reduce to quantum interactions inside the brain, or anything else. What counts is the emergent behaviour, which is best treated at its own level. As Nobel laureate physicist Robert Laughlin notes, 'physical law is a rule of collective behavior, it is a consequence of more primitive rules of behavior underneath (although it need not have been), and it gives one predictive power over a limited range of circumstances. Outside this range, it becomes irrelevant, supplanted by other rules that are either its children or its parents in a hierarchy of descent.'[15] Just as quantum effects can appear as emergent properties of physical systems, so emergent social properties may sometimes be best expressed using a quantum formalism.

Another connection between Koestler's holons and quantum physics, which in part inspired his approach, is that the quantum formalism neatly encapsulates the ideas of the whole and the part, and the tension between unity and plurality. A physical example of a holon discussed already in Chapter 1 is the super-particle known as a phonon, which consists of collectively excited atoms as caused

* The main approach here therefore differs slightly from other common alternatives, which (in order of strength) are to treat quantum physics as just a metaphor, to use the quantum formalism as a mathematical toolbox, and to assert that social phenomena can at least in principle be reduced to quantum physics (though I see merit in all, and sometimes draw on them as should be clear from context).

by low-energy sound waves in a metal bar. Similarly, an individual photon of light may seem to exist in isolation, but in reality its wave function is entangled and shared with other particles and its surroundings in general. Context matters, so there is feedback between the different levels. The whole and the part – or the system wave function and its individual particles – are therefore co-emergent phenomena. Furthermore, the complexity of quantum interactions, at the micro or macro level, vastly expands the space of possible structures that might emerge. On computers, it is straightforward to produce a conventional agent-based model of a market and show that it has emergent properties which resemble those of a real market; but in the quantum version, there is another level of feedback where the behaviour of the market changes the nature of the agents, just as living in a market economy changes us.[16]

The US psychologist Paul Piff has shown, for example, how wealth can affect people's attitudes and behaviour, reinforcing their sense of self-entitlement and reducing empathy for others.[17] Conversely, the physical and psychological stresses of poverty and scarcity sap mental capacity: according to behavioural economist Sendhil Mullainathan, 'if I made you poor tomorrow, you'd probably start behaving in many of the same ways we associate with poor people'.[18] There is a reason why people who can least afford it often become drug addicts. (Economics calls itself the science of scarcity, even though its model of rational behaviour applies least well under conditions of scarcity.) Indeed, according to a Goldman Sachs report, the financial crisis is likely to have worsened the current opioid crisis in the US.[19] Our social context, such as living in an unequal society, therefore influences us as much as a shared wave function affects the behaviour of an electron.

Again, it is puzzling that quantum physics is frequently described as bizarre and counterintuitive, when it seems to have so much in common with social relationships. One reason people like to participate in group events – from demonstrations, to riots, to drug-fuelled raves – is because they enjoy the sensation of, not just joining, but actually *becoming part of* a crowd, and in so doing losing part of their individual identity. This effect approximates certain group quantum behaviours of particles that are routinely exploited in technology. One example is superconductivity, which is described by physicist Robert Laughlin as a collective 'tendency of electrons to lock arms and move as one gigantic body'.[20] Another is plasma, an electrically charged form of gas where, as David Bohm wrote: 'The whole system is undergoing a co-ordinated movement more like a ballet dance than like a crowd of unorganized people … closer to the organized unity of the parts of a living being than it is to the kind of unity that is obtained by putting together the parts of a machine.'[21]

These descriptions of quantum phenomena resemble that of sociologists Donald MacKenzie and Taylor Spears, though they were talking about the quantitative finance industry: 'Perhaps the modelling of derivatives in investment banking always has an aspect of what one of our interviewees memorably called a "ballet," in which highly-paid quants are needed not just to try to capture the way the world is, but also to secure co-ordinated action. Perhaps the quant is actually a dancer, and the dance succeeds when the dancers co-ordinate.'[22] Again there is a feedback between the group behaviour and the individuals, the dance and the dancers, the holon and its parts.

While money has two sides, though, it also has a preferred direction. As the historian Fernand Braudel wrote of the penetration of money into medieval society: 'What did it actually bring? Sharp variations in prices of essential foodstuffs; incomprehensible relationships in which man no longer recognized either himself, his customs or his ancient values. His work became a commodity, himself a "thing".'[23] Money may not be a 'thing' in the mechanistic sense of a solid object, but it has a way of bringing out the particle-like aspects of the world.

Measurement error

While we have focused so far on the question *how much* as it applies to financial transactions, it is appropriate then to ask how this quantum-like behaviour at the individual level, or the macroeconomic level, feeds up to the highest levels not just of the economy, but of the world system as a whole.

As we have seen, money is a measuring device – a way of collapsing the fuzzy concept of value to produce a single number. One of the emergent effects of money is therefore to put a number on the value of the world. Perhaps the best example of this is the continued reliance of economists on the metric known as gross domestic product or GDP. This is defined as the total amount spent for all final goods and services produced within a country. (A final good such as a car includes intermediate goods, i.e. the parts, that are not included separately. Adding it up isn't easy – the UN System of National Accounts, a manual which describes the process, has over 600 pages.[24]) Natural resources such as oil or water do not count unless they are extracted and used as part of some economic transaction. Nor do 'negative externalities' such as pollution. Nor does any kind of work performed for free in the home such as cooking, looking after children, etc.

Simon Kuznets, who founded the GDP in the 1930s as a way to measure the impact of the Great Depression, wanted to exclude spending on things like financial speculation, advertising, and armaments on the basis that they did not contribute to human well-being, but such subtle distinctions were soon dropped. In fact in the US during the Cold War, economic growth became a kind of proxy indicator of growth in military supremacy, with quality of life an added but secondary benefit. In a 1953 article for *Foreign Affairs*, the economist P.D. Wiles wrote that 'in a long cold war, the rate of growth is the most important thing, for in the end the country that grows most becomes biggest, and every economic advantage belongs to it, be it military power, dominance in world markets or even a higher standard of living'.[25]

Because GDP is based on measured transactions, it has the virtues of logical and aesthetic consistency. An additional benefit, if you believe in the wonders of efficient markets and think that the economy is a rational machine for optimising utility, is that it hands over the job of valuing the economy to the markets. But as many have pointed out, its answer to the question *how much* is also highly misleading. For example, Canada's GDP has done quite well in recent years – but if you subtract the effects of resource depletion, the apparent growth all but disappears. A 2016 report on Canada from the International Institute for Sustainable Development, which covered the years 1980 to 2013, found that: 'After taking inflation and population growth into consideration, comprehensive wealth grew at an annual rate of 0.19 per cent over the period' – which doesn't sound very impressive.[26]

Many alternatives to GDP have been proposed which attempt to make up for these and other missing factors. One example is the Genuine Progress Indicator which also accounts for things like social inequality and crime rates, and apparently reached its global peak back in 1978.[27] But a problem with all such metrics is that they include estimates that are not based on transactions – and because money is a measurement device, that means the numbers have to be made up. The reason GDP does not include natural resources that are still in the ground is that they haven't yet been sold, so there is no price. Pollution doesn't count because – apart from in artificial markets for things like carbon emissions – it isn't something that is typically bought or sold (though cleaning it up is, so that adds to GDP). Similarly, unpaid labour doesn't appear exactly because it is unpaid, so it hasn't been measured.

As with any quantum system, the measurement process also affects the system being measured. By measuring any activity that produces numerical wealth, while ignoring or downplaying problems such as resource depletion or pollution, GDP biases the economy towards activities that damage the environment. After all, what better way is there to boost GDP than to extract wealth from the earth and dump the pollution as cheaply as possible? (This business model historically accounts for much of the wealth of my home city Toronto, a major centre for the global mining industry.[28])

As Frederick Soddy pointed out, though, all human activity including the economy is subject to a greater set of laws, which are the laws of thermodynamics, quantum or otherwise.[29] The economy can be viewed as a way of extracting energy from ordered, useful, low-entropy sources (e.g. solar energy stored in plants) and dumping it as disordered, unuseful, high-entropy waste. Economists have traditionally modelled things like pollution as 'externalities', but the choice of word betrays their mechanistic mindset, and helps to explain why the environmental crisis has been allowed to unfold with little intervention from the mainstream. Neoclassical economists are wont to compare heterodox economists with climate change deniers (see box below), but that may reflect anxiety about their history on this topic, back before there was a status quo. Milton Friedman, for example, wrote that 'Ecological values can find their natural space in the market, like any other consumer demand', which put environmental sustainability on the same plane as a new toaster.[30]

When economists do engage with the climate debate, they typically frame it in terms of a cost-benefit approach, where the utility of reducing climate emissions – based on estimates from climate models – is balanced against the costs of implementing the required policies, such as lost output. The effects of climate change – such as extreme weather, flooding, forest fires, species extinctions, mass displacement of populations, loss of human lives, and so on – are somehow aggregated down to a single dollar value, which represents our average happiness with it all. As the Australian academic Clive Hamilton puts it, the image is of the economist as 'the ultimate economic technocrat with his hand on the global thermostat, checking his modelling results and fiddling with the knob, checking again and adjusting further, all so that the planet's atmospheric layer may be tuned optimally to suit the majority of human inhabitants.'[31] However, there are a few problems with this approach.

One, as Hamilton observes, is that the climate is 'more like a wild beast than a thermostat that can be controlled'. Another, as I have written elsewhere, is that the predictive capability of such models – coupling as they do the unpredictable economy with the unpredictable climate – is approximately zero, and the models can be adjusted to give any answer you want.[32] This is particularly a problem given that economists have traditionally been less than up-front about declaring conflicts of interest, for example with mining or oil companies.*

---

* As Richard Denniss, chief economist for The Australia Institute, told the CBC in 2016: 'Economists are often pretending to be impartial. They're often pretending to be putting their intellectual credibility forward in defence of something, and if they just want to be sales people then they should admit that. They should come clean with journalists, they should come clean with politicians, they should come clean with public servants, and say look I am here on behalf of someone, my opinions are irrelevant, these are the opinions I am presenting to help my client get their way.' Kennedy, P. (5 January 2016), 'It's The Economists, Stupid' (CBC). Retrieved from: http://www.cbc.ca/radio/ideas/it-s-the-economists-stupid-1.3219471

But a more basic problem is that the aggregating approach works no better here than for things like trade policy. The climate/economy system isn't a tub of water, which adjusts in a smooth and continuous way to policy refinements. It is a complex, connected system where changes in one part can have a sudden and dramatic effect somewhere else. And we can't put a price on the climate, or collapse it down to a dollar value, because in a very literal sense it's *not for sale*.

The tragedy of economics

Perhaps the main driver of the environmental crisis – which of course is excluded from models – is our debt-based money system. As discussed earlier, because most of the money supply is created through loans for private banks, the vast majority of the money we use ultimately represents somebody's debt. That debt bears interest, so if the economy were to stop growing, and the money supply tapered off, then it would be impossible to pay off the debt. To keep pace, the implication is that the economy must grow for ever as well, which brings us up against natural limits.

One solution would be to change our money system towards something like full-reserve banking, in which private banks can only loan what they actually have.[33] Endorsed over the years, for different reasons, by economists as varied as David Ricardo, Frederick Soddy, Irving Fisher, Milton Friedman, Herman Daly, and Martin Wolf of the *Financial Times*, this would have the added benefits of reducing taxes and decreasing inequality, since seigniorage and interest payments would be captured by the state rather than the highly-paid financial sector. While the system has its disadvantages – some fear, for example, that it could drive loan activity to unregulated shadow institutions – the fact that no country has adopted it since the nineteenth century probably speaks more to the power of the banking sector than to any flaw in the idea.

Another solution, though, is to create and foster places where money is taken out of the picture altogether, by reclaiming the old idea of the shared commons. In medieval England, for example, large areas of land were set aside as collectively managed commons and were used for purposes such as animal grazing and collecting firewood. As the feudal system broke down with the spreading use of money, tenants were increasingly evicted from common land as part of the privatisation process known as enclosure. The practice spread to Scotland, Ireland, and the colonies. Today wealthy hedge funds and national governments continue to take over remaining arable land around the world, in what has been called the global land grab.[34]

The idea of the commons obviously doesn't fit well with economics, since the whole point of the economy is to attach a number to things by putting them up for sale. It also seems to have a basic flaw, for as Aristotle noted: 'that which is common to the greatest number has the least care bestowed upon it. Every one thinks chiefly of his own, hardly at all of the common interest; and only when he is himself concerned as an individual.'[35] The same point was raised by ecologist Garrett Hardin in a 1968 paper called 'The Tragedy of the Commons', which described a kind of parable.[36] A number of individual animal herders all have access to an area of common pasture. For each herder, rational self-interest dictates that they should exploit as much of the land as possible; but if they all do this, then the result is over-grazing, so no one benefits. A real-world example is the collapse of fisheries like Grand Banks off Nova Scotia, Canada, in 1992, where as economists Ronald Colman and Hans Messinger observed, 'Economic performance of Newfoundland and Nova Scotia benefited from record fish landings up to the very moment of the collapse of the Atlantic ground-fish stocks'.[37]

At the same time, though, there is also ample evidence from forestries, fisheries, irrigation systems, grasslands, and so on around the world that commons can be successfully and sustainably managed, for the reason that users are not independent atoms but entangled social beings who tend to develop shared rules and norms. The political scientist Elinor Ostrom won her economics Nobel – the only one at the time of writing to have been awarded to a woman – for her work in this area.

Today, the power of the shared commons is particularly evident in the digital domain. Much of the software which drives computers, smartphones, and the internet was developed under a general public licence (GPL). Instead of asserting the right to exclusive use, it asserts that the resource must remain in the digital commons. The legal framework was emulated in academia by open-access online journals, and by Creative Commons licences for things like Wikipedia – admittedly a bad development for the publishers of encyclopaedias, but in general far from tragic. As with other commons throughout history, the digital commons constantly has to resist enclosure from digital giants such as Facebook, who try to corral users into their own monetised platforms.

The same principle of treating shared resources as commons applies to managing things like the climate system. After all, we all breathe the same air, and you can't put a price on it. As Ostrom emphasised, people don't need to be told by economists how to manage commons, because they have been doing it themselves for centuries.[38] In fact, interventions by economists are often more likely to destroy sustainability than enhance it.[39] The climate system is different only because of its global scale, which certainly makes it a daunting problem that will involve every level of government, industry, and society in general in order to solve; but it is one where economists should play a supporting as opposed to a leading role.

The approach of quantum economics towards the environment is therefore refreshingly simple – it has no idea what it's talking about (because the environment is not based on money, and economists have enough trouble understanding the economy as it is) but it can work with other fields that do. This might seem a radical approach, given that economic reformers usually talk in terms of expanding economics so that it can better account for the value and dynamics of natural systems. However, critics also call for economics to be more humble; and empirically speaking, the development of areas such as environmental economics has done little to slow actual damage to the environment in recent decades. According to the philosopher Michael Sandel: 'As markets reach into spheres of life traditionally governed by nonmarket norms, the notion that markets don't touch or taint the goods they exchange becomes increasingly implausible.'[40] The same can be said of economics, when it attempts to make up for nature's lack of market mechanisms by introducing proxy versions. By putting a numerical value on nature, it is devaluing it in another way. And by couching the problem in terms of its own abstract mathematical models, it actually hides its assumptions – or rather renders them obscure to the uninitiated – rather than clarifying them.

Money is not a natural system, it is a human invention which by its nature brings us into conflict with natural systems. An ecological economist, in this view, is someone who understands ecology and economics, while appreciating that – although they have aspects in common – they are not the same thing. In fact something like this seems to be what differentiates the otherwise apparently similar fields of environmental and ecological economics – the ecological economist Herman Daly, for example, argues that we should control resource use by capping the physical amount extracted and selling the extraction rights to the highest bidder, while environmental economists would tackle the same problem by performing a cost-benefit analysis and imposing taxes.[41]

Since most aspects of the economy affect the environment in one way or another, economists will of course have to learn to design the economy to work within its constraints. But we shouldn't trust economists to optimise planetary health by themselves any more than we should trust them to manage our personal health. And instead of extending economics, we should enclose it.

The veil of money

A similar valuation problem occurs when we look at the other side of the ledger, and ask what we are actually buying with all this economic activity. According to neoclassical economics, the economy consists of rational agents who perform transactions in order to maximise their individual utility. Because utility is additive and linear, the net effect is therefore to maximise overall utility as well.

The subject's founders explicitly associated utility with a form of pleasure energy – or as Francis Edgeworth called it in his 1881 *Mathematical Psychics*, 'a sort of hedonico-magnetic field'.[42] More modern textbooks define utility as 'The satisfaction or well-being that a consumer receives from consuming some good or service' (Ragan and Lipsey) or 'the level of happiness or satisfaction that a person receives' (Mankiw).[43] This connection between utility and happiness leads to the assumption that economic growth makes people happy.[44] Sometimes this assumption is explicit – Olivier Blanchard, for example, noted in a textbook: 'Economists take for granted that higher output per capita means higher utility and increased happiness' – but more often it is implicit in the economic models used to make decisions.[45]

Given that the connection between economic growth and happiness is a basic principle of mainstream economic thought – or as one book put it, 'Economics is about happiness' – one might think that there would be a great deal of empirical evidence to show that it is true.[46] But in fact the relationship between societal wealth and reported happiness levels is weak, except in the poorest countries.[47] In wealthy countries such as the US, happiness seems to have peaked some time back in the 1960s. Japan went from being one of the poorest countries in the world in the late 1950s to one of the richest in the space of a few decades without any significant change in reported happiness.[48]

Instead, what seems far more important, at least as an economic factor, is social status or rank. One side-effect of having a society based on money is that it makes it very easy to compare ourselves with others on a linear scale. A 2010 study by British researchers found that 'Rank of income, not income, affects life satisfaction'.[49] As one of the authors, Chris Boyce from the University of Warwick's Department of Psychology, summarised: 'Earning a million pounds a year appears to be not enough to make you happy if you know your friends all earn 2 million a year.'[50] Or as a 1907 essay, usually but probably incorrectly attributed to John Stuart Mill, put it: 'Men do not desire to be rich, but to be richer than other men.'[51]

In fact, inequality seems to affect even our physical well-being. A 2014 study based on British data concluded 'that social position rather than material conditions may explain the impact of money on human health'.[52] This concurs with a famous 1991 study of British civil servants, which showed that the strongest predictor for heart disease was job status, apparently because low-status workers experienced more stress so had more heart problems.[53] From a purely mechanistic perspective, these findings are hard to understand: why should one inert rational independent economic agent care about what the other agents are up to? But when we view the economy as an entangled system, in which people have direct influence over one another, it makes perfect sense.

Financial entanglement is not symmetric, because it encodes a power relationship – the creditor over the debtor – which is backed by law. This property has meant that, throughout history, debt has been a major reason for people falling into slavery or peonage. Conversely, the historian Carl Wennerlind wrote how England's involvement in the eighteenth-century slave trade meant that 'a closer mental association was forged between the urban milieu of London, the slave forts on the African coast, and the colonial towns of New Spain. This sophisticated time-space compression transferred value from the future to the present, from the sphere of commerce to public finance, and from the Atlantic world to the city of London.'[54] Even today, slave labour plays a role in the global supply chains of many firms (in the UK it has been estimated as up to 11 per cent), even if it no longer weighs so heavily on the minds of most consumers.[55] More apparent is that much of the economy relies on the efforts of highly-indebted 'wage slaves' who only earn enough to service their debts and pay for their upkeep. Unfortunately it appears that another side-effect of our increasingly entangled economy is a rise in inequality.

The arrow of money

While global poverty has been trending down in recent years, inequality within many countries has been sharply increasing. This was epitomised in 2017 by Oxfam's claim that eight men now hold as much wealth as half of the world's population (down from 388 people in 2010).[56] It seems that if, instead of a coffee cup, you put a small group of extremely rich people into the centre of the world economy, their wealth doesn't dissipate out, or trickle down – it just grows larger, as if the arrow of time is pointing backwards.

This rise in inequality has been widely documented, mostly by non-neoclassical economists such as Thomas Piketty but also more recently by organisations including the OECD and IMF, and has become an important political issue in many countries.[57] Yet mainstream economists have on the whole had surprisingly little to say about topics such as the distribution of wealth or income. Or rather, as Dani Rodrik noted in 2016, they have 'consistently minimized distributional concerns'.[58] According to Branko Milanovic, former lead economist at the World Bank, until a few years ago 'even the word inequality was not politically acceptable, because it seemed like something wild or socialist or whatever'.[59]

While Rodrik describes this state of affairs as 'curious', it is actually *designed into* economic models. Distributional problems are seen as a distortion to the model, which, as we have seen, is based on the idea of the average man and ignores financial entanglements – and indeed the financial system – altogether.[60] Some economists have been very explicit about this. Lionel Robbins wrote in the 1930s that because the subjective utility of one person cannot be measured versus that of another, the whole question of fair distribution is 'entirely foreign to the assumptions of scientific Economics' (not sure how this lack of interest in distribution relates to his famous definition of economics as the science of scarcity).[61] More recently, Robert Lucas wrote in 2004: 'Of the tendencies that are harmful to sound economics, the most seductive, and in my opinion the most poisonous, is to focus on questions of distribution.'[62] And of course, if you believe that markets are efficient, inequality just reflects differences in ability. An example is CEO pay, the poster boy of pay inequality. As Gregory Mankiw wrote in a 2013 paper, 'the most natural explanation of high CEO pay is that the value of a good CEO is extraordinarily high'.[63] (Some of them must be very talented indeed.)

An explanation of low pay for everyone else, meanwhile, was supplied by co-discoverer of DNA James Watson in 2003: 'this growing inequality of income may in some sense be a reflection of some people being more strong and healthy than others. Some people, no matter how much schooling you give them, will never really be up to what is now considered a necessary degree of effective intelligence.'[64] Or as then-London mayor Boris Johnson reminded his hedge fund-owning supporters in a 2013 speech: 'Whatever you may think of the value of IQ tests, it is surely relevant to a conversation about equality that as many as 16 per cent of our species have an IQ below 85, while about 2 per cent have an IQ above 130.'[65] (Those numbers just reflect the definition of the IQ scoring system, which is designed to roughly follow a normal distribution with a mean of 100 and a standard deviation of 15. Inequality is of course far more skewed.)

This idea dates back to the Social Darwinists of the nineteenth century, who compared economic survival to the law of the jungle.[66] But even without the genetic/IQ narrative, implicit in the hands-off approach of mainstream economics is a stance which says that economists should not interfere with distribution in order to make the economy appear less unfair, because the market – at least in its idealised form – is a better judge of such matters than them. If people are independent atoms, responsible for their own decisions, then they are also responsible for their economic fate. It has even been claimed that the fact that economic models treat all individuals on an equal basis reflects the field's egalitarian and cosmopolitan world view.[67]

However, this seems to be making a virtue out of necessity. The real reason economists have traditionally paid little attention to distributional issues is because they violate the symmetry conditions at the heart of the reductionist approach. Economic models see the economy in terms of a tepid kind of thermodynamic bath, and with these tools economists couldn't model things like extreme inequality even if they wanted to.

This is not to say that all economists tilt right politically, only that their symmetry-based theories are not good at handling inequality.[68] At the same time, by ignoring or downplaying the importance of money and debt, mainstream economics has helped to create both the debt and the inequality problems in the first place – for only by seeing a problem and treating it seriously can we do something about it. Instead, according to Dean Baker, 'There is overwhelming pressure to produce work that supports the status quo (for example, redistributing to the rich), that doesn't question authority, and that is needlessly complex. The result is a discipline in which much of the work is of little use, except to legitimate the existing power structure.'[69] Baker points out, for example, that free trade agreements focus on making labour and capital mobile, while placing restrictions on things like intellectual property and professional licences that restrict competition in protected sectors such as health care.[70] The finance sector is meanwhile ignored, despite the fact that its exorbitant pay structure, along with its tendency to blow up asset bubbles, is itself a major creator of inequality.

The pursuit of happiness

If happiness is truly the goal of economics, it would therefore make more sense for economists to optimise distribution, rather than economic growth. And yet most effort is focused on the latter, while little is known about the former. At a deeper level, though – should economics be about happiness at all?

As Robert Putnam wrote in his 2000 book *Bowling Alone*: 'The single most common finding from a half century's research on the correlates of life satisfaction, not only in the United States but around the world, is that happiness is best predicted by the breadth and depth of one's social connections.'[71] And just as money bears interest, happiness also breeds happiness, with the difference that it is shared. This was borne out by a 2008 US study which followed a cohort of 4,700 people over twenty years and found that having a happy friend or neighbour boosts your own feelings of happiness by an estimated 9 per cent. As one of the co-authors of the study, political scientist James Fowler, concluded: 'The pursuit of happiness is not a solitary goal. We are connected, and so is our joy.'[72] We are part of something larger, whether we like it or not. Wealth is just a sideshow.

Again, just as observing a quantum state changes it, so it seems the 'pursuit of happiness' can actually make us less happy. One Australian study showed, according to social psychologist Brock Bastian, that 'Depression rates are higher in countries that place a premium on happiness. Rather than being the by-product of a life well-lived, feeling happy has become a goal in itself. Smiling faces beam at us from social media and happiness gurus flog their latest emotional quick fixes, reinforcing the message that we should aim to maximize our positive emotions and avoid our negative ones.'[73]

While happiness is affected by economic factors such as inequality, part of that is because we live in a number-based economic system which encourages us to rank ourselves against others according to metrics such as salary, house price or net worth. In other words, instead of making us happy as economists claim, economics is probably doing the opposite. Rather than pretending that it knows the route to true happiness, economics should stick to problems that it can actually help with, such as making economic opportunity more fair. For example, if economic models were to replace Pareto optimality with a constraint that each citizen should be able to make a living wage, then policies such as a universal basic income, which are currently being debated and tested in a number of countries, would certainly look a lot more acceptable.[74] And if growth targets were capped by the restrictions of environmentalists and systems scientists, we might or might not be happier, but at least the outlook for our children would improve.

While quantum economics may not have much to say about happiness, it does have something to say about a related issue, which is that of a sense of meaning and purpose in life. This is related to happiness, but it isn't quite the same thing – artists suffer for their art, parents suffer for their children, and so on. The story from mainstream economics is that we are utility-optimising machines, so a job is just a way to earn money to spend on stuff, which doesn't seem very meaningful. By bringing consciousness into the equations, the quantum approach invites us to think of the economy as a creative, participatory, and above all meaningful process.

Boundary issues

The long course of our Western scientific project, while tremendously successful in many respects, has by its nature involved a gradual usurping of our mental processes by number-based reductionism. Nowhere is this more evident than in neoclassical economics, which set itself the goal of rationally optimising happiness, and went so far as to omit money from its calculations exactly because it didn't fit with this narrative. But if we stand back to look at the modern economy from a distance – like the Apollo astronauts looking back at the Earth – we see that far from optimising utility, it is sacrificing both the environment and human happiness in order to maintain a highly distorted status quo. Economists speak of money as an inert means of exchange, but it seems to have become something of a toxic substance that is leading to a breakdown in what Arthur Koestler called the holon's integrative tendency. Instead of uniting us, as a shared currency is supposed to do, it is pulling us apart.

While the idea of building a quantum economics model that merges the human economy with the Earth system, based on sound principles of physics, sounds like a good idea for an academic grant proposal, as argued above, big models of complex systems always end up having so many sensitive parameters and interlocking feedback loops that you can make them tell any story you want. A simpler approach is to take the conclusions of quantum economics at face value. One of these is that value is a fuzzy social concept that collapses to a single number only when measured through transactions. Price measurements are therefore emergent features of the economy that are subject to intrinsic uncertainty, but just as importantly they are *only* price measurements. They might have meaning for us, but in themselves they don't have physical relevance for the planet. In particular, while prices are influenced to an extent by scarcity, they are nothing like a measurement of scarcity. The fact that the price of oil surges or collapses in the space of months is not an indicator of the amount of oil left in the ground.

In order to reintegrate the economy, we can therefore take a page from the structure of our own brains. As Iain McGilchrist notes, the left hemisphere pretends to be an expert on things like utility – it is imperturbably optimistic – but in fact its main talent is in reducing everything to logical bits of information, such as numbers and letters. In contrast, 'The right hemisphere's particular strength is in understanding meaning as a whole and in context'.[75] According to McGilchrist, if the left hemisphere were to have its way, the world would be seen as something 'relatively mechanical, an assemblage of more or less disconnected "parts"; it would be relatively abstract and disembodied; relatively distanced from fellow-feeling; given to explicitness; utilitarian in ethic; over-confident of its own take on reality, and lacking insight into its problems – the neuropsychological evidence is that these are all aspects of the left hemisphere world as compared with the right'.[76]

The left hemisphere would see itself 'as the passive victim of whatever it is not conscious of having willed' (a random external shock, perhaps). And of course there would be an emphasis on 'Numbers, which the left hemisphere feels familiar with and is excellent at manipulating', and '"measurability", in other words the insistence on quantification, not qualification'.[77]

That has already happened – it is called mainstream economics. In 1936, the economist Friedrich Hayek asked rhetorically: 'How can the combination of fragments of knowledge existing in different minds bring about results which, if they were to be brought about deliberately, would require a knowledge on the part of the directing mind which no single person can possess?'[78] He found his answer in the market pricing system (as did his admirer Margaret Thatcher), which he saw as a kind of super-brain. As Matt Ridley wrote, 'We live in a world richly furnished with technological and cultural marvels, because we have networked our minds as a collective brain. It was exchange and specialisation that enabled us to do so. That's Hayek's great discovery.'[79] However, this number-based 'collective brain' is one in which only the left hemisphere is functioning – and which has convinced itself that the multi-dimensional information in the economy can somehow be compressed down to a single number, namely price. (Hayek, it should be pointed out, was writing before the invention of information theory, which might have tempered his outlook somewhat.)

So to bring the system back into balance, we don't necessarily need economists to give up their numbers, or go to art school, or get in touch with their feelings (though it might help if they read more fiction, which has a lot to teach about human behaviour).[80] Economics is about a particular money-based social institution known as the market economy. It has nothing to say about the energy flows that characterise our relationship with the environment – its units of money are not compatible with the units of physics (a long-standing criticism of economists is that they pay little attention to things like units) – and it has even less to say about the 'psychic energy' of happiness. Economics can learn a great deal from sciences such as ecology or psychology or thermodynamics, and tools such as the Genuine Progress Indicator (GPI) can provide useful indicators; but Gary Becker's statement that 'the economic approach is a comprehensive one that is applicable to all human behavior' is completely wrong.

Instead, we need a social version of a corpus callosum – from the Latin for 'tough body' – to keep economic reductionism in its place, and protect against seizures and other malfunctions. In particular, it is ecologists and environmentalists who should establish firm boundary conditions for economic activity, such as how much pollution or other disruption can be absorbed by an ecosystem – because for them, as for the planet, money really is a veil. And as for being happiness gurus, economists shouldn't even try.

A main critique of neoclassical economics has long been that it doesn't include things like the environment or accurate metrics of social well-being, and the usual solution is that economics needs to broaden its domain. However, this approach doesn't work so well in practice, because it doesn't account for the natural bias of the money system. So maybe instead of becoming bigger, economics should become smaller. After all, if economists can't predict financial crashes, they are not well placed to advise on things like environmental crises or social tipping points either.

This is not of course to say that economists should *ignore* environmental or social factors and constraints when making predictions or designing economic policy; rather it is that their calculations should always be done in recognition of those inputs, which is not the same thing (see box below). In the final chapter, we show how acknowledging the powerful, entangled, and also unstable nature of our quantum economy, and setting some boundaries on it, can help to restore the economic system to a state of health.

Coffee with bankers

The American physicist Robert Millikan spent ten years trying to test and disprove Einstein's quantum theory of the photo-electric effect; he could find no fault, but maintained his belief that 'the physical theory upon which the equation is based is totally untenable.'[81] Classical economists are likely to be even more resistant to quantum ideas than were physicists.[82] The standard arguments against change of any sort were on display during a 2015 debate between economics professor Pieter Gautier and two Dutch students (Joris Tieleman and Lorenzo Fränkel) about the need for diversity in economics education.[83]

Echoing V.V. Chari's testimony, Gautier said that 'There is one large mainstream approach, which about 98 per cent of economists work in. The group split from the mainstream, the heterodox economists … is actually a group that wants to rid itself of the order and discipline of the mainstream … you also see this happening in the other sciences; in biology you have intelligent design, in climate science you have the climate skeptics.' Christopher Auld from the University of Victoria similarly wrote in 2013: 'Every mainstream science which touches on political or religious ideology attracts more than its fair share of deniers: the anti-vaccine crowd v mainstream medicine, GMO fearmongers v geneticists, creationists v biologists, global warming deniers v climatologists. Economics is no different.'[84] The Cambridge economist Pontus Rendahl told the *Financial Times* in 2016 that calling for more pluralism in economics is 'the same argument as the creationists in the US who say that natural selection is just a theory', while in

2017 Michael Ben-Gad from the University of London mocked student groups as wanting to be 'liberated from neoclassical economics' dogmatic insistence on internal logic, mathematical rigour and quantification ... Still, we do not teach astrology or creationism in our universities, though some students might enjoy them more than physics.'[85]

When one of the ~~creationists~~ students (Tieleman) observes that topics such as power, culture, and the environment are largely excluded from the analysis, Gautier replies: 'I think you see economics as a lot more narrow than it actually is. Culture is included.' The idea that 'neoclassical economics considers the economy separately from the planet' is, according to Gautier, 'absolutely not true' (despite the fact that this has long been a criticism of mainstream economists, including from climate scientists).[86] On the other hand, 'you have to abstract from all the noise, all the irrelevant issues. And that is what we do with models.'

When Tieleman brings up the lack of emphasis on field work – no economist 'had the idea to go to "Ground Zero", London City, and talk to the bankers' – Gautier finally agrees that this is excluded, on purpose.[87] 'To me it doesn't seem wise to ask the bankers what we have to do ... What *you* want is to do field work, to drink coffee with bankers ... we believe that you don't learn very much from those conversations. You might learn just enough to form a hypothesis, but eventually you want to look at hard data.' Or as Robert Lucas put it in *Lives of the Laureates*, 'Economic theory *is* mathematical analysis. Everything else is just pictures and talk.'[88]

Debates such as this between orthodox and heterodox economists often seem almost religious in nature and therefore impossible to resolve; but an advantage of the quantum approach is that it has room in its culture for mathematical and non-mathematical ideas, and the interplay between them.[89] For example, it is true that models need to be simple in order to be effective, and by their nature involve a particular kind of mathematical analysis; but the argument then is about what you can leave out, and how valid the conclusions will be, which can't always be deduced from logical principles. Finding this balance between simplicity and complexity is key to the art of mathematical modelling and forecasting.[90] I don't think (and I suspect some neoclassical economists might agree) that economics should 'include' culture or the environment – instead it should be in negotiation with those things – but it should include money.

So while quantum economics may be fundamentally incompatible with key tenets of the neoclassical approach, economists should continue to drink coffee with bankers – and with each other. Alternatively, of course, quantum economists could build an incredibly elaborate quantum model of the world economy which only people with the proper training can understand, blame any prediction errors on quantum uncertainties, and start drafting their biographies for *Lives of the Laureates*. But as argued in this book, that would be exactly the wrong approach.

CHAPTER 10

WE-CONOMICS

The love of money is the root of all evil.
The Bible (King James version)

Money is the root of all good.
Ayn Rand, *Atlas Shrugged* (1957)

Good and evil are one.
Heraclitus

When quantum physics was in its early days, a common objection was that it seemed to impart a degree of agency to subatomic particles, as if they had a choice in what they did. 'I find the idea quite intolerable', wrote Albert Einstein in a 1924 letter to Max Born, 'that an electron exposed to radiation should choose of its own free will, not only its moment to jump off, but also its direction.' What is strange, though, is that the same prejudice seems to be applied to human beings. Economists have long modelled the economy as a mechanistic machine, in which people behave like inanimate cogs. One implication is that ethics has been dropped from the subject. This final chapter sums up the argument for a new economics inspired by the insights of quantum physics.

During the late 1960s, Western countries such as America were experiencing a countercultural revolution, led by hippies, feminists, environmentalists, anti-nuclear groups, and visionaries such as Stewart Brand, who founded the Whole Earth Catalog, and Timothy Leary, who extolled the benefits of psychedelic drugs. In part, the movement was a reaction to the Cold War and the Vietnam War, which were absorbing American lives and treasure. But it also seemed to promise an alternative to the machine aesthetic of modern life. Much to the horror of most physicists, New Age culture began to incorporate ideas from quantum physics in the 1970s with the appearance of books such as Fritjof Capra's *The Tao of Physics* and Gary Zukav's *The Dancing Wu Li Masters*.[1] (The idea of quantum economics gave some physicists an attack of the vapours too, at least until they learned what it was.[2])

However, not everyone was attracted to the idea of blissful collectivism, or bought into the hippie ethos of tuning in and tripping out. One hold-out was the Russian-born author Alisa Zinov'yevna Rosenbaum – more commonly known by her penname Ayn Rand. Her first book, the semi-autobiographical *We the Living*, didn't set the world on fire. Perhaps blaming the title, she then wrote a novella called *Anthem* (her working title was *Ego*) which – some 75 years before the selfie stick – celebrated the idea of individuality: 'I am done with the monster of "we," the word of serfdom, of plunder, of misery, falsehood and shame. And now I see the face of god, and I raise this god over the earth, this god whom men have sought since men came into being, this god who will grant them joy and peace and pride. This god, this one word: "I."'[3]

Rand's first hit, *The Fountainhead*, published in 1943, was about an architect genius called Howard Roark. This was followed in 1957 by *Atlas Shrugged*, which was about a corporate titan called John Galt, trapped in a dystopian future in which collectivism had triumphed. Her books took a while to take off, but went on to sell millions of copies and be highly influential especially among conservative movements in the US and UK.

The theme of Rand's books can be summed up by what she called 'the morality of rational self-interest', which she turned into a philosophy known as objectivism.[4] This asserted that reality has an objective existence independent of consciousness; that one can attain knowledge about this objective reality through the use of inductive logic; that the purpose of life is the pursuit of one's own happiness; that respect for individual rights is paramount; and that laissez-faire capitalism is the only way to achieve these ends. As she wrote in 1961, 'The choice is clear-cut: either a new morality of rational self-interest, with its consequences of freedom, justice, progress and man's happiness on earth – or the primordial morality of altruism, with its consequences of slavery, brute force, stagnant terror and sacrificial furnaces.'[5]

Rand had a circle of admirers whom she teasingly called the Collective. This included her much younger lover Nathaniel Blumenthal, who unselfishly changed his last name to Branden so it would include hers.[6] He went on to write some twenty books on psychology, ten of which had 'self' in the title. Another young member of the Collective was Alan Greenspan, who later wrote that 'Ayn Rand became a stabilizing force in my life … I was intellectually limited until I met her … we agreed on the importance of mathematics and rigor'.[7] According to a 1999 profile in *Time* magazine, 'During long nights at Rand's apartment and through her articles and letters, Greenspan found in objectivism a sense that markets are an expression of the deepest truths about human nature and that, as a result, they will ultimately be correct'. It followed that 'trying to defy global market forces is in the end futile'.[8] Greenspan's belief in rational self-interest became something of a talking point after the 2007–08 crisis, when he testified to Congress that 'those of us who have looked to the self-interest of lending institutions to protect shareholders' equity (myself especially) are in a state of shocked disbelief'.[9] (This mea culpa didn't last long, and he was soon back to arguing in favour of what he called 'the global "invisible hand".[10])

Rand is still in the news today because of her continued popularity with leaders, both in politics and business. Donald Trump doesn't claim to be a big reader, but still found time for *The Fountainhead*: 'It relates to business, beauty, life and inner emotions. That book relates to ... everything', he told *USA Today*. Former Secretary of State Rex Tillerson, meanwhile, once listed *Atlas Shrugged* as his favourite book.[11] Speaker of the House Paul Ryan said: 'It's inspired me so much that it's required reading in my office for all my interns and my staff.'[12] Clearly, reading Rand is the key to world domination (though problems do seem to occur when there is more than one admirer competing within an organisation). It is no surprise that her book sales amount to hundreds of thousands annually and tripled after the financial crisis.[13]

Rand seems to be especially popular among technology CEOs. A *Vanity Fair* piece interviewing Silicon Valley leaders concluded that Rand is 'Perhaps the most influential figure in the industry'.[14] According to Apple co-founder Steve Wozniak, Steve Jobs described *Atlas Shrugged* as one of his 'guides in life'. The same would appear to hold, at least anecdotally, for many in the quantitative finance industry. Robert Mercer, the billionaire quant who helped bankroll Trump's election, has been described as having a philosophy akin to Rand's objectivism. One former colleague told the *New Yorker*: 'Bob believes that human beings have no inherent value other than how much money they make. A cat has value, he's said, because it provides pleasure to humans. But if someone is on welfare they have negative value. If he earns a thousand times more than a schoolteacher, then he's a thousand times more valuable.'[15] (It's not compulsory: when Elon Musk was grappling with an 'existential crisis' at the age of fourteen he turned to *The Hitchhiker's*

Guide to the Galaxy by Douglas Adams for enlightenment, which seemed to work.[16])

In fact, Rand's celebration of what Nietzsche called the Apollonian *principium individuationis* (principle of individuation) is just the latest phase of a long trend towards increased social atomism which stretches back centuries.[17] Back in the early 1800s, words such as 'ego' and 'self-love' were only beginning to be used in their modern sense, and 'atoms' were for scientists. Two centuries later, a 1995 survey showed that most Americans saw others (but not themselves) as 'increasingly atomized [and] selfish'.[18] It's not just that we identify with rational economic man; it is that we identify with the (wrong) classical picture of atoms that inspired his creation. It is often said that atomic physics does not scale up to the human level, but its ideas certainly do.

Part of this effect may be due to the enlarged role of money; numerous studies by behavioural economists have shown that priming people to think about money makes them behave in a more selfish way.[19] But the effect seems particularly strong in Western culture, which according to philosopher and geographer Yi-Fu Tuan, 'encourages an intense awareness of self and, compared with other cultures, an exaggerated belief in the power and value of the individual ... This isolated, critical and self-conscious individual is a cultural artifact. We may well wonder at its history. Children, we know, do not feel and think thus, nor do nonliterate and tradition-bound peoples, nor did Europeans in earlier times.'[20]

This emphasis on self seems especially curious given that one of humanity's distinguishing features is exactly our talent for empathy, altruism, and the development of social norms, which – far from the 'stagnant terror and sacrificial furnaces' of Rand's imagination – 'allows us to engage in the kind of large-scale cooperation seen uniquely in humans', as an article in the journal *Frontiers in Psychology* observed.[21] One reason that suggests itself for this cultural disposition is the dominance of an economic theory that prizes the power of individual atomistic agents, and puts the parts above the whole. As Joseph Stiglitz notes, behavioural economics shows that 'embedding individuals within a culture of selfishness (where that is taken as the norm) leads to changes in behavior in that direction'.[22] And for a culture of selfishness, neoclassical economics is hard to beat.

However, both Rand's objectivism and mainstream economics have a basic flaw, for they make sense only when applied to classical objects as opposed to quantum objects, which is a problem because we live in a quantum universe. According to conventional game theory of the sort used in economics, for example, each person is assumed to act rationally to optimise their own utility – their aim is to be a winner. This contrasts with quantum game theory, where, as Alexander Wendt notes, strategy has 'an irreducibly collective aspect, such that players are at least partly in "We-mode" rather than just "I-mode"'.[23] Winning seems slightly less attractive if you are entangled with the loser. In other words, collectivism isn't just a hippie lifestyle choice – it's in our nature. And to ignore it will lead to problems.

Quantum objectivism

One problem with individualism is that it isn't always clear where the line should be drawn for the word 'I'. In biology, the basic unit of life is usually considered to be not the person, but the cell. For example, if you agree with David Deutsch that life is about DNA, then each cell carries its own copy of the DNA which would seem to make it an individual. However, if you are a selfish-gene person then you might want to go down another level to individual genes, which according to this theory assemble bodies only as a means to propagate themselves. Either way, a human being begins to look something more like a superorganism. This is especially the case when you think that the human body relies on large colonies of micro-organisms in our gut, skin and elsewhere without which we could not survive.

Of course, most biologists would not say that a cell is conscious – but then consciousness isn't really a feature of mechanistic science, as we've seen. But if you can work down towards genes, then why can't you also work in the other direction? People are part of societies, and along with other species we are part of the holon known as the living planet. As James Lovelock points out, the Earth has many attributes in common with a living organism, for example in the way that it actively maintains conditions in the atmosphere and oceans in a way that is suitable for life.[24]

More generally, our sense of self is intimately tied up with relationships. When we interact with other people, we don't just bounce off them and emerge on the other side unchanged: we get under each other's skins, and we are different people as a result (even if we don't change our names to include theirs, like Branden did). As in a quantum system, in which particles are entangled and therefore in effect share their wave functions, it doesn't really make sense to speak of individuals as something separate from their context. The family you grow up in changes you, makes you a different person, as does the country or the society (even if we don't change our names to sound American, like Rand did). Descartes wrote that 'there is a great difference between the mind and the body, inasmuch as the body is by its very nature always divisible, while the mind is utterly indivisible'.[25] He used this to justify his belief that mind and body are separate, independent entities. But when we form relationships, our consciousness remains unified, but it is not unchanged; and conversely, as quantum physics shows, atoms have a way of merging together to form a coherent whole. The mind/body, unity/plurality divide breaks down with quantum entities.[26]

When neoclassical economics was founded in the nineteenth century, its founders didn't set out to promote the importance of untrammelled individuality. Instead their work seems to have been motivated by a genuine impulse to improve people's living conditions. Even today, while the economics profession is commonly associated with conservative politics, many economists describe themselves in surveys as being politically moderate.[27] At the same time, though, the logic of economic models has a way of asserting itself. One such effect has been to promote the idea that optimising individual utility automatically leads, through the invisible hand etc., to optimising the greater good. But another has been to expunge ethics from the field altogether. As Milton Friedman wrote in 1953, economics is 'in principle independent of any particular ethical position or normative judgments ... [It] is, or can be, an "objective" science, in precisely the same sense as any of the physical sciences.'[28] (Though he wasn't above such judgements himself, describing Rand as 'an utterly intolerant and dogmatic person who did a great deal of good'.[29]) Neoclassical economists may have borrowed their money creation story from Aristotle, but they left out the ethical distinction he drew between what he called 'natural' uses of monetary exchange, and 'unnatural' uses such as usury.[30] Utility theory makes no distinction between good uses or bad, and gross domestic product is indifferent to what is being produced.

Mainstream economics, in its quest for the appearance of scientific objectivity, therefore perfectly prepares the soil for Randian objectivism to bloom (see box below). On the one hand it gives an apparently scientific explanation for the benefits of restraining the kinds of collective forces – such as unions, governments, financial or environmental regulations, and so on – which so frustrated the fictional likes of Howard Roark and John Galt in her books. On the other hand it incapacitates the kind of non-numerical ethical arguments which might provide a counterbalance. Economics is therefore an enabler of Randianism, even if most mainstream economists would not subscribe to it themselves. (And certainly, behaviours such as the quest for tenure, avoiding accountability for mistakes, and sucking at the teat of the financial sector don't sound *exactly* like what she had in mind.)

If quantum economics has a central principle, though, it is that it is not possible to take this kind of detached, impersonal view of the economy. We are entangled with each other and with the economy as a whole, and our subjective judgements about value both define the economy, and are shaped by the economy. The quantum 'I' has an independent, localised, 'particle aspect', but also a diffuse and entangled 'wave aspect' – in a very real sense, we are not just influenced by, but are actually formed by our relationships, especially when money is involved. This quantum objectivism, if we call it that, might sound a bit mystical, but really it is a more realistic version of Randian objectivism: reality has a quantum nature that is dependent on consciousness; one cannot always attain knowledge about this reality through the use of inductive logic; the purpose of life is more than the pursuit of one's own happiness; individuals are entangled. And as we have already seen, it has a number of practical implications for the field of economics.

What's cooking?

The Greek philosopher Democritus' atomic theory was inspired, it is said, by baking. How is it possible that we can smell a loaf of bread that is cooking in an oven? The answer must be that particles of the bread – the atoms – escape from the oven. Subjective sensations like taste and smell were nothing but the interplay between the atoms of our body and those of the environment: 'Sweet exists by convention, bitter by convention, color by convention; but in reality atoms and the void alone exist.[31]

An atomistic theory of another sort was forged some two millennia later by René Descartes, who while stationed as a young French soldier in a German town during the winter of 1619, spent the night actually sleeping in an oven, and experienced a number of visions that led, among other things, to the formulation of analytical geometry, and his famous statement 'I think, therefore I am'. He was a thinking atom.

A corollary to the belief that one is the centre of the universe, is the feeling that the other people might not be completely real. As Descartes later wrote in his *Meditations on First Philosophy*, 'if I look out of the window and see men crossing the square, as I just happen to have done, I normally say that I see the men themselves ... Yet do I see any more than hats and coats which could conceal automatons?'[32] (As a young man, Alan Greenspan had a similar interest in logical positivism – as Nathaniel Branden wrote: 'In his 20s he's sitting there in my apartment and saying that he cannot say with certainty that he exists.'[33])

Finally, the quantum revolution in physics began with another oven-based experiment, when Max Planck analysed the light emitted from ovens, and found that it was emitted in discrete quanta. The eventual conclusion was that the universe is not neatly partitioned into atoms and the void, as Democritus had said. Instead, the quantum version of the 'void' was pregnant with potential forms of matter; and atoms weren't as solid as they seemed.

These ideas took a long time to rise, but are now working their way into the social sciences. Quantum social science takes the position that not only do we all exist, and are not automatons, but we are to a degree entangled, so that in some sense we contain one another. In other words, I exist in part because you do (thanks!), and vice versa. Nowhere is that more true than in the economy, where money only has value because it is backed by a network of people and institutions.

Good versus evil

While I have referred to neoclassical economics somewhat loosely throughout this book, the exact definition is naturally a topic of debate. One paper described it as being based on the 'Holy Trinity' of Rationality, Selfishness, and Equilibrium.[34] Another said its three basic axioms are methodological instrumentalism (so theories are viewed as instruments for some practical purpose), methodological individualism, and methodological equilibration.[35] In *Economyths*, I argued that we should instead define it in line with neoclassical art, as representing a 'revival of aesthetic principles from classical Greece and Rome, such as simplicity, balance and symmetry'. At the same time, neoclassical economics has proved adept at incorporating ideas from other areas, while being careful to neuter them first. As one survey notes: 'At the edges of neoclassical economics, new theoretical fields have emerged, such as behavioural economics and complexity economics, which soften and modify the traditional neoclassical assumptions such as the rationality of agents, perfect information or the isolation of actors.' However, 'these are often developed within the framework of standard neoclassical economics', with the result that 'the basic system of axioms, terms and categories, i.e. the paradigmatic foundation, remains untouched by these changes'.[36]

Quantum economics, in contrast, questions the most basic concept of neoclassical economics, which is that of the atomistic self. Without a well-defined individualistic 'I' it makes no sense to speak of purely individual rationality or selfishness or instrumentalism. And when entanglement and nonlinearities are brought into the picture, ideas such as symmetry and equilibrium similarly fall away. Quantum economics is therefore not an adjustment to mainstream economics that can be safely ignored just as weather forecasters or plumbers can ignore the quantum behaviour of water molecules. Instead it means that every conclusion from economics has to be rethought.

In particular, the entangled nature of the money system means that we can't use money to optimise our own utility – and Pareto optimality doesn't make mathematical sense – because there is nothing coherent to optimise. We don't get to have our own special well-defined, boxed-in existence which doesn't interact or overlap with anyone else's; part of it always leaks out. Questions about money therefore have an intrinsic ethical component. Like medieval philosophers who developed the idea of the 'just price', economics needs to ask not just what is 'efficient' according to its models, but also what is reasonable and serves the greater aims of society. A related issue is that the economics profession needs to examine its own strong entanglements with corporations and in particular the financial sector. There is a reason why economists keep saying that the global invisible hand is rational, efficient, and fair, and it's not just from reading too much Ayn Rand like Greenspan.

Rather than a collection of individuals who interact only through trade, society is made up of a fractal structure of overlapping holons, including individuals, companies, ethnic groups, regions, countries, international alliances, and so on. These in turn are embedded within, and rely on, a highly complex planetary ecosystem. So what might seem like a good idea when you model the world as a uniform and balanced quasi-thermodynamic machine, like an elaborately complicated steam engine, might not seem so brilliant when you model it as a delicate quantum system. Indeed, the whole argument around things like globalisation or the role of the financial sector changes rather quickly. It is possible to sympathise in turn with John Maynard Keynes when he wrote in 1933: 'I sympathise with those who would minimise, rather than with those who would maximise, economic entanglement among nations … let goods be homespun whenever it is reasonably and conveniently possible, and, above all, let finance be primarily national.'[37]

Another conclusion of the quantum approach is that, while numerical prices are a way of reducing a system to a number, it does not necessarily follow that the number is particularly meaningful. Prices are produced by transactions, and they may say as much about the exact circumstances of the transaction as they do about what is being bought. On the other hand, it is impossible to put an exact price on things like inequality, societal happiness, and environmental issues, because they aren't traded (except in an artificial way, as with carbon permits). Economists can add epicycles to account for these and other 'externalities' but the numbers are easily fixed by whoever is in power, which is one reason the environmental and social crises have continued unabated and largely unaddressed by the mainstream. We therefore need to counter the bias of favouring anything that can be reduced to price. Part of this will involve new metrics such as GPI; but more important will be putting boundaries on how economics is used to make decisions.

Too much mathematics

The idea that the economy is a kind of entangled quantum system also challenges the core assumption in neoclassical economics that the economy can be accurately simulated using mathematical equations. A common defence of mathematical models is that they force the user to make their assumptions clear. As Dani Rodrik wrote in 2015, 'We still have endless debates today about what Karl Marx, John Maynard Keynes, or Joseph Schumpeter really meant. … By contrast, no ink has ever been spilled over what Paul Samuelson, Joe Stiglitz, or Ken Arrow had in mind when they developed the theories that won them their Nobel.'[38] Noah Smith similarly wrote in 2016: 'People will forever argue about what Minsky meant, or John Maynard Keynes, or Friedrich Hayek' because they avoided equations (Keynes and Minsky initially trained in mathematics, which is an interesting clue for non-mathematicians).[39] Pieter Gautier notes that an important advantage of mathematical models is that 'You say "these are my assumptions". You make it very easy for people to attack them, because you're being explicit and clear. And I think that is the only way to make progress. Many of those heterodox schools try to use muddled language to say what they mean. But it is very hard to falsify that, because it is formulated so vaguely that you can go in any direction with it.'[40] According to Pontus Rendahl: 'The model is the cross-check on whether you actually know what you're talking about.'[41] Or as Adam Smith's friend, the philosopher David Hume put it in 1777, 'If we take in our hand any volume; of divinity or school metaphysics, for instance; let us ask, "Does it contain any abstract reasoning concerning quantity or number?" No. "Does it contain any experimental reasoning concerning matter of fact and existence?" No. Commit it then to the flames: for it can contain nothing but sophistry and illusion.'[42]

Speaking as a mathematician, I certainly appreciate the strengths of mathematical models, when properly applied. However, such models also introduce a subtle bias, because their insistence on the Apollonian qualities of clarity and definiteness put a restriction on the kind of assumptions that can be made, and the questions that can be asked. Any mathematical model of a system needs to introduce simplifications in order to make progress, and biases the user towards a mechanistic approach. This is seen clearly in the traditional models favoured by neoclassical economists, but switching to a quantum viewpoint won't in itself make this problem go away, as discussed in Chapter 8. And the fact that we still debate the work of thinkers such as Keynes or Minsky doesn't mean their ideas have lost relevance, quite the opposite: physicists and philosophers still debate the correct interpretation of quantum physics too. It is a little like literature; people don't debate what subtle message Rand was trying to convey through her character-objects, but they debate Shakespeare.

An emphasis on abstract mathematics also leads easily to arrogance and hubris, acts as an imposing barrier to change, and can hide problems: as Wassily Leontief put it in 1971, 'uncritical enthusiasm for mathematical formulation tends often to conceal the ephemeral substantive content of the argument behind the formidable front of algebraic signs'.[43] The oft-repeated claim that heterodox schools 'use muddled language', meanwhile, is very unfair: for one thing, many heterodox economists have been trained in mathematics or physics and do use mathematical models; but the fact that someone does not use mathematics does not imply that their thinking is muddled. Finally, one of the main problems with most economic models is that they contain too many unknown parameters, which makes them unfalsifiable, extremely difficult even for specialists to understand, and very easy to abuse. An example is quantitative finance, where complex risk models are often used not so much to accurately calculate risk, or provide clarity for clients or regulators, but the exact opposite: to justify trades and deter investigation.[44]

Mathematical models excel in areas such as engineering where the parameters can be precisely controlled. However, one of the lessons of complexity science is that what works in human-designed machines doesn't always carry over to other areas. The transition from what physicist Robert Laughlin calls the Age of Reductionism to the Age of Emergence 'brings to an end the myth of the absolute power of mathematics. This myth is still entrenched in our culture, unfortunately, a fact revealed routinely in the press and popular publications promoting the search for ultimate laws as the only scientific activity worth pursuing, notwithstanding massive and overwhelming experimental evidence that exactly the opposite is the case.'[45] He was speaking primarily about Theories of Everything in physics, but the same applies in economics, where the naiveté of mainstream apologists is sometimes equally concerning. As Aristotle wrote in *Nicomachean Ethics*, 'it is the mark of an educated man to look for precision in each class of things just so far as the nature of the subject admits' – and in economics it isn't that far.[46] Mathematics is to economics as number is to money: one side of the coin.

Economics needs to open up. 'Economics has been unusually insular and trust in economists is low', observes a 2017 Bank of England paper.[47] But as the Austrian economist Ludwig von Mises wrote in 1949, 'Economics must not be relegated to classrooms and statistical offices and must not be left to esoteric circles. It is the philosophy of human life and action and concerns everybody and everything.'[48] Instead of obsessing over slight changes to GDP figures, as is currently often the case, economists should communicate what these figures represent for society, and debate with others whether the gains are being borrowed from future generations through debt or environmental damage. Economics education, which currently focuses almost exclusively on narrow technical problem-solving, should also be broadened to encourage critical thinking and insights from different disciplines, as student groups such as Rethinking Economics argue. And if economists are going to learn abstract mathematical topics such as game theory and probability theory, then these should include their quantum versions. As Werner Heisenberg wrote, modern physics, through its openness to a variety of concepts, raises the hope that 'many cultural traditions may live together and may combine different human endeavors into a new kind of balance between thought and deed, between activity and meditation.'[49] Or as David Bohm later put it: 'What is called for is not an integration of thought, or a kind of imposed unity, for any such imposed point of view would itself be merely another fragment. Rather, all our different ways of thinking are to be considered as different ways of looking at the one reality, each with some domain in which it is clear and adequate.'[50] And while quantum physics is often described as our most successful scientific theory, the fact that there is no settled interpretation for it is also 'deeply, deeply humbling', as Gabriela Barreto Lemos and Kathryn Schaffer note; an attribute which could usefully rub off on economics.[51]

Finally, if quantum economics has a single central demand, it is that economists need to put money – and the question *how much* – at the centre of economics. This need was demonstrated by the 2007–08 crisis where money creation, complex derivatives, and loan defaults all played a key role, except in conventional models. To address broad problems of societal significance such as financial instability, inequality, the environmental crisis, and corruption in business, government, and economics itself, a first step is to follow the money. Mainstream economists have long ignored, downplayed, or actively misrepresented the role of money, and ridiculed anyone who brought up the subject as a 'monetary crank.'[52] But the reason for these attacks is of course that their field cannot handle the topic of money. Incorporating money fully into the picture will mean rethinking all the fundamental principles of mainstream economics, such as rationality, stability, efficiency, atomism, and so on. It will mean adopting alternative mathematical approaches, and opening up to ideas from other disciplines such as biology and ecology. And as Roman Chlupatý and I argued in *The Evolution of Money*, we also need to explore new ideas about money, including alternative currencies such as cybercurrencies, but also forms of organisation (such as the commons) that omit money altogether.

The land of the free

This book has focused on quantum economics, rather than on what the implications for the economy might look like. But the economy is shaped, like everything else, by the way that we see it; and this in turn shapes us. The traditional vision of economics as the science of scarcity has led to an economy that itself produces scarcity, by stripping the Earth and pitting people in competition against one another in order to maximise numbers. The image of rational economic man, combined with the ideal of perfectly competitive markets, has acted as a model that legitimises and encourages selfish behaviour. The theory of efficient markets has turned us into passive victims of the financial gods. The emphasis on numerical growth has brought us into conflict with environmental limits. Extensions to mainstream theory such as environmental economics have attempted to solve the planet's problems by monetising them, while ignoring the fact that it was money that got us into this spot in the first place.

Quantum economics reminds us of the creative nature of money, recognises the dynamic and sometimes fragile link between value and number at its heart, and points the way towards an economy which serves social and environmental values instead of dictating to them. Instead of rational economic man as an ideal, we have quantum economic person; instead of perfectly competitive markets, we have markets that combine competition with cooperation; instead of intrinsic value, we have a spectrum of eigenvalues; instead of random economic shocks that come out of nowhere, we have uncertainty combined with shared responsibility. And instead of treating money as a passive intermediary, it is seen as probably the most powerful technology we have ever invented. When physicists unlocked the quantum power of the atom, it took only a few short decades for that power to be realised in the form of atomic weapons. Quantum money has been on a longer and slower burn, but it too has enormous potential for either good or evil. Rather than letting it run free, we need to harness and control its energy – to make a reactor rather than a bomb.

One way to insert some control rods into this reaction process is to limit the role of money, by concentrating on what is free. A basic premise of mainstream economics, as captured in the title of a 1975 book by Milton Friedman, is that *There's No Such Thing as a Free Lunch*.[53] Efficient market theory, for example, implies a lack of free lunch because everything is correctly priced. Coupled with this is the idea that there is no genuine creativity, only the rearranging of objects or ideas.[54] As Ayn Rand put it: 'The power to rearrange the combinations of natural elements is the only creative power man possesses. It is an enormous and glorious power – and it is the only meaning of the concept "creative".'[55] Or as economist Paul Romer explained in a 1997 interview: 'Value creation and wealth creation in their most basic senses have to do with taking physical objects and rearranging them.'[56] Mark Twain: 'There is no such thing as a new idea. It is impossible. We simply take a lot of old ideas and put them into a sort of mental kaleidoscope. We give them a turn and they make new and curious combinations. We keep on turning and making new combinations indefinitely; but they are the same old pieces of colored glass that have been in use through all the ages.'[57]

While there is certainly some truth in these remarks (this book is in large part an exercise in rearrangement, lining quantum physics up against economics to see how it looks), the quantum universe doesn't play by such rigid rules – it may be bound by conservation laws, subject to the uncertainty principle, but it is also profoundly generous and creative, and not just in Rand's sense of moving the furniture around. The cosmologist Alan Guth famously remarked: 'It is said that there's no such thing as a free lunch. But the universe is the ultimate free lunch.'[58] Instead of scarcity there is – the universe. In the economy too there is a free lunch, in the sense that money objects are constantly appearing out of the void and disappearing back into it as credit is issued or cancelled. But the lunch buffet is becoming increasingly bountiful in other categories as well. We have open-source software and open-source design that can be used to send ideas around the world at zero marginal cost. As Stewart Brand said: 'Information wants to be free.'[59] We have solar power and wind power that is supplied for free, even if it costs money to harness. We have artificial intelligence and robots. We have increasingly efficient efforts at recycling materials and sharing resources. And then there is the tasty but unhealthy item known as fossil fuels, which we found prearranged in the earth for free.

Other things we often get for free, as feminist economists have long pointed out, include running the household, caring for children and the elderly, and other unpaid tasks that on a global basis are usually carried out by women. People volunteer their time for free. In fact, the harder you look, the more you see that a lot in the economy is actually free. For example, corporations get all kinds of tax breaks for free. Landowners see the value of their holdings increase for free. The financial sector was bailed out after the crisis, and has since been lunching for free off policies such as quantitative easing. So the question becomes, how to balance free stuff with free numbers; real freedom with virtual freedom. To do this we need to change the design parameters of the economy.

Some existing ideas which are consistent with a quantum approach, and which many people including myself have written about elsewhere, include:

- A universal basic income to give money to people, for free (being tested in a number of countries).
- Governments to print their own money for free instead of renting it from banks (it is their money, after all).
- Taxes to be shifted from human labour to things like resource use, as ecological economists have long proposed, and financial assets including land.*
- A financial transactions tax to limit the role of the financial sector.
- Corporations to be remodelled to reflect entanglements with society and the environment.
- Expansion and protection of the commons, both virtual (e.g. intellectual property) and real (e.g. shared resources).
- An ecosystem of alternative currencies to experiment with new ideas (this is well underway).
- Non-money-based metrics of things like environmental impacts and social well-being to be adopted as alternatives to GDP.
- An ethical code of conduct for economists and quants.[60]

All of these ideas have been around for a long time, but have struggled to make headway under an economic paradigm dominated

---

* On land taxes, see Lloyd George's Limehouse Speech from 1909, where he notes that land prices around the Port of London, much of which used to be 'sodden marsh', had increased by a factor of a thousand due to development. 'Who created that increment? Who made that golden swamp? Was it the landlord? Was it his energy? Was it his brains – a very bad look out for the place if it were – his forethought? It was purely the combined efforts of all the people engaged in the trade and commerce of the Port of London – trader, merchant, shipowner, dock labourer, workman, everybody except the landlord.'

by neoclassical thinking. So to change the system, a first step is to change the story we tell ourselves about the economy.

The path not taken

As discussed earlier, the traditional test for a scientific theory is its ability to make accurate predictions; however, in the social sciences, the inability to control the system means that the 'predictions' are usually based on what is known already, so are tied to the theory's assumptions. The fact that efficient market theory, which assumes the inability to predict, is held up as the ultimate predictive success in the social sciences is an almost comical demonstration of this. Neoclassical theory assumes and predicts that money is just an inert medium of exchange of little importance to the economy, which is why it has been largely excluded from models. The theory also assumes and predicts that the economy is self-stabilising, which is why the models are built around the concept of equilibrium. And it assumes and predicts outcomes that are fundamentally fair, apart from random effects, which is why models pay so little attention to distribution. The effect of these assumptions/predictions has been to produce an unstable and unfair economy where money plays an outsized role, and financial crises such as the one of 2007–08 always come as a surprise.

The quantum approach, in contrast, assumes and predicts that money has dualistic properties which have a powerful effect on both the human psyche, and the stability of markets. It assumes and predicts that people's behaviour depends on infinitely many factors and that their preferences are often constructed at the time of decision. And it assumes and predicts that the economy will be creative but also inherently unstable. It may not be able to accurately forecast the timing of financial crises, but it doesn't dangerously underestimate their likelihood. We have seen how different versions of quantum models have proved useful for explaining empirical results in cognitive psychology, can capture things like the effect of investor entanglement on markets, and are being used to make trading decisions. The quantum viewpoint has also explained how new forms of money such as cybercurrencies could be booted up out of the void and remain viable, even if they are unbacked by metal or the state and are not very useful for everyday exchange, despite assertions to the contrary from mainstream economists and central bankers alike.

When it comes to predictions, quantum economics is therefore at least starting from a better place. However, while it would be nice to assume that the chance of a new economic approach establishing itself will depend on something like a prediction test, this is far from being the case; neoclassical economics has deterred competitors and remained in place for a century and a half without much of a predictive track record to boast of. Max Planck said that 'Science progresses one funeral at a time', but as Steve Keen notes, even that isn't enough in economics: 'Without controlled experiments that can flatly contradict a superficially appealing theory, it continues to promulgate its beliefs, regardless of its manifest real-world failures.'[61] The fact that the theory survived the 2007–08 crisis is proof of that. Instead a theory is likely to be accepted if it provides a narrative which benefits a powerful constituency, either within the profession or outside it (e.g. the government, the financial sector).[62]

For quantum economics, its natural constituency is perhaps similar to that which fuelled the anti-nuclear protests: people who have lived through the recent financial crisis and its aftermath, and want to prevent it from happening again. However, while economics is clearly overdue for an update, 'revolution' doesn't seem to be quite the right word, because the revolution already happened a century ago. What we need is a *recognition* (from the Latin verb *recognoscere* for 'know again, recall to mind') that the financial system is a type of quantum system.

The main contribution of quantum economics is to provide something which heterodox approaches have previously lacked, which is a narrative to challenge the mechanistic story of orthodox economics. Since the dawn of science (and coin money) in ancient Greece over two thousand years ago, we have tried to understand and predict the world by breaking it down into individual parts, figuring out the mathematical laws which govern those parts, and computing the solution. Underpinning this approach is the idea that phenomena can be reduced to atomistic numbers, which can be abstracted from the system and handled using the tools of mathematics.

The economy seems a perfect application of this approach, based as it is on money. But as the Pythagoreans knew, not everything is consonant with the linear demands of number. Physicists were reminded of this when they were confronted with the confounding behaviour of quantum matter, but – uncomfortable with implications such as the role for consciousness – they chose to handle it by wrapping it in abstract mathematics, and repeating the mantra that it was too complex for non-specialists to ever understand.[63] A collateral effect was to retard development in other areas such as the social sciences. Economics therefore remained wedded to ideas from nineteenth-century physics, despite the fact that money is our own version of a quantum system.

The only respectable message that was allowed to escape from quantum theory, or in particular the nuclear programme, was that nature is probabilistic. A debased version of this appeared in finance as the random walk theory, and in macroeconomics as ergodic random shocks; but these only had the effect of giving the mechanistic approach an extra lease of life, by providing an excuse for forecast error. The resulting misunderstanding of risk was a major cause of financial catastrophes such as the 2007–08 crisis. The lesson: if you are going to import methods and ideas from quantum physics, make sure you do it properly. Meanwhile, heterodox approaches, which are more consonant with the idea that prices are the emergent result of complex dynamics rather than the result of an optimisation problem, were marginalised.

There were signs of change after the crisis, where heterodox ideas often proved more useful and relevant than mainstream techniques. However, while neoclassical economists have tinkered around the edges with ideas from areas such as behavioural economics, the field has proved impressively resistant to any genuine transformation. As Cambridge University's Ha-Joon Chang remarked in 2017, 'If you had a similar disaster like the 2008 financial crisis in any other subject, people who used to be the mainstream of the subject would all have been purged', which doesn't seem to have happened; and in general the effect of the reform movement on economics has been 'not a lot'.[64]

One reason for the lack of progress to date is that heterodox economics has long consisted of a scattered and diffuse set of different schools. Quantum economics promises to help break the log jam by providing – not a single unified mathematical model – but a common framework that can encompass or at least accommodate these diverse approaches, just as quantum cognition provides a framework for different behavioural models. Techniques from quantum mechanics, quantum thermodynamics, and other fields studying the dynamics of complex quantum systems, including the quantum agent-based approach contemplated in Chapter 7, enlarge the space of possible models, by allowing efficient ways to incorporate factors such as entanglement and context. But from a modelling perspective, the main conclusion from quantum economics is that the economy is an emergent, entangled, nonlinear system – which makes it rather like other systems that emerge from quantum principles, such as life, or the universe. That is why models developed for the study of living systems can transport easily to economics, but not the other way round. The quantum approach also makes it clear why models that rely on conventional techniques such as equilibrium and aggregation are incapable of handling things like financial instability or inequality, and should equally be kept away from issues such as the environment or social happiness. And it warns us that while models may give a sense of clarity and precision, those qualities may be not just misleading, but also open to misuse.

Perhaps the best way to view the current turning point is in terms of aesthetics, where the traditional machine aesthetic is slowly being overturned by one that is inspired by living organic systems, but also by a slow familiarisation with the consequences of quantum theory, such as indeterminacy and a role for consciousness, that collide directly with the machine approach but also suggest a different kind of beauty. The shift seems to have been anticipated by Keynes in 1926 when he wrote, in a biography of the neoclassical economist Francis Edgeworth, that 'The atomic hypothesis which has worked so splendidly in Physics breaks down in Psychics [i.e. mental phenomena]. We are faced at every turn with the problems of Organic Unity, of Discreteness, of Discontinuity – the whole is not equal to the sum of the parts, comparisons of quantity fail us, small changes produce large effects, the assumptions of a uniform and homogeneous continuum are not satisfied.'[65] By the 'atomic hypothesis' he was presumably referring to the classical version of physics, rather than the quantum one which was still being hammered out. (When Keynes lectured in Berlin the same year, one of the listeners he met was Einstein, and it seems the title for his *General Theory of Employment, Interest and Money* was influenced by Einstein's general theory of relativity.[66]) Those insights were lost along the way, as neoclassical economists such as Paul Samuelson scrubbed the subject of any such vague uncertainties; but economics could so easily have taken a different path.*

As Marshall McLuhan wrote in 1992: 'I do not think that philosophers in general have yet come to terms with this declaration from quantum physics: the days of the Universe as Mechanism are over.'[67] Nowhere has that been more true than in economics. The time has come for it to let go of established beliefs, put down its mechanistic tools, channel an echo version of the intellectual excitement of the early twentieth century, and take its own belated leap into the indeterminate, quantum future.

---

* 'Samuelson's view of Keynesianism resulted in aborting Keynes's revolutionary analysis from altering the foundation of mainstream macroeconomics. Consequently what passes as conventional macroeconomic wisdom of mainstream economists at the beginning of the 21st century is nothing more than a high-tech and more mathematical version of 19th century classical theory.' Davidson, P. (2015), 'What was the primary factor encouraging mainstream economists to marginalize post Keynesian theory?', *Journal of Post Keynesian Economics*, 37 (3), pp. 369–83.

Appendix

Calculating an option

In the coin-tossing game described in Chapter 6, you toss a coin three times in a row and each time you get heads, your friend pays you a dollar, and each time you get tails, you pay him a dollar. What is the fair price of an option to only win at the game?

The horizontal axis below shows the step in the game, from the starting point which is 0, to the final toss which is 3, while the vertical axis shows the game's current state, in terms of wins minus losses. So after one throw of the dice (i.e. at step 1) the score can move up to 1 if you roll heads, or down to –1 if you roll tails. In the next step the options are 2 (two heads), 0 (a head and a tail), or –2 (two tails). After the third toss the options are 3 (three heads), 1 (two heads and a tail), –1 (one head and two tails), and –3 (three tails).

The number in each position represents the expected payoff of the option when the game is in that state. We can calculate the fair price for the option by working our way backwards in time. Starting at the right of the graph, i.e. after all three tosses, the payoff is $3 if you got three heads in a row, $1 if you got two heads and one tail, or nothing otherwise, because the option protects against losses. Next, we can solve for how much the option would be worth for each state of the game at step 2. If the current score is 2, then you would pay $2 for the option, because that equals the expected payout at step 3, which is the average of $3 and $1. Continuing in this manner, and taking the average at each step, we find that the fair price of the option at the start of the game is $0.75.

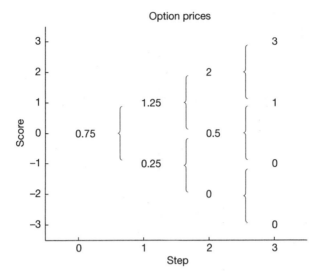

Figure 6. Diagram of option prices for the coin-tossing game, for different times and scores. Horizontal axis shows the step, which has values from 0 to 3. Vertical axis is the score in dollars, which starts at 0, can be –1 or 1 at step 1, and finishes in the range –3 to 3. The numbers at each point are the option prices for each step and score. The option price at time 3 is equal to the payout, so is the same as the score if that is positive, and zero otherwise. The option prices at step 2 are found by averaging (indicated by brackets) the adjacent values at time 3, and so on.

The order effect

For the order effect problem discussed in Chapter 7, the quantum model is quite simple and can be visualised without the use of equations as shown in the figures below. The grey line in diagram A shows the person's state when answering the Clinton question. It therefore represents a snapshot of a probabilistic wave function, which is in a superposition of two states, trust and mistrust. If the person was sure of her trust in Clinton, then this line would align closely with the horizontal YES axis; if she was very distrustful, it

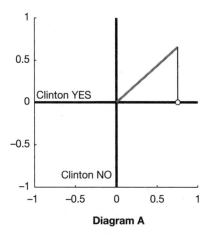

Diagram A

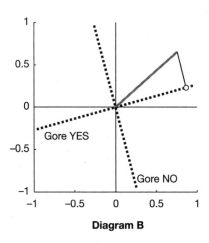

Diagram B

Figure 7. Diagram A shows a quantum model for response to the question on Clinton's trustworthiness, with possible answers yes (horizontal axis) or no (vertical axis). The initial state of the person is shown by the grey line. The response is indeterminate, and the decision to select YES or NO is indicated by projecting from the state onto the corresponding axis. The probability is found by taking the square of the projection length, which here gives a result of 0.57, or 57 per cent. Diagram B shows the same configuration for Gore, but now the dashed axes lines have been rotated to favour a positive response, with a probability of 81 per cent.

would align with the vertical NO axis. This person – like an electron of indeterminate spin – is rather unsure so she holds the two
options in superposition with roughly equal strength, and the line
is nearly diagonal. She still has to supply a definite yes/no answer
at the time of measurement, though (think of a mental version of
a quantum coin toss). A decision to answer yes is equivalent to
a collapse of the uncertain superposed state, and is represented
mathematically by projecting onto the YES axis, to the point shown
by the white circle. The probability of this choice, according to the
quantum model, is then the square of the distance of that point
from the centre, which gives 57 per cent. A decision to answer no
(not shown) is represented by projecting left onto the NO axis,
which has a probability of 43 per cent.

Diagram B shows the same person's mental state when answering the Gore question. The axes have rotated around by about
10 degrees, because this person trusts Gore a little more than
Clinton. The probability of selecting yes, which is found again by
projecting onto the YES axis, has now improved to 81 per cent,
while the probability of selecting no is 19 per cent. Note that if the
person has a definite response to Clinton – say, for example, her
state is aligned with the horizontal YES axis – then the response to
the Gore question is necessarily uncertain (since the axes do not
line up), and vice versa: the uncertainty principle in action.

Now, suppose that the person receives two questions in a row,
without any other question or information being supplied between
them. If the first question is about Clinton, and she answers yes,
that projects the person's mental state as before onto the white
circle in diagram C. But this is now her state when she gets the
next question which is about Gore (one can say that the response
to the second question is entangled with the response to the first).
So to find the probability of answering yes again, we project onto
the point marked with a black circle on the YES axis for Gore. The

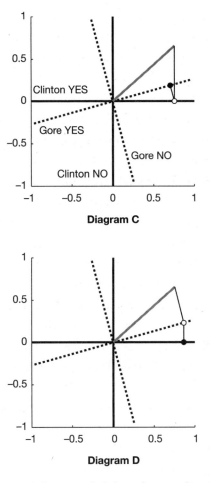

Figure 8. Diagram C shows probability of responding YES to Clinton (projection to white circle) followed by YES to Gore (black circle) which is 53 per cent. Diagram D shows probability of reverse order, which is 75 per cent.

probability, given again by the distance from the centre, is 53 per cent. On the other hand, if the Gore question comes first, then the sequence is that shown in diagram D, and we get a probability of 75 per cent – an increase of 22 per cent.

Finally, the same calculations can be performed for the case where people vote no for each. The model for this person gives a probability of 40 per cent for voting no for Clinton, followed by no for Gore; but only 18 per cent for voting no for Gore, and then no for Clinton – a decrease of 22 per cent. This balances the change in number of people voting yes–yes, and it can be shown that this always holds for any situation. This simple model therefore explains the observed symmetry.

For more information on quantum economics, including a technical description of some of the mathematics used, please see davidorrell.com/quantumresources.html

Notes

Introduction

1. Robbins, L. (1932), *An Essay on the Nature and Significance of Economic Science* (London: Macmillan). This has been described as 'perhaps the most commonly accepted current definition of the subject' in Backhouse, R.E., and Medema, S. (2009), 'Retrospectives: On the Definition of Economics', *Journal of Economic Perspectives*, 23 (1), p. 225; and the 'dominant definition' in Keen, S. (2017), 'Ricardo's Vice and the Virtues of Industrial Diversity', *American Affairs*, 1 (3), pp. 85–98.
2. Mankiw, N.G. (2016), *Principles of Economics* (8th edn) (Boston, MA: Cengage Learning), p. 4.
3. Martin, F. (2013), *Money: The Unauthorised Biography* (London: Random House), p. 224.
4. Samuelson, P.A., and Nordhaus, W.D. (2001), *Economics* (17th edn) (Boston, MA: McGraw-Hill), p. 511.
5. Bouchaud, J.-P. (2008), 'Economics needs a scientific revolution', *Nature*, 455, p. 1181.
6. Chang, H.-J., and Aldred, J. (11 May 2014), 'After the crash, we need a revolution in the way we teach economics', *The Observer*.
7. Economic and Social Research Council (20 April 2017), *Innovative new network will 'revolutionise' how we study the economy*. Retrieved from http://www.esrc.ac.uk/news-events-and-publications/news/news-items/innovative-new-network-will-revolutionise-how-we-study-the-economy/
8. Orrell, D. (2010), *Economyths: Ten Ways That Economics Gets It Wrong* (London: Icon Books).
9. Bohm, D. (1974), in J. Lewis, *Beyond Chance and Necessity* (London: Garnstone Press), pp. 128–35.
10. See for example: Busemeyer, J., and Bruza, P. (2012), *Quantum Models of Cognition and Decision* (Cambridge: Cambridge University Press); Wendt, A. (2015), *Quantum Mind and Social Science: Unifying Physical and Social Ontology* (Cambridge: Cambridge University Press).
11. Quoted in Buchanan, M. (5 September 2011), 'Quantum minds: Why we think like quarks', *New Scientist*.

12. Barad, K. (2007), *Meeting the Universe Halfway: Quantum Physics and the Entanglement of Matter and Meaning* (Durham, NC: Duke University Press).

13. Orrell, D., and Chlupatý, R. (2016), *The Evolution of Money* (New York: Columbia University Press). See also Orrell, D. (2016), 'A quantum theory of money and value', *Economic Thought*, 5 (2), pp. 19–36; Orrell, D. (2017), 'A Quantum Theory of Money and Value, Part 2: The Uncertainty Principle', *Economic Thought*, 6 (2), pp. 14–26; and Orrell, D. (2015), *Marshall McLuhan Lecture 2015: Money is the Message* (Transmediale), retrieved from https://www.youtube.com/playlist?list=PL9olnMFdRIwshkq3nfaF2nBzbFAQRvLmy

14. Letter from Einstein to D. Lipkin, 5 July 1952, Einstein Archives. In: Fine, A. (1996), *The Shaky Game* (Chicago: University of Chicago Press).

15. Carroll, S. (2016), *The Big Picture: On the Origins of Life, Meaning, and the Universe Itself* (New York: Dutton).

16. Gell-Mann, M. (1994), *The Quark and the Jaguar: Adventures in the Simple and the Complex* (New York: Freeman).

17. Samuelson, P.A. (11 December 1970), 'Maximum Principles in Analytical Economics', *Prize Lecture, Lecture to the memory of Alfred Nobel*, p. 69.

18. Samuelson, P.A. (1979), 'A quantum theory model of economics: is the co-ordinating entrepreneur just worth his profit?', in *The collected scientific papers of Paul A. Samuelson* (Vol. 4, pp. 104–10) (Cambridge, MA: MIT Press). Mirowski, P. (1989), *More Heat Than Light: Economics as Social Physics, Physics as Nature's Economics* (Cambridge: Cambridge University Press), p. 383.

19. Mirowski, P. (1989), *More Heat Than Light: Economics as Social Physics, Physics as Nature's Economics* (Cambridge: Cambridge University Press), p. 221.

20. Penrose, R. (1989), *The Emperor's New Mind: Concerning Computers, Minds and The Laws of Physics* (Oxford: Oxford University Press).

21. Lambert, N., Chen, Y.-N., Cheng, Y.-C., Li, C.-M., Chen, G.-Y., and Nori, F. (2013), 'Quantum biology', *Nature Physics*, 9 (1), pp. 10–18.

22. See e.g. Zohar, D., and Marshall, I. (1993), *The Quantum Society* (London: Flamingo), p. 16.

23. For a discussion, see for example: Atmanspacher, H., Römer, H., and Walach, H. (2002), 'Weak quantum theory: Complementarity and entanglement in physics and beyond', *Foundations of Physics*, 32 (3), pp. 379–406.

24. Schrödinger, E. (1935), 'Discussion of probability relations between separated systems', *Mathematical Proceedings of the Cambridge Philosophical Society*, 31 (4), pp. 555–63. For a more recent discussion of financial entanglement, see: China Center for International Economic Exchanges (11 November 2016), 'Economic quantum entanglement may subvert the traditional concept of international competition'. Retrieved from: http://english.cciee.org.cn/archiver/ccieeen/UpFile/Files/Default/20161202084100609671.pdf

25. Institute of International Finance (June 2017), *Global Debt Monitor*. Retrieved from https://www.iif.com/publication/global-debt-monitor/global-debt-monitor-june-2017

26. The expression 'bounded rationality' was coined by Herbert A. Simon, who wrote that 'The first consequence of the principle of bounded rationality is that the intended rationality of an actor requires him to construct a simplified model of the real situation in order to deal with it.' Simon, H.A. (1957), *Models of Man: Social and Rational* (New York: John Wiley), p. 198.

27. Oxfam (16 January 2017), *Just 8 men own same wealth as half the world*. Retrieved from http://oxf.am/ZLE4.

Chapter 1

1. Lightman, A.P. (2005), *The Discoveries: Great Breakthroughs in 20th-Century Science, Including the Original Papers* (Toronto: Alfred A. Knopf Canada), p. 8.

2. Michelson, A.A. (1896), Dedication of Ryerson Physical Laboratory. In *Annual Register* (Chicago: University of Chicago Press).

3. Unpublished letter from Max Planck to R.W. Wood, Berlin (1931).

4. Lucas, R. (2003), 'Macroeconomic Priorities', *American Economic Review*, 93 (1), pp. 1–14.

5. Einstein, A. (1905), 'Über einen die Erzeugung und Verwandlung des Lichtes betreffenden heuristischen Gesichtspunkt (On a heuristic viewpoint concerning the production and transformation of light)', *Annalen Der Physik*, 17 (6), pp. 132–48.

6. Bohr, N. (1913), 'On the Constitution of Atoms and Molecules', *I. Phil. Mag.*, 26, p. 1.

7. Pauli, W. (1925), 'Über den Zusammenhang des Abschlusses der Elektronengruppen im Atom mit der Komplexstruktur der Spektren (On the Connection between the Completion of Electron Groups in an Atom with the Complex Structure of Spectra)', *Z. Phys.*, 31, p. 765.

8. Zohar, D. (1990), *The Quantum Self* (London: Flamingo), p. 206.

9. Young, T. (1807), 'On the Nature of Light and Colours'. In *A Course of Lectures on Natural Philosophy and the Mechanical Arts* (Vol. 1, p. 359) (London: Joseph Johnson).

10. Taylor, G.I. (1909), 'Interference Fringes with Feeble Light', *Proc. Cam. Phil. Soc.*, 15, p. 114.

11. Einstein, A. (20 April 1924), 'Das Komptonsche Experiment (The Compton Experiment)', *Berliner Tageblatt*.

12. De Broglie, L. (1963), *Recherches sur la théorie des quanta* (Paris: Masson), p. 4.

13. Moore, W.J. (1989), *Schrödinger, life and thought* (Cambridge: Cambridge University Press), p. 202.

14. Born, M. (1926), 'Zur Quantenmechanik der Stoßvorgänge (Quantum Mechanics of Collision)', *Z. Phys.*, 37, p. 863.

15. Dirac, P. (1942), Bakerian Lecture, 'The Physical Interpretation of Quantum Mechanics', *Proceedings of the Royal Society A: Mathematical, Physical and Engineering Sciences*, 180 (980), pp. 1–39.

16. Heisenberg, W. (1925), 'Über quantentheoretische Umdeutung kinematischer und mechanischer Beziehungen (Quantum-Theoretical Re-Interpretation of Kinematic and Mechanical Relations)', *Z. Phys.*, 33, p. 879.

17. Heisenberg, W. (1927), 'Über den anschaulichen Inhalt der quantentheoretischen Kinematik und Mechanik (The Actual Content of Quantum Theoretical Kinematics and Mechanics)', *Z. Phys.*, 43, p. 172.

18. Ananthaswamy, A. (22 June 2011), 'Quantum magic trick shows reality is what you make it', *New Scientist*.

19. Aristotle (2009), *Metaphysics* (W.D. Ross, trans.) (Sioux Falls, SD: NuVision Publications), p. 51.

20. Buckley, P., and Peat, F.D. (1996), 'Werner Heisenberg 1901–1976', in *Glimpsing Reality: Ideas in Physics and the Link to Biology* (Toronto: University of Toronto Press).

21. Kumar, M. (2008), *Quantum: Einstein, Bohr and the Great Debate About the Nature of Reality* (London: Icon Books), p. 220.

22. Kumar, M. (2008), *Quantum: Einstein, Bohr and the Great Debate About the Nature of Reality* (London: Icon Books), p. 125.

23. Trimmer, J.D. (1980), 'The Present Situation in Quantum Mechanics: A Translation of Schrödinger's "Cat Paradox" Paper', *Proceedings of the American Philosophical Society*, 124 (5), pp. 323–38.

24. Von Neumann, J. (1955), *The Mathematical Foundations of Quantum Mechanics* (Princeton, NJ: Princeton University Press).

25. Einstein, A., Podolsky, B., and Rosen, N. (1935), 'Can quantum-mechanical description of physical reality be considered complete?', *Phys. Rev.*, 47, p. 777.

26. Trimmer, J.D. (1980), 'The Present Situation in Quantum Mechanics: A Translation of Schrödinger's "Cat Paradox" Paper', *Proceedings of the American Philosophical Society*, 124 (5), pp. 323–38.

27. Bell, J.S. (1964), 'On the Einstein-Podolsky-Rosen paradox', *Physics*, 1, pp. 195–200.

28. Popkin, G. (2017), 'Spooky action achieved at record distance', *Science*, 356 (6343), pp. 1110–11.

29. Conover, E. (27 March 2017), 'Millions of atoms entangled in record-breaking quantum tests'. Retrieved from *Science News*: https://www.sciencenews.org/article/millions-atoms-entangled-record-breaking-quantum-tests

30. Romero-Isart, O., Juan, M., Quidant, R., and Cirac, J. (2010), 'Toward quantum superposition of living organisms', *New Journal of Physics*, 12 (3), p. 033015.

31. Mermin, N.D. (April 1985), 'Is the moon there when nobody looks? Reality and the quantum theory', *Physics Today*, pp. 38–47.

32. Hillmer, R., and Kwiat, P. (2007), 'A Do-It-Yourself Quantum Eraser', *Scientific American*, 296 (5), pp. 90–95.

33. Feynman, R. (1964), *The Feynman Lectures on Physics* (Vol. 3) (Reading, MA: Addison Wesley).

34. Barad, K. (2007), *Meeting the Universe Halfway: Quantum Physics and the Entanglement of Matter and Meaning* (Durham, NC: Duke University Press), p. 254.

35. Farmelo, G. (2009), *The Strangest Man: The Hidden Life of Paul Dirac, Quantum Genius* (London: Faber), p. 178; Dirac, P. (1930), *The Principles of 'Quantum' Mechanics* (Oxford: Clarendon Press).

36. Kumar, M. (2008), *Quantum: Einstein, Bohr and the Great Debate About the Nature of Reality* (London: Icon Books), p. 356.

37. For a discussion of entanglement in the social sciences, see: Aerts, D., Arguëlles, J.A., Beltran, L., Geriente, S., Bianchi, M.S., Sozzo, S., and Veloz, T. (2017), 'Spin and Wind Directions II: A Bell State Quantum Model', *Foundations of Science*, pp. 1–29. For its role in quantum economics, see 'Introduction to the mathematics of quantum economics', available at davidorrell.com/quantumeconomics math.pdf

38. Von Baeyer, H.C. (2016), *QBism: The Future of Quantum Physics* (Cambridge, MA: Harvard University Press).

39. Barad, K. (2007), *Meeting the Universe Halfway: Quantum Physics and the Entanglement of Matter and Meaning* (Durham, NC: Duke University Press), p. 24.
40. Anderson, P.W. (1972), 'More is different', *Science*, 177 (4047), pp. 393–6.
41. Laughlin, R.B. (2005). *A Different Universe: Reinventing physics from the bottom down*. New York: Basic Books, p. 108.
42. Folger, T. (2001), 'Quantum Shmantum', *Discover*, 22 (9).
43. Aerts, D. (2009), 'Quantum Particles as Conceptual Entities: A Possible Explanatory Framework for Quantum Theory', *Foundations of Science*, 14 (4), pp. 361–411.
44. Rupp, R. (9 February 2015), 'Is a Tomato a Fruit? It Depends on How You Slice It', *National Geographic*.
45. Aerts, D. (2010), 'Interpreting Quantum Particles as Conceptual Entities', *International Journal of Theoretical Physics*, 49 (12), pp. 2950–70.

Chapter 2

1. Simmel, G. (2004), *The Philosophy of Money* (T. Bottomore and D. Frisby, trans.) (London: Routledge).
2. According to Gallup, 'Half of Americans have substantial financial anxiety'. Saad, L. (20 April 2015), *Americans' Money Worries Unchanged from 2014*. Retrieved from Gallup: www.gallup.com/poll/182768/americans-money-worries-unchanged-2014.aspx
3. See for example: Martin, F. (2013), *Money: The Unauthorised Biography* (London: Random House), p. 52.
4. British Museum (9 November 2017), *The first writing: counting beer for the workers*. Retrieved from: https://www.google.com/culturalinstitute/beta/asset/early-writing-tablet-recording-the-allocation-of-beer/fgF9ioy89DC2Uw
5. Tymoigne, É., and Wray, L.R. (2007), 'Money: An Alternative Story', in P. Arestis, and M.C. Sawyer (eds.), *A Handbook of Alternative Monetary Economics* (Northampton, MA: Edward Elgar), pp. 1–16.
6. Jevons, W.S. (1875), *Money and the Mechanism of Exchange* (New York: D. Appleton and Co.), p. 5.
7. Davies, G. (2002), *A History of Money: From Ancient Times to the Present Day* (3rd edn) (Cardiff: University of Wales Press), p. 52.
8. Aristotle (2000), *Politics* (Mineola, NY: Dover Publications), p. 42.
9. For example: 'All sorts of commodities have been used as money at one time or another, but gold and silver proved to have great advantages … Before the invention of coins, it was necessary to carry the metals in bulk … The invention of coinage eliminated the need to

weigh the metal at each transaction, but it created an important role for an authority, usually a king or queen, who made the coins and affixed his or her seal, guaranteeing the amount of precious metal that the coin contained. This was clearly a great convenience ...' Ragan, C.T., and Lipsey, R.G. (2011), *Economics* (13th edn) (Toronto: Pearson Education Canada), pp. 672-3.

10. Innes, A.M. (May 1913), 'What is Money?', *The Banking Law Journal*, pp. 377-408.

11. Ragan, C.T., and Lipsey, R.G. (2011), *Economics* (13th edn) (Toronto: Pearson Education Canada), pp. 672-3.

12. Quoted in: Graeber, D. (2011), *Debt: The First 5000 Years* (Brooklyn, NY: Melville House), p. 29.

13. Ragan, C.T., and Lipsey, R.G. (2011), *Economics* (13th edn) (Toronto: Pearson Education Canada), pp. 672-3.

14. Menger, K. (1892), 'On the origins of money', *Economic Journal*, 2 (3), pp. 239-55.

15. Schaps, D. (2006). The Invention of Coinage in Lydia, in India, and in China. *XIV International Economic History Congress*. Helsinki.

16. Crawford, M.H. (1970), 'Money and exchange in the Roman world', *Journal of Roman Studies*, 60, pp. 40-48.

17. Guthrie, W. (1962), *A History of Greek Philosophy: The earlier Presocratics and the Pythagoreans* (Vol. 1) (Cambridge: Cambridge University Press), p. 207.

18. Guthrie, W. (1962), *A History of Greek Philosophy: The earlier Presocratics and the Pythagoreans* (Vol. 1) (Cambridge: Cambridge University Press), p. 221.

19. As feminist philosophers have noticed, there is a distinct ordering to this list. Gatens, M. (1991), *Feminism and Philosophy: Perspectives on Difference and Equality* (Bloomington, IN: Indiana University Press); Korsmeyer, C. (2017), *Feminist Aesthetics* (E.N. Zalta, ed.). Retrieved from T*he Stanford Encyclopedia of Philosophy* (Spring 2017 edition): https://plato.stanford.edu/archives/spr2017/entries/feminism-aesthetics/

20. Orrell, D. (2012), *Truth or Beauty: Science and the Quest for Order* (New Haven, CT: Yale University Press).

21. The term was introduced by philosopher and psychologist William James in the late nineteenth century. Holton, G. (1970), 'The roots of complementarity', *Daedalus*, 99, pp. 1015-55.

22. In this scheme, 'hard' currencies based on materials such as gold or silver are therefore feminine, which might seem strange until you consider that these soft metals have traditionally been used

for ornamentation of the female body. On this topic of gender, the feminist theologian and psychologist Catherine Keller notes a correspondence between the theory of the solid Newtonian atom and the male sense of self: 'It is separate, impenetrable, and only extrinsically and accidentally related to the others it bumps into in its void.' Roszak, T. (1999), *The Gendered Atom: Reflections on the Sexual Psychology of Science* (Berkeley, CA: Conari Press), p. 88. In contrast, according to the author Danah Zohar whose 1990 book *The Quantum Self* was inspired in part by her experience of pregnancy and early motherhood, 'There is something deeply feminine about seeing the self as part of a quantum process … Selecting things out, seeing them as separate, naming them and structuring them logically are male attributes. They follow, if you like, from the "particle aspect" of our intelligence. Seeing the connections between things is more feminine. It mirrors the "wave aspect" of the psyche.' (Of course people of either gender share these attributes, just as a healthy brain uses both hemispheres.) Zohar, D. (1990), *The Quantum Self* (London: Flamingo), pp. 133–4. If Zohar is correct, then the well-documented male bias in economics – according to the American Economics Association, less than 15 per cent of full professors in US economics departments are women – may present a significant obstacle to the acceptance of a quantum viewpoint. Committee on the Status of Women in the Economics Profession (21 March 2017), *CSWEP: Survey & Annual Report*. Retrieved from American Economic Association: https://www.aeaweb.org/about-aea/committees/cswep/survey

23. Wendt, A. (2015), *Quantum Mind and Social Science: Unifying Physical and Social Ontology* (Cambridge: Cambridge University Press), p. 19. Mershon Center (24 February 2015), *Wendt Again Named Top Scholar In International Relations*. Retrieved from: https://mershoncenter.osu.edu/index.php/news/mershon-news/wendt-again-named-top-scholar-in-international-relations. The philosopher Mary Midgley wrote that the word 'subjective' has become 'a simple term of abuse directed at any mention of thoughts or feelings, and the word "objective" a potent compliment for any approach which ignores them.' Midgley, M. (1985), *Evolution as a Religion: Strange hopes and stranger fears* (London: Methuen), p. 25. According to Iain McGilchrist, impersonal facts of the sort favoured by the left hemisphere are 'the only kind of knowledge permitted by science'. McGilchrist, I. (2009), *The Master and his Emissary* (London: Yale University Press), p. 95.

24. Graeber, D. (2011), *Debt: The First 5000 Years* (Brooklyn, NY): Melville House.

Chapter 3

1. 'If you consider the whole army of legionnaires and auxiliaries at the time of Augustus, 250,000 men, the total annual requirement of the army for silver denarii (or equivalent copper coins) was at least 75,000,000 per year!' Pense, A. (1992), 'The Decline and Fall of the Roman Denarius', *Materials Characterization*, 29 (2), pp. 213-22.

2. Eagleton, C., and Williams, J. (2007), *Money: A History* (Firefly Books), p. 51.

3. Weatherford, J. (1997), *The History of Money* (New York: Three Rivers Press), p. 52. For comparison, the modern Italian army employs about 180,000.

4. According to Matthew 20:2. Wages for a Roman legionary soldier changed from 225 denarii under Caesar (c. 46 BC) to 1,800 denarii under Maximinus (AD 235-8). Eagleton, C., and Williams, J. (2007), *Money: A History* (Firefly Books), p. 54.

5. Harris, W. (2008), *The Monetary Systems of the Greeks and Romans* (Oxford: Oxford University Press), p. 205.

6. Spiegel, H.W. (1991), *The Growth of Economic Thought* (3rd edn) (Durham, NC: Duke University Press), pp. 88-9.

7. The technique was codified by the mathematician Luca Pacioli in his 1494 book *Summa de arithmetica*, though by that time it had already been in use for over a century. Davies, G. (2002), *A History of Money: From Ancient Times to the Present Day* (3rd edn), (Cardiff: University of Wales Press), p. 235.

8. Bloch, M. (1965), *Feudal Society* (L. Manyon, trans.) (Chicago: University of Chicago Press).

9. Le Goff, J. (2012), *Money and the Middle Ages* (Oxford: Polity Press), p. 115.

10. From the 12th-century treatise *The Dialogue Concerning the Exchequer*.

11. Graeber, D. (2011), *Debt: The First 5000 Years* (Brooklyn, NY: Melville House), p. 268.

12. Polo, M., and Yule, H. (1903), *The book of Ser Marco Polo, the Venetian, concerning the kingdoms and marvels of the East* (London: Murray).

13. When Venetian authorities discovered in 1321 that merchants were practising fractional reserve banking, they passed legislation saying

that banks had to be able to meet all requests for withdrawal within three days. Martin, F. (2013), *Money: The Unauthorised Biography* (London: Random House), p. 104. See also: Kindleberger, 1984, p. 51.

14. Fairs were highly organised, and followed fixed schedules over the course of a few weeks, with days for settlement at the end. Kindleberger, C.P. (1984), *A Financial History of Western Europe* (London: Allen & Unwin), p. 36.

15. Weatherford, J. (1997), *The History of Money* (New York: Three Rivers Press), p. 99.

16. Forero, J. (25 September 2012), *Bolivia's Cerro Rico: The Mountain That Eats Men*. Retrieved 22 January 2014, from NPR.org: http://www.npr.org/2012/09/25/161752820/bolivias-cerro-rico-the-mountain-that-eats-men

17. Cocker, M. (1998), *Rivers of Blood, Rivers of Gold* (New York: Grove Press), p. 88.

18. Graeber, D. (2011), *Debt: The First 5000 Years* (Brooklyn, NY: Melville House), p. 339.

19. Milton Friedman for example wrote that 'nothing is so unimportant as the quantity of money expressed in terms of the nominal monetary unit … let the number of dollars in existence be multiplied by 100; that, too, will have no other essential effect, provided that all other nominal magnitudes (prices of goods and services, and quantities of other assets and liabilities that are expressed in nominal terms) are also multiplied by 100.' Friedman, M. (1969), 'The Optimum Quantity of Money', in M. Friedman (ed.), *The Optimum Quantity of Money and Other Essays* (Chicago: Macmillan), pp. 1–50, p. 1.

20. Häring, N. (2013), 'The veil of deception over money', *Real World Economics Review*, 63, pp. 2–18.

21. Morgan, J. P. (1912), Testimony before the Bank and Currency Committee of the House of Representatives. Retrieved 20 November 2017 from: https://memory.loc.gov/service/gdc/scd0001/2006/200 60517001te/20060517001te.pdf

22. Innes, A.M. (May 1913), 'What is Money?', *The Banking Law Journal*, pp. 377–408.

23. Pozadzki, A. (11 November 2017), 'Bitcoin investors party like it's 1999', *Globe and Mail*.

24. McKenna, B. (14 December 2017), 'Poloz says Canada's economy in "sweet spot"; warns of cryptocurrency's allure', *Globe and Mail*.

25. Carstens, A. (6 February 2018), 'Money in the digital age: what role for central banks?' Retrieved from Bank for International Settlements: https://www.bis.org/speeches/sp180206.pdf

26. Bessa, O. (8 November 2015), 'Nobel Prize Winner Eugene Fama on Bitcoin'. Retrieved from CoinTelegraph: http://cointelegraph.com/news/115593/nobel-prize-winner-eugene-fama-on-bitcoin

27. Davies, H. (27 February 2018), 'Hawk or dove? Bitcoin is forcing central banks to take sides', *The Guardian*.

28. Santos, M. (27 August 2015), 'David Orrell: "Cryptocurrency is the future, but the future might be a long time coming"'. Retrieved from 99bitcoins: https://99bitcoins.com/david-orrell-cryptocurrency-is-the-future-but-the-future-might-be-a-long-time-coming/

29. Chun, R. (September 2017), 'Big in Venezuela: Bitcoin Mining', *The Atlantic*.

30. Or approximately 4 million bolivars.

31. Alabi, K. (2017), 'Digital blockchain networks appear to be following Metcalfe's Law', *Electronic Commerce Research and Applications*, 24, pp. 23–9.

32. Satoshi has not been heard from since 2011, and the digital forensics firm Chainalysis treats his holdings – possibly a million bitcoins in all – as lost. Roberts, J.J., and Rapp, N. (25 November 2017), 'Exclusive: Nearly 4 Million Bitcoins Lost Forever, New Study Says'. Retrieved from *Fortune*: http://fortune.com/2017/11/25/lost-bitcoins/

Chapter 4

1. Mill, J.S. (1848), *Principles of Political Economy* (London: Parker).

2. Samuelson, P.A. (1973), *Economics* (9th edn) (New York: McGraw-Hill), p. 55.

3. Smith, A. (1776), *An Inquiry into the Nature and Causes of the Wealth of Nations* (London: W. Strahan and T. Cadell). Retrieved from: http://socserv.mcmaster.ca/econ/ugcm/3ll3/smith/wealth/wealbk01

4. Say, J.-B. (11 September 2017), *A Treatise on Political Economy* (C.R. Prinsep, trans. and Clement C. Biddle, ed.), 1855. Retrieved from Library of Economics and Liberty: http://www.econlib.org/library/Say/sayT15.html

5. Samuelson, P.A. (1973), *Economics* (9th edn) (New York: McGraw-Hill).

6. Marx, K. (1887), *Capital: A Critique of Political Economy* (Vol. 1) (F. Engels, ed., S. Moore, and E.B. Aveling, trans.) (Moscow: Progress Publishers).

7. Cohan, W.D. (2011), *Money and Power: How Goldman Sachs Came to Rule the World* (New York: Doubleday).

8. Jevons, W.S. (1957), *The Theory of Political Economy* (5th edn) (New York: Kelley and Millman).

9. Bentham, J. (1907), *An Introduction to the Principles of Morals and Legislation* (Oxford: Clarendon Press), p. 1.

10. McGilchrist, I. (2009), *The Master and his Emissary* (London: Yale University Press), p. 340.

11. Jevons, W.S. (1957), *The Theory of Political Economy* (5th edn) (New York: Kelley and Millman), p. 11.

12. Ibid., pp. xvii–xviii.

13. Robbins, L. (1932), *An Essay on the Nature and Significance of Economic Science* (London: Macmillan).

14. McCauley, J.L. (2004), *Dynamics of markets: Econophysics and finance* (Cambridge: Cambridge University Press), p. 11.

15. See for example Mankiw, N.G. (2016), *Principles of Economics* (8th edn) (Boston, MA: Cengage Learning), p. 434.

16. Mankiw, N.G. (2016), *Principles of Economics* (8th edn) (Boston, MA: Cengage Learning), p. 86.

17. Bauman, Y. (January 2009), *Quantum Microeconomics*. Retrieved from: http://www.smallparty.org/yoram/quantum/quantum.pdf. I looked at this open-source textbook because of the title. It turns out that the word 'quantum' refers to the 'optimising individual' which is seen as the smallest unit of the economy. That seems to be almost the opposite of the way it is used here.

18. Samuelson and Nordhaus, for example, write that 'the law' that demand curves always slope downward has been 'empirically tested and verified for practically all commodities' (though the example given is labelled as hypothetical). Samuelson, P.A. and Nordhaus, W.D. (2010), *Economics* (New Delhi: Tata McGraw-Hill), p. 57. In 2018, Bloomberg's Noah Smith wrote that 'The lines on the graph are totally hypothetical!' Smith, N. (13 April 2018), 'Econ Majors Graduate With a Huge Knowledge Gap'. Retrieved from Bloomberg: https://www.bloomberg.com/view/articles/2018-04-13/econ-majors-graduate-with-a-huge-knowledge-gap

19. Pickford, J. (26 May 2017), 'House prices – sellers forced to offer discounts', *Financial Times*.

20. 'Only in special cases can an economy be expected to act as an "idealized consumer".' Shafer, W., and Sonnenschein, H. (1993), 'Market Demand and Excess Demand Functions', in K. Arrow, and M. Intriligator (eds.), *Handbook of Mathematical Economics*

(Amsterdam: Elsevier), pp. 671–2. 'Even if individual behaviour were perfectly understood, it would be impossible to draw useful conclusions about macroeconomics directly from that understanding, due to the aggregation problem.' Ackerman, F. (2002), 'Still dead after all these years: interpreting the failure of general equilibrium theory', *Journal of Economic Methodology*, 9 (2), pp. 119–39.

21. Robbins, L. (1932), *An Essay on the Nature and Significance of Economic Science* (London: Macmillan), p. 112.

22. Albert, H., Arnold, D., and Maier-Rigaud, F. (2012), 'Model Platonism: Neoclassical economic thought in critical light', *Journal of Institutional Economics*, 8 (3), pp. 295–323.

23. Krugman, P. (5 January 2018), 'Good enough for government work? Macroeconomics since the crisis', *Oxford Review of Economic Policy*, 34 (1–2), pp. 156–68.

24. Emery, N. (2017), 'Against Radical Quantum Ontologies', *Philosophy and Phenomenological Research*, 95 (3), pp. 564–91.

25. As an example of this approach, see Sarkissian, J. (2016), *Quantum theory of securities price formation in financial markets.* Retrieved from: https://ssrn.com/abstract=2765298. See also: Schaden, M. (2002), 'Quantum finance', *Physica A*, 316 (1), pp. 511–38.

26. In the quantum jargon, price and momentum are conjugate variables. See, for example: Zhang, C., and Huang, L. (2010), 'A quantum model for the stock market', *Physica A: Statistical Mechanics and its Applications*, 389 (24), pp. 5769–75.

27. Kumar, M. (2008), *Quantum: Einstein, Bohr and the Great Debate About the Nature of Reality* (London: Icon Books), p. 231.

28. Holton, G.J., and Brush, S.G. (2001), *Physics, the human adventure: from Copernicus to Einstein and beyond* (New Brunswick, NJ: Rutgers University Press), p. 418.

29. Samuelson, P.A. (1969), 'Classical and Neoclassical Theory', in R. Clower (ed.), *Monetary Theory* (London: Penguin), p. 184.

30. Anonymous (12 August 2017), 'Say's law: supply creates its own demand', *The Economist*. Krugman, P. (10 February 2015), 'There's Something About Money (Implicitly Wonkish)'. Retrieved from: http://krugman.blogs.nytimes.com/2015/02/10/theres-something-about-money-implicitly-wonkish/

31. As Robert Nelson notes, this is rarely made explicit, but is 'most powerfully communicated in their manner of doing and presenting their economic research'. Nelson, R.H. (2017), *Why Economic Progress Requires Economic Religion* (Copenhagen: Copenhagen Business School).

32. McGilchrist, I. (2009), *The Master and his Emissary* (London: Yale University Press), p. 330.
33. Ibid., p. 82.
34. Sperry, R.W. (9 August 1975), 'Left-brain, right-brain', *Saturday Review*, pp. 30–33.
35. McGilchrist, I. (2009), *The Master and his Emissary* (London: Yale University Press), p. 281.
36. Ibid., p. 279.
37. Ibid., p. 321.
38. Ibid., p. 233.

Chapter 5

1. Nicolaisen, J. (25 April 2017), 'Jon Nicolaisen: What should the future form of our money be?'. Retrieved from Bank of Norway: http://www .norges-bank.no/en/published/speeches/2017/2017-04-25-dnva/
2. An exception was the Bank of France, founded in 1800. Kindleberger, C.P. (1984), *A Financial History of Western Europe* (London: Allen & Unwin), p. 98.
3. Monaghan, A. (2 February 2018), 'Bitcoin biggest bubble in history, says economist who predicted 2008 crash', *The Guardian*; Buck, J. (2 December 2007), 'Billionaire Carl Icahn Doesn't Get Bitcoin, Sees A Bubble'. Retrieved from: Cointelegraph: https://cointelegraph .com/news/billionaire-carl-icahn-doesnt-get-bitcoin-sees-a-bubble
4. Lemay, J.A. (2006), *The Life of Benjamin Franklin, Volume 1: Journalist, 1706–1730* (Philadelphia: University of Pennsylvania Press), p. 399.
5. Davies, G. (2002), *A History of Money: From Ancient Times to the Present Day* (3rd edn) (Cardiff: University of Wales Press), p. 483.
6. Federal Reserve (2017), 'Who owns the Federal Reserve?'. Retrieved 20 November 2017, from: http://www.federalreserve.gov/faqs/ about_14986.htm
7. Soddy, F. (1926), *Wealth, Virtual Wealth and Debt: The Solution of the Economic Paradox* (New York: Dutton).
8. Soddy, F. (2003), *The Role of Money: What It Should Be, Contrasted with What It Has Become* (London: Routledge).
9. Soddy, F. (1926), *Wealth, Virtual Wealth and Debt: The Solution of the Economic Paradox* (New York: Dutton).
10. McLeay, M., Radia, A., and Thomas, R. (14 March 2014), 'Money Creation in the Modern Economy', *Quarterly Bulletin 2014 Q1* (Bank of England).

11. Schumpeter, J. (1934), *The Theory of Economic Development: An Inquiry into Profits, Capital, Credit, Interest and the Business Cycle* (Cambridge, MA: Harvard University Press), p. 73.

12. Schumpeter, J. (1954), *History of Economic Analysis* (London: Allen & Unwin), p. 1114.

13. Werner, R.A. (2016), 'A lost century in economics: Three theories of banking and the conclusive evidence', *International Review of Financial Analysis*, 46, pp. 361–79. Norbert Häring similarly noted in 2013 that 'Cursory observation suggests that credit creation or money creation are taboo words in the leading journals.' Häring, N. (2013), 'The veil of deception over money', *Real World Economics Review*, 63, pp. 2–18.

14. McLeay, M., Radia, A., and Thomas, R. (14 March 2014), 'Money Creation in the Modern Economy', *Quarterly Bulletin 2014 Q1* (Bank of England).

15. Turner, A. (10 November 2014), 'Printing money to fund deficit is the fastest way to raise rates', *Financial Times*.

16. Werner, R.A. (2014), 'Can banks individually create money out of nothing? – The theories and the empirical evidence', *International Review of Financial Analysis*, 36, pp. 1–19.

17. McLeay, M., Radia, A., and Thomas, R. (14 March 2014), 'Money Creation in the Modern Economy', *Quarterly Bulletin 2014 Q1* (Bank of England).

18. Turner, A. (10 November 2014), 'Printing money to fund deficit is the fastest way to raise rates', *Financial Times*.

19. Clarke, D. (27 October 2017), 'Poll Shows 85% of MPs Don't Know Where Money Comes From'. Retrieved from Positive Money: http://positivemoney.org/2017/10/mp-poll/

20. Werner, R.A. (2014), 'How do banks create money, and why can other firms not do the same? An explanation for the coexistence of lending and deposit-taking', *International Review of Financial Analysis*, 36, pp. 71–7.

21. Werner, R.A. (2016), 'A lost century in economics: Three theories of banking and the conclusive evidence', *International Review of Financial Analysis*, 46, pp. 361–79.

22. Neal, T. (7 February 2017), 'Hard times ahead for first-time buyers', *Beach Metro Community News*.

23. Kirby, J. (31 March 2017), 'Stephen Poloz: "No one wins a trade war. Everybody loses"', *Maclean's*.

24. Salter, M. (15 July 1988), 'Hot hot houses', *The Globe and Mail*.

25. Minsky, H.P. (1972), 'Financial instability revisited: the economics of disaster', in *Reappraisal of the Federal Reserve Discount Mechanism* (Washington, DC: Board of Governors of the Federal Reserve System), pp. 95–136.

26. Kuroda, H. (20 March 2014), 'Aiming at 2 Per Cent Inflation. Why? Speech at the Japan Chamber of Commerce and Industry'. Retrieved from Bank of Japan: https://www.boj.or.jp/en/announcements/press/koen_2014/data/ko140320a1.pdf

27. Fleming, S. (4 October 2017), 'Fed has no reliable theory of inflation, says Tarullo', *Financial Times*. See also: Giles, C. (11 October 2017), 'Central bankers face a crisis of confidence as models fail', *Financial Times*.

28. Bouchaud, J.-P., Gualdi, S., Tarzia, M., and Zamponi, F. (15 September 2017), 'Optimal Inflation Target: Insights from an Agent-Based Model'. Retrieved from: https://arxiv.org/pdf/1709.05117.pdf

29. Wingrove, J., and Argitis, T. (16 October 2017), 'Poloz Says Canada's Economy Entered "Sweet Part" of Business Cycle'. Retrieved from Bloomberg: https://www.bloomberg.com/news/articles/2017-10-16/poloz-says-canada-economy-entered-sweet-part-of-business-cycle

30. See Keen, S. (2017), *Can We Avoid Another Financial Crisis?* (Cambridge: Polity), p. 77.

31. Bezemer, D., and Hudson, M. (2016), 'Finance Is Not the Economy: Reviving the Conceptual Distinction', *Journal of Economic Issues*, 50 (3), pp. 745–68.

32. White, W. (11 February 2014), 'Central Banking … Not a Science'. Retrieved from YouTube: https://www.youtube.com/watch?v=tCx-lKdRrPs

33. Central Intelligence Agency (1 August 1975), 'An Evaluation of Jay Forrester's "Systems Dynamics" Methodology'. Retrieved from: https://www.cia.gov/library/readingroom/docs/CIA-RDP80B01495R000600180019-0.pdf

34. Bouchaud, J.-P., Gualdi, S., Tarzia, M., and Zamponi, F. (15 September 2017), 'Optimal Inflation Target: Insights from an Agent-Based Model'. Retrieved from: https://arxiv.org/pdf/1709.05117.pdf

35. For an application from another area, see: Snell, C., Orrell, D., Fernandez, E., Chassagnole, C., and Fell, D. (2011), 'Systems Biology Approaches to Cancer Drug Development', in A. Cesario, and F. Marcus, *Cancer Systems Biology, Bioinformatics and Medicine* (London: Springer), pp. 367–80.

36. This is the principle of so-called stock-flow consistent modelling. Caverzasi, E. and Godin, A. (2013), 'Stock-flow consistent modeling through the ages', Working Paper, Levy Economics Institute.
37. Smith, N. (25 August 2016), 'Data Geeks Are Taking Over Economics'. Retrieved from Bloomberg.com: https://www.bloomberg.com/view/articles/2016-08-25/data-geeks-are-taking-over-economics
38. Hannam, J. (2009), *God's Philosophers: How the Medieval World Laid the Foundations of Modern Science* (London: Icon Books), p. 174.

Chapter 6

1. Pearson, K. (1905), 'The problem of the random walk', *Nature*, 72, pp. 294, 318, 342.
2. Editorial (September 2004), 'Einstein=Man of Conscience2'. *Scientific American*, 291, p. 10.
3. Bachelier, L. (1900), 'Théorie de la spéculation', *Annales Scientifiques de l'École Normale Supérieure*, 3 (17), pp. 21–86.
4. Clark, M. (director), (1999), *The Midas Formula* (motion picture).
5. Fama, E.F. (1965), *Random walks in stock-market prices* (Chicago: Graduate School of Business, University of Chicago).
6. Fama, E.F. (1991), 'Efficient capital markets II', *The Journal of Finance*, 46 (5), pp. 1575–1617. Cochrane, J.H. (2011), 'Presidential address: Discount rates', *The Journal of Finance*, 66 (4), pp. 1047–1108.
7. Jensen, M. (1978), 'Some Anomalous Evidence Regarding Market Efficiency', *Journal of Financial Economics*, 6, pp. 95–102.
8. Lo, A.W., and MacKinlay, A.C. (2002), *A Non-Random Walk Down Wall Street* (Princeton, NJ: Princeton University Press), p. 4.
9. Lo, A.W. (2008), 'Efficient Markets Hypothesis', in S.N. Durlauf, and L.E. Blume (eds), *The New Palgrave Dictionary of Economics, Second Edition* (Basingstoke: Palgrave Macmillan).
10. According to economists David Vines and Samuel Wills, there are 'two critical assumptions underpinning DSGE models: the efficient market hypothesis, and rational expectations'. Vines, D. and Wills, S. (5 January 2018), 'The rebuilding macroeconomic theory project: an analytical assessment', *Oxford Review of Economic Policy*, 34 (1–2), pp. 1–42.
11. Cochrane, J. (2011), 'How did Paul Krugman get it so wrong?', *IEA Economic Affairs*, (June), pp. 36–40.
12. Sewell, M. (2011), 'History of the Efficient Market Hypothesis', Research Note RN/11/04 20, UCL Department of Computer Science.
13. Anonymous (16 July 2009), 'Efficiency and beyond', *The Economist*.

14. Mackenzie, D. (2006), *An Engine, Not a Camera: How Financial Models Shape Markets* (Cambridge, MA: MIT Press), p. 120.

15. Mackenzie, D. (2006), *An Engine, Not a Camera: How Financial Models Shape Markets* (Cambridge, MA: MIT Press), p. 158.

16. Albrecht, A., and Phillips, D. (2014), 'Origin of probabilities and their application to the multiverse', *Physical Review D*, 90 (12), p. 123514.

17. There are plenty of papers exploring the relationship between these equations, such as: Haven, E. (2003), 'A Black-Scholes Schrödinger option price: "bit" versus "qubit"', *Physica A*, 324, pp. 201–06. However, they are fundamentally different in that the Black-Scholes equation is a version of a dissipative heat equation, while the Schrödinger equation is an oscillatory wave equation, and it is only possible to translate between them by making numerous assumptions.

18. Baaquie, B.E. (2007), *Quantum Finance: Path Integrals and Hamiltonians for Options and Interest Rates* (Cambridge: Cambridge University Press), p. 99. See also: Schaden, M. (2002), 'Quantum finance', *Physica A*, 316 (1), pp. 511–38.

19. Paul Wilmott, private communication, 2017.

20. Sarkissian, J. (2016), 'Risk valuation for securities with limited liquidity'. Retrieved from: https://ssrn.com/abstract=2891669

21. Everett, H. (1957), 'Relative state formulation of quantum mechanics', *Rev. Mod. Phys.*, 29, pp. 454–62.

22. Deutsch, D. (1997), *The Fabric of Reality* (London: Penguin), p. 51.

23. Birkhoff, G., and von Neumann, J. (1936), 'The Logic of Quantum Mechanics', *Annals of Mathematics*, 37, pp. 823–43.

24. Khrennikov, A. (2009), 'Classical and Quantum-Like Randomness and the Financial Market', in M. Faggini (ed.), *Coping with the complexity of economics* (New York: Springer), pp. 67–77.

25. Feynman, R. (1982), 'Simulating physics with computers', *International Journal of Theoretical Physics*, 21 (6–7), pp. 467–88. See also: Boghosian, B. (1998), 'Simulating quantum mechanics on a quantum computer', *Physica D*, 120 (1–2), pp. 0–42.

26. Wilson, E.K. (2000), 'Quantum Computers', *Chemical and Engineering News*, 78 (45), pp. 35–9.

27. Asmundsson, J. (14 June 2017), 'Quantum Computing Might Be Here Sooner Than You Think'. Retrieved from: Bloomberg.com

28. Wilmott, P., and Orrell, D. (2017), *The Money Formula: Dodgy Finance, Pseudo Science, and How Mathematicians Took Over the Markets* (Chichester: Wiley).

29. Baaquie, for example, writes of his book that 'No attempt is made to apply quantum theory in re-working the fundamental principles of finance'. Baaquie, B.E. (2007), *Quantum Finance: Path Integrals and Hamiltonians for Options and Interest Rates* (Cambridge: Cambridge University Press), p. 1.

30. Kunte, S. (6 August 2015), 'The Herding Mentality: Behavioral Finance and Investor Biases'. Retrieved from CFA Institute: https://blogs.cfainstitute.org/investor/2015/08/06/the-herding-mentality-behavioral-finance-and-investor-biases/

31. Zyga, L. (6 June 2014), 'Herding in the stock market may inspire human-guided trading algorithms'. Retrieved from phys.org: https://phys.org/news/2014-06-herding-stock-human-guided-algorithms.html

32. For a discussion of such simple modelling approaches, see: Bouchaud, J.-P. (2009), 'The (unfortunate) complexity of the economy', *Physics World*, 22, pp. 28–32.

33. Black, F., and Scholes, M. (1973), 'The Pricing of Options and Corporate Liabilities', *Journal of Political Economy*, 81 (3), pp. 637–54.

34. Jones, S.L., and Netter, J.M. (28 October 2017), 'Efficient Capital Markets' (Library of Economics and Liberty). Retrieved from The Concise Encyclopedia of Economics: http://www.econlib.org/library/Enc/EfficientCapitalMarkets.html

35. Wilmott, P., and Orrell, D. (2017), *The Money Formula: Dodgy Finance, Pseudo Science, and How Mathematicians Took Over the Markets* (Chichester: Wiley).

Chapter 7

1. Leibniz, G.W. (1902), *Discourse on Metaphysics* (Chicago: The Open Court).

2. Jevons, W.S. (1957), *The Theory of Political Economy* (5th edn) (New York: Kelley and Millman), pp. xvii–xviii.

3. Fisher, I. (1892), *Mathematical investigations in the theory of value and prices* (New Haven, CT: Connecticut Academy of Arts and Sciences), p. 85.

4. Quetelet, L.A. (1984), *Research on the propensity for crime at different ages* (Cincinnati, OH: Anderson), p. 3.

5. Edgeworth, F.Y. (1881), *Mathematical psychics: an essay on the application of mathematics to the moral sciences* (London: C.K. Paul), p. 16.

6. Robbins, L. (1932), *An Essay on the Nature and Significance of Economic Science* (London: Macmillan), p. 112.

7. Von Neumann, J., and Morgenstern, O. (1944), *Theory of Games and Economic Behavior* (Princeton, NJ: Princeton University Press).

8. Heims, S. (1980), *John Von Neumann and Norbert Wiener: from mathematics to the technologies of life and death* (Cambridge, MA: MIT Press), p. 295.

9. Bockman, J. (2011), *Markets in the Name of Socialism: The Left-Wing Origins of Neoliberalism* (Stanford, CA: Stanford University Press), p. 47.

10. Arrow, K.J., and Debreu, G. (1954), 'Existence of a Competitive Equilibrium for a Competitive Economy', *Econometrica*, 22, pp. 65–90.

11. See: Varoufakis, Y., Halevi, J., and Theocarakis, N. (2011), *Modern Political Economics: Making Sense of the Post-2008 World* (New York: Routledge), pp. 253–4. The authors discuss the 'propaganda value' of the Arrow-Debreu model, while emphasising that this use was not the intention of the modellers. Bouchaud also notes that 'The supposed omniscience and perfect efficacy of a free market stems from economic work done in the 1950s and 1960s, which with hindsight looks more like propaganda against communism than plausible science'. Bouchaud, J.-P. (2008), 'Economics Needs a Scientific Revolution', *Nature*, 455, p. 1181.

12. Akerlof, G.A., and Shiller, R.J. (2016), *Phishing for Phools: The Economics of Manipulation and Deception* (Princeton, NJ: Princeton University Press), pp. 5, 186.

13. Deutsch, D. (1997), *The Fabric of Reality* (London: Penguin), p. 175.

14. Monod, J. (1971), *Chance and Necessity: An Essay on the Natural Philosophy of Modern Biology* (New York: Knopf).

15. Becker, G.S. (1976), *The Economic Approach to Human Behavior* (Chicago: University of Chicago Press), pp. 5–8.

16. Committee on Financial Services, US House of Representatives (20 July 2006), 'Monetary Policy And The State of the Economy'. Retrieved from: https://www.gpo.gov/fdsys/pkg/CHRG -109hhrg31539/html/CHRG-109hhrg31539.htm

17. Lucas, R. (2003), 'Macroeconomic Priorities', *American Economic Review*, 93 (1), pp. 1–14.

18. Solow, R.M. (2003), 'Dumb and Dumber in Macroeconomics'. Festschrift for Joe Stiglitz, Columbia University.

19. Earle, J., Moran, C., and Ward-Perkins, Z. (2016), *The Econocracy: The Perils of Leaving Economics to the Experts* (Manchester: Manchester University Press).

20. Morgan, M.S. (2012), *The World in the Model: How Economists Work and Think* (Cambridge: Cambridge University Press), p. 157.

21. Raworth, K. (2017), *Doughnut Economics: Seven Ways to Think Like a 21st-Century Economist* (White River Junction, VT: Chelsea Green Publishing), p. 82.

22. Thaler, R.H. (8 May 2015), 'Unless You Are Spock, Irrelevant Things Matter in Economic Behavior', *New York Times*.

23. Thaler, R.H. (2015), *Misbehaving: The Making of Behavioral Economics* (New York: W.W. Norton & Company), pp. 42, 260.

24. Kahneman, D. (9 September 2017), 'Daniel Kahneman – Biographical'. Retrieved from Nobelprize.org: https://www.nobelprize.org/nobel_prizes/economic-sciences/laureates/2002/kahneman-bio.html

25. Thaler, R.H. (2015), *Misbehaving: The Making of Behavioral Economics* (New York: W.W. Norton & Company), p. 269.

26. Cochrane, J. (22 May 2015), '*Homo economicus* or *homo paleas?*'. Retrieved from The Grumpy Economist: http://johnhcochrane.blogspot.ca/2015/05/homo-economicus-or-homo-paleas.html

27. BBC (31 October 2017), 'Russia-linked posts "reached 126m Facebook users in US"'. Retrieved from BBC.com: http://www.bbc.com/news/world-us-canada-41812369

28. Chicago Booth Review (30 June 2016), 'Are Markets Efficient?'. Retrieved from: http://review.chicagobooth.edu/economics/2016/video/are-markets-efficient

29. https://en.wikipedia.org/wiki/List_of_cognitive_biases

30. See for example: Pastor, L., and Veronesi, P. (2006), 'Was there a NASDAQ bubble in the late 1990s?', *Journal of Financial Economics*, 81 (1), pp. 61–100. As George Cooper notes: 'The intellectual contortions required to rationalize all of these prices beggars belief, but the contortions are performed, none the less, in the name of defending the Efficient Market Hypothesis.' Cooper, G. (2008), *The Origin of Financial Crises: Central banks, credit bubbles and the efficient market fallacy* (London: Harriman House), p. 10.

31. Akerlof, G.A., and Shiller, R.J. (2016), *Phishing for Phools: The Economics of Manipulation and Deception* (Princeton, NJ: Princeton University Press), p. 171. See also p. 164.

32. Hoff, K., and Stiglitz, J.E. (2016), 'Striving for balance in economics: Towards a theory of the social determination of behavior', *Journal of Economic Behavior & Organization*, 126, pp. 25–57.

33. Tversky, A., and Simonson, I. (1993), 'Context-Dependent Preferences', *Management Science*, 39 (10), pp. 1179–89.

34. Quoted by: Jammer, M. (1974), *The Philosophy of Quantum Mechanics* (New York: Wiley), p. 151.

35. Qadir, A. (1978), 'Quantum Economics', *Pakistan Economic and Social Review*, 16 (3/4), pp. 117–26. Qadir's use of the phrase 'quantum economics' was predated by French economist Bernard Schmitt, whose version gained its name in the 1950s from the idea that production is an instantaneous event that quantises time into discrete units. However, a key assumption was that money is nothing more than a means of payment, so the theory has little in common with the approach here.

36. Busemeyer, J., and Bruza, P. (2012), *Quantum Models of Cognition and Decision* (Cambridge: Cambridge University Press).

37. Quoted in: Wendt, A. (2015), *Quantum Mind and Social Science: Unifying Physical and Social Ontology* (Cambridge: Cambridge University Press), p. 158.

38. As Zheng Wang from Ohio State University summarised, 'the number of people who switch an answer one way are always offset by the number of people who switch in the opposite direction'. Ohio State University (16 June 2014), 'Quantum theory reveals puzzling pattern in how people respond to some surveys'. Retrieved from ScienceDaily: www.sciencedaily.com/releases/2014/06/140616151347.htm. See also: Wang, Z., Solloway, T., Shiffrin, R.S., and Busemeyer, J.R. (2014), 'Context effects produced by question orders reveal quantum nature of human judgments', *Proceedings of the National Academy of Sciences*, 111 (26), pp. 9431–6.

39. Gorder, P. F. (2015, September 14). *You're not irrational, you're just quantum probabilistic*. Retrieved from Ohio State News: https://news.osu.edu/news/2015/09/14/youre-not-irrational-youre-just-quantum-probabilistic/

40. Anonymous (8 July 2014), 'Equal and opposite', *The Economist*.

41. Tversky, A., and Shafir, E. (1992), 'The disjunction effect in choice under uncertainty', *Psychological Science*, 3, pp. 305–09.

42. Busemeyer, J.R., Wang, Z., and Shiffrin, R.S. (2015), 'Bayesian model comparison favors quantum over standard decision theory account for dynamic inconsistency', *Decision*, 2, pp. 1–12.

43. Busemeyer, J., and Bruza, P. (2012), *Quantum Models of Cognition and Decision* (Cambridge: Cambridge University Press), p. 267.

44. Tversky, A., and Thaler, R.H. (1990), 'Anomalies: preference reversals', *Journal of Economic Perspectives*, 4, pp. 201–11.

45. Yukalov, V.I., and Sornette, D. (2015), 'Preference reversal in quantum decision theory', *Frontiers in Psychology*, 6, pp. 1–7.

46. Franzen, J. (4 November 2017), 'Is it too late to save the world?', *The Guardian*.

47. For a discussion, see Wendt, A. (2015), *Quantum Mind and Social Science: Unifying Physical and Social Ontology* (Cambridge: Cambridge University Press), p. 172.

48. McGilchrist, I. (2009), *The Master and his Emissary* (London: Yale University Press), p. 146.

49. Mendes, R.V. (2005), 'The Quantum Ultimatum Game', *Quantum Information Processing*, 4 (1), pp. 1–12.

50. Van Wolkenten, M., Brosnan, S.F., and de Waal, F.B. (2007), 'Inequity responses of monkeys modified by effort', *Proceedings of the National Academy of Sciences*, 104, pp. 18854–9.

51. In physics, to quote one textbook from Alastair Rae, 'the word "entanglement" refers to a quantum state of two or more variables, where the probabilities of the outcome of measurements on one of them depend on the state of the other – even though there is no interaction between them'. Rae, A.I.M. (2008), *Quantum Mechanics* (5th edn) (London: Taylor & Francis), p. 268.

52. Wendt, A. (2015), *Quantum Mind and Social Science: Unifying Physical and Social Ontology* (Cambridge: Cambridge University Press), p. 166.

53. Ibid., p. 33.

54. Carter, S.P. and Skiba, P.M. (2012), 'Pawnshops, Behavioral Economics, and Self-Regulation', *Review of Banking & Financial Law*, 32 (1), pp. 193–220.

55. See: 'Introduction to the mathematics of quantum economics', available at davidorrell.com/quantumeconomicsmath.pdf

56. Fougères, A-J. (2016), 'Towards quantum agents: the superposition state property', *International Journal of Computer Science Issues*, 13, pp. 20–27. Kitto, K. and Boschetti, F. (2013), 'Attitudes, ideologies and self-organization: Information load minimization in multi-agent decision making', *Advances in Complex Systems*, 16, pp. 1–37. For a discussion of mortgage default, see Wilkinson-Ryan, T. (2011), 'Breaching the Mortgage Contract: The Behavioral Economics of Strategic Default', *Vanderbilt Law Review*, 64 (5), pp. 1547–83. It appears, for example, that homeowners who are underwater on their mortgages are more likely to default if the default is framed as a kind of option in the contract, which removes some of the stigma.

57. Sterman, J.D. (2000), *Business Dynamics: Systems Thinking and Modeling for a Complex World* (New York: McGraw-Hill), pp. 13–14.

58. Zúñiga, M. (12 February 2018), '"It's humiliating": plight of Venezuelan middle class is pawn shops' gain', *The Guardian*.

59. Wendt, A. (2015), *Quantum Mind and Social Science: Unifying Physical and Social Ontology* (Cambridge: Cambridge University Press), p. 164.

60. Yukalov, V.I. and Sornette, D. (2014), 'Conditions for Quantum Interference in Cognitive Sciences', *Topics in Cognitive Science*, 6, pp. 79–90.

61. Busemeyer, J.R., Wang, Z., and Shiffrin, R.S. (2015), 'Bayesian model comparison favors quantum over standard decision theory account for dynamic inconsistency', *Decision*, 2, pp. 1–12.

62. See for example: Favre, M., Wittwer, A., Heinimann, H.R., Yukalov, V.I., and Sornette, D. (2016), 'Quantum Decision Theory in Simple Risky Choices', *PLOS ONE*, 11 (12), e0168045.

63. Hubbard, W.H. (2017), *Quantum Economics, Newtonian Economics, and Law* (Chicago: University of Chicago Law School).

64. Mankiw, N.G. (2016), *Principles of Economics* (8th edn) (Boston, MA: Cengage Learning), pp. 462–3.

65. Cochrane, J. (22 May 2015), '*Homo economicus* or *homo paleas?*' Retrieved from The Grumpy Economist: http://johnhcochrane .blogspot.ca/2015/05/homo-economicus-or-homo-paleas.html

66. Levy, A. (1 February 2006), 'Mapping the trader's brain', *Bloomberg Markets*, 15 (3), pp. 34–45.

67. Akerlof, G.A., and Shiller, R.J. (2016), *Phishing for Phools: The Economics of Manipulation and Deception* (Princeton, NJ: Princeton University Press), p. 17.

68. For example, Busemeyer and Bruza's *Quantum Models of Cognition and Decision* mentions money only a few times when it appears in experiments. Ironically, the reason for neglecting money is probably that quantum cognition has focused on reproducing the results of behavioural economics.

69. Hanauske, M., Kunz, J., Bernius, S., and Konig, W. (2010), 'Doves and hawks in economics revisited: An evolutionary quantum game theory based analysis of financial crises', *Physica A*, 389 (21), pp. 5084–5102.

70. Cadwalladr, C. (30 July 2017), 'Al Gore: "The rich have subverted all reason"', *The Guardian*.

71. Rethinking Economics NL (19 September 2015), 'VPRO Buitenhof: Rethinking Economics'. Retrieved from YouTube: https://www .youtube.com/watch?v=x7uITEBqQvM

72. Wendt, A. (2015), *Quantum Mind and Social Science: Unifying Physical and Social Ontology* (Cambridge: Cambridge University Press), p. 282.

73. Cheal, D. (16 September 2017), 'Top of the pops', *Financial Times*.
74. Raworth, K. (2017), *Doughnut Economics: Seven Ways to Think Like a 21st-Century Economist* (White River Junction, VT: Chelsea Green Publishing), p. 88.
75. Sedláček, T., Orrell, D. and Chlupatý, R. (2012), *Soumrak Homo Economicus* (Prague: 65.pole).
76. Friedman, M. (1962), *Capitalism and Freedom* (Chicago: University of Chicago Press), pp. 133–4.
77. Lazonick, W., Hopkins, M., Jacobson, K., Sakinç, M.E., and Tulum, Ö. (2017), *US Pharma's Financialized Business Model, Working Paper No. 60* (New York: Institute for New Economic Thinking).
78. Global Strategy Group (2018), 'Call to Action in the Age of Trump'. Retrieved from: http://www.globalstrategygroup.com/ thought-leadership/business-and-politics/

Chapter 8

1. Von Helmholtz, H. (1853), 'On the Conservation of Force', in J. Tyndall, and W. Francis (eds), *Scientific memoirs* (London: Taylor and Francis).
2. Castelvecchi, D. (29 March 2017), 'Battle between quantum and thermodynamic laws heats up', *Nature*, 543 (7647), pp. 597–8.
3. Wolchover, N. (16 April 2014), 'Time's Arrow Traced to Quantum Source'. Retrieved from *Quanta Magazine*: https://www .quantamagazine.org/quantum-entanglement-drives-the-arrow-of -time-scientists-say-20140416/
4. Lambert, N., Chen, Y.-N., Cheng, Y.-C., Li, C.-M., Chen, G.-Y., and Nori, F. (2013), 'Quantum biology', *Nature Physics*, 9 (1), pp. 10–18. Mihelic, F.M. (2013), 'Model of Biological Quantum Logic in DNA', *Life: Open Access Journal*, 3 (3), pp. 474–81. McFadden, J. (29 October 2014), 'Life is quantum'. Retrieved from Aeon: https:// aeon.co/essays/quantum-weirdness-is-everywhere-in-the-living -world
5. Or as Joseph Stiglitz put it, 'DSGE models seem to take it as a religious tenet that consumption should be explained by a model of a representative agent maximizing his utility over an infinite lifetime without borrowing constraints. Doing so is called micro-founding the model.' Stiglitz, J.E. (11 September 2017), 'Where Modern Macroeconomics Went Wrong'. Retrieved from: https://www8. gsb.columbia.edu/faculty/jstiglitz/sites/jstiglitz/files/Where%20 Modern%20Macroeconomics%20Went%20Wrong_0.pdf

6. Samuelson, P.A. (1972 [1969]), 'The Way of an Economist', in R.C. Merton (ed.), *The Collected Scientific Papers of Paul A. Samuelson* (Vol. III, pp. 675–85) (Cambridge, MA: MIT Press), p. 683.

7. Schumacher, R. (2013), 'Deconstructing the theory of comparative advantage', *World Social and Economic Review*, (2), p. 83.

8. Ricardo, D. (11 September 2017), *On the Principles of Political Economy and Taxation* (1821). Retrieved from Library of Economics and Liberty: http://www.econlib.org/library/Ricardo/ricP.html

9. Hausmann, R., Hidalgo, C.A., Bustos, S., Coscia, M., Simoes, A., and Yildirim, M.A. (2014), *The Atlas of Economic Complexity: Mapping Paths to Prosperity* (Cambridge, MA: MIT Press), p. 6. Ricardo, D. (11 September 2017), *On the Principles of Political Economy and Taxation* (1821). Retrieved from Library of Economics and Liberty: http://www.econlib.org/library/Ricardo/ricP.html

10. Committee on Science and Technology (20 July 2010), 'Building a Science of Economics for the Real World'. Retrieved from: https://science.house.gov/sites/republicans.science.house.gov/files/documents/hearings/072010_charter.pdf. See also: Arora, V. (December 2013), 'An Evaluation of Macroeconomic Models for Use at EIA'. Retrieved from US Energy Information Administration: https://www.eia.gov/workingpapers/pdf/macro_models-vipin-wappendix.pdf

11. Blanchard, O. (2014), 'Where Danger Lurks', *Finance & Development*, 51 (3), pp. 28–31.

12. As William White wrote in 2013: 'An important practical aspect of [DSGE] models is that they make no reference to money or credit, and they have no financial sector.' White, W. (2013), 'Is Monetary Policy a Science? The Interaction of Theory and Practice Over the Last 50 Years', in M. Balling, and E. Gnan (eds.), *50 Years of Money and Finance – Lessons and Challenges* (Vienna: SUERF).

13. Barad, K. (2007), *Meeting the Universe Halfway: Quantum Physics and the Entanglement of Matter and Meaning* (Durham, NC: Duke University Press), p. 239.

14. Institute of International Finance (June 2017), 'Global Debt Monitor'. Retrieved from: https://www.iif.com/publication/global-debt-monitor/global-debt-monitor-june-2017

15. Bernanke, B. (1995), 'The Macroeconomics of the Great Depression: A Comparative Approach', *Journal of Money, Credit, and Banking*, 27 (1), pp. 1–28.

16. Krugman, P. (2012), *End This Depression Now!* (New York: W.W. Norton & Co.), p. 112.

17. In a representative agent model of the sort typically used in macroeconomics, 'debt (held domestically) nets out, and therefore should have no role'. Stiglitz, J.E. (11 September 2017), 'Where Modern Macroeconomics Went Wrong'. Retrieved from: https://www8.gsb.columbia.edu/faculty/jstiglitz/sites/jstiglitz/files/Where%20Modern%20Macroeconomics%20Went%20Wrong_0.pdf

18. According to Notre Dame sociologist Robert M. Fishman, the country came under 'unfair and arbitrary pressure from bond traders, speculators and credit rating analysts' which forced it to seek a bailout. Fishman, R.M. (12 April 2011), 'Portugal's Unnecessary Bailout', *New York Times*.

19. Haldane, A. (29 October 2014), 'Managing global finance as a system – speech by Andrew Haldane'. Retrieved from Bank of England: http://www.bankofengland.co.uk/publications/Documents/speeches/2014/speech772.pdf

20. According to Haldane's above-cited speech, 'Other things equal, a common global factor potentially accounts for perhaps 70–90% of the movements in advanced country asset prices'.

21. Battiston, S., Delli Gatti, D., Greenwald, B. and Stiglitz, J.E. (2007), 'Credit Chains and Bankruptcy Propagation in Production Networks', *Journal of Economic Dynamics and Control*, 31 (6), pp. 2061–84.

22. International Monetary Fund (April 2006), 'Global Financial Stability Report: Market Developments and Issues' (Washington, DC), p. 51.

23. Bernanke, B. (18 May 2006), 'Basel II: Its Promise and Its Challenges'. Retrieved from: http://www.federalreserve.gov/newsevents/speech/bernanke20060518a.htm

24. Wilmott, P., and Orrell, D. (2017), *The Money Formula: Dodgy Finance, Pseudo Science, and How Mathematicians Took Over the Markets* (Chichester: Wiley).

25. The Bank for International Settlements, for example, noted in 2017 that the borrowing through foreign exchange swaps and forwards contracts by non-banks outside the United States was similar in size to the $10.7 trillion of on-balance-sheet dollar debt. Borio, C., McCauley, R.N., and McGuire, P. (17 September 2017), 'FX swaps and forwards: missing global debt?' Retrieved from Bank for International Settlements: https://www.bis.org/publ/qtrpdf/r_qt1709e.htm

26. Wilmott, P. (2000), 'The use, misuse and abuse of mathematics in finance', *Philosophical Transactions of the Royal Society of London*.

Series A: Mathematical, Physical and Engineering Sciences, 358 (1765), pp. 63–73.

27. As Joseph Stiglitz noted, 'The Congressional inquiry into the 2008 crisis called itself the Financial Crisis Inquiry Commission and focused on aspects of the financial sector like credit rating agencies and the role of CDS's, derivatives, and other complex financial instruments. The standard DSGE models have nothing to say about either of these.' Stiglitz, J.E. (11 September 2017), 'Where Modern Macroeconomics Went Wrong'. Retrieved from: https://www8. gsb.columbia.edu/faculty/jstiglitz/sites/jstiglitz/files/Where%20 Modern%20Macroeconomics%20Went%20Wrong_0.pdf

28. Jevons, W.S. (1957), *The Theory of Political Economy* (5th edn) (New York: Kelley and Millman).

29. Lewis, J. (2005), 'Roots of Ensemble Forecasting', *Monthly Weather Review*, 133 (7), pp. 1865–85.

30. Unlike observation error, model error does not lend itself easily to the ensemble approach, because if the equations have the wrong form it is not clear what type of perturbation is appropriate. Orrell, D. (2007), *Apollo's Arrow: The Science of Prediction and the Future of Everything* (Toronto: HarperCollins).

31. For an example of a machine learning approach from a non-weather organisation, see Grover, A., Kapoor, A., and Horvitz, E. (2015), 'A Deep Hybrid Model for Weather Forecasting', *KDD '15 Proceedings of the 21th ACM SIGKDD International Conference on Knowledge Discovery and Data Mining* (New York: ACM Press), pp. 379–86. Retrieved from https://www.microsoft.com/en-us/research/ publication/deep-hybrid-model-weather-forecasting/. As David Gold, Chief Meteorologist of IBM-Global Business Services, notes: 'Largely driven by the widespread belief that ensemble based dynamical forecast systems offer the best possible predictions, the modern day meteorological community has largely shunned/ abandoned purely statistical/ML approaches.' Gold, D. (5 June 2013), 'Are machine learning algorithms used in weather forecasting? If so, which ones? If not, why?' Retrieved from Quora: https://www.quora.com/Are-machine-learning-algorithm s-used-in-weather-forecasting. For a machine learning approach to climate forecasting, see Fildes, R., and Kourentzes, N. (2011), 'Validation and forecasting accuracy in models of climate change', *International Journal of Forecasting*, 27, pp. 968–95. As the authors note, while there have been many studies of climate models, 'few, if any, studies have made a formal examination of their comparative

forecasting accuracy records, which is at the heart of forecasting research.'

32. Constâncio, V. (25 September 2017), 'Developing models for policy analysis in central banks'. Retrieved from European Central Bank: http://www.ecb.europa.eu/press/key/date/2017/html/ecb.sp170925. en.html

33. Independent Evaluation Office (November 2015), 'Evaluating forecast performance'. Retrieved from Bank of England: https:// www.bankofengland.co.uk/independent-evaluation-office/ forecasting-evaluation-november-2015

34. Meakin, L., Goodman, D., and Tartar, A. (17 January 2018), 'Which Central Bank is the Most Accurate Forecaster?' Retrieved from Bloomberg: https://www.bloomberg.com/amp/news/ articles/2018-01-17/which-central-bank-is-the-most-accurate -forecaster

35. Keynes, J.M. (1923), *A Tract on Monetary Reform* (London: Macmillan), p. 80.

36. Bernanke, B. (5 June 2007), 'The Housing Market and Subprime Lending'. Retrieved from: https://www.federalreserve.gov/news-events/speech/bernanke20070605a.htm. Hudson, M. (20 April 2006), 'The New Road to Serfdom – An illustrated guide to the coming real estate collapse'. Retrieved from: http://michael-hudson .com/2006/04/the-new-road-to-serfdom-an-illustrated-guide-to -the-coming-real-estate-collapse/

37. Inman, P. (5 January 2017), 'Chief economist of Bank of England admits errors in Brexit forecasting', *The Guardian*.

38. Diane Coyle, for example, described it in 2017 as a staple of a new 'literary genre' that criticises mainstream economics. My 2010 book *Economyths* was an early example. Coyle, D. (23 June 2017), 'Economics in Transition'. Retrieved from Project Syndicate: https:// www.project-syndicate.org/onpoint/economics-in-transition-by -diane-coyle-2017-06

39. Stewart, H. (26 July 2009), 'This is how we let the credit crunch happen, Ma'am ...', *The Guardian*.

40. Quoted is David Stockton, Director of the Division of Research and Statistics. Federal Open Market Committee (11 December 2007), 'Federal Open Market Committee transcript'. Retrieved from: https://www.federalreserve.gov/monetarypolicy/files/ FOMC20071211meeting.pdf

41. OECD (2008), 'OECD Economic Outlook', Volume 2008, Issue 1 (Paris: Organisation for Economic Cooperation and Development).

42. Ahir, H., and Loungani, P. (March 2014), 'Can economists forecast recessions? Some evidence from the Great Recession'. Retrieved from The Oracle.

43. Greenspan, A. (23 October 2008), 'Testimony of Dr Alan Greenspan', House Committee of Government Oversight and Reform (Washington, DC).

44. Melnick, D. (producer), Jackson, M. (director), and Martin, S. (screenwriter) (1991), *L.A. Story* (motion picture) (United States: Carolco Pictures).

45. Lucas, R. (6 August 2009), 'In defence of the dismal science', *The Economist*.

46. Chari, V.V. (20 July 2010), 'Testimony before the Committee on Science and Technology, Subcommittee on Investigations and Oversight', US House of Representatives. Retrieved from: http://people.virginia.edu/~ey2d/Chari_Testimony.pdf

47. Anton Korinek of Johns Hopkins for example writes: 'Curiously, a majority of the critics of dynamic stochastic general equilibrium macroeconomics agree that it is, in principle, desirable for macroeconomic models (i) to incorporate dynamics, i.e. a time dimension, (ii) to deal with stochastic uncertainty, and (iii) to study general equilibrium effects.' Korinek, A. (15 July 2017), 'Thoughts on DSGE Macroeconomics: Matching the Moment, But Missing the Point?' Retrieved from SSRN: https://ssrn.com/abstract=3022009

48. As Ricardo Caballero notes, 'there has been an enormous collective effort in recent decades in building such models, with an increasing number of bells and whistles representing various microeconomic frictions. The research departments of central banks around the world have become even more obsessed than academics with this agenda.' Of course, lots of money is spent on modelling in other areas, but rarely to such little effect. Caballero, R.J. (2010), 'Macroeconomics after the Crisis: Time to Deal with the Pretense-of-Knowledge Syndrome', *Journal of Economic Perspectives*, 24 (4), pp. 85–102.

49. MSNBC (6 March 2015), 'Thomas Piketty, Paul Krugman and Joseph Stiglitz: The Genius of Economics'. Retrieved from YouTube: https://www.youtube.com/watch?v=Si4iyyJDa7c. The last remark was possibly a reference to his 1998 prediction, much celebrated by the IT community, that 'The growth of the Internet will slow drastically ... ten years from now, the phrase information economy will sound silly'. Krugman, P. (June 1998), 'Why most economists' predictions are wrong', *The Red Herring*. He later said he was trying to be 'fun and provocative'. Yarow, J. (30 December 2013), 'Tech People

Are Passing Around This Paul Krugman Quote on the Internet After He Called Bitcoin "Evil"', *Business Insider*.

50. Rethinking Economics NL (19 September 2015), 'VPRO Buitenhof: Rethinking Economics'. Retrieved from YouTube: https://www.youtube.com/watch?v=x7uITEBqQvM

51. See www.systemsforecasting.com. The book is *Apollo's Arrow*, which in the US has the title *The Future of Everything*.

52. Quoted in: Bezemer, D. (2010), 'Understanding Financial Crisis Through Accounting Models', *Accounting, Organizations and Society*, 35 (7), pp. 676-88.

53. Bernanke, B. (22 May 2009), 'Commencement address at the Boston College School of Law', Newton, MA. For a critique of the butterfly effect, see Orrell, D. (2007), *Apollo's Arrow: The Science of Prediction and the Future of Everything* (Toronto: HarperCollins).

54. Sargent, T. (September 2010), 'Interview with Thomas Sargent' (A. Rolnick, interviewer), Federal Reserve Bank of Minneapolis. Retrieved from: https://www.minneapolisfed.org/publications/the-region/interview-with-thomas-sargent

55. Edge, R.M., and Gürkaynak, R. (2010), 'How Useful Are Estimated DSGE Model Forecasts for Central Bankers?', Brookings Papers on Economic Activity, 41 (2), pp. 209-59.

56. I discussed economic forecasting in: Orrell, D. (2017), *Economyths: 11 Ways That Economics Gets it Wrong* (London: Icon Books).

57. BBC (13 December 2012), 'Queen questions financial crisis'. Retrieved from BBC: http://www.bbc.com/news/uk-20716299

58. Parker, G. (14 April 2016), 'Veteran of Treasury battles tots up a decade's wins and losses', *Financial Times*.

59. Reisz, M., Auld, C., Bateman, V., Keen, S., and Oswald, A. (6 July 2017), 'New horizons: economics in the 21st century', *Times Higher Education*.

60. Attanasio, O., Bandiera, O., Blundell, R., Machin, S., Griffith, R. and Rasul, I. (20 December 2017), 'Dismal ignorance of the "dismal science" – a response to Larry Elliot', *Prospect*.

61. Hughes, L. (6 January 2017), 'Michael Fish jokes that his forecasts are better than the Bank of England's dire Brexit predictions'. Retrieved from *The Daily Telegraph*: http://www.telegraph.co.uk/news/2017/01/06/michael-fish-jokes-forecasts-better-bank-englands-dire-brexit/

62. Krugman, P. (5 January 2018), 'Good enough for government work? Macroeconomics since the crisis', *Oxford Review of Economic Policy*, 34 (1–2), pp. 156-68.

63. Akerlof, G.A., and Shiller, R.J. (2016), *Phishing for Phools: The Economics of Manipulation and Deception* (Princeton, NJ: Princeton University Press), pp. 164–5.
64. Leonhardt, D. (21 August 2005), 'Be Warned: Mr. Bubble's Worried Again', *New York Times*.
65. Kocherlakota, N. (2016), *Toy Models*. Retrieved from: https://docs. google.com/viewer?a=v&pid=sites&srcid=ZGVmYXVsdGRvbW Fpbnxrb2NoZXJsYWtvdGEwMDl8Z3g6MTAyZmIzODcxNGZi OGY4Yg
66. Mayeda, A., and Torres, C. (18 November 2016), 'The Rebel Economist Who Blew Up Macroeconomics'. Retrieved from Bloomberg: https://www.bloomberg.com/news/articles/2016-11-18/ blah-blah-blah-a-renowned-economist-sums-up-the-state-of -macro
67. Constâncio, V. (11 May 2017), 'Speech at the second ECB Macroprudential Policy and Research Conference, Frankfurt am Main'. Retrieved from European Central Bank: https://www.ecb. europa.eu/press/key/date/2017/html/ecb.sp170511.en.html
68. Stiglitz, J.E. (11 September 2017), 'Where Modern Macroeconomics Went Wrong'. Retrieved from: https://www8.gsb.columbia. edu/faculty/jstiglitz/sites/jstiglitz/files/Where%20Modern%20 Macroeconomics%20Went%20Wrong_0.pdf
69. Hume, D. (1987), *Essays, Moral, Political, and Literary* (E.F. Miller, ed.). Retrieved 22 April 2015, from Library of Economics and Liberty: http://www.econlib.org/library/LFBooks/Hume/hmMPL26. html. Say, J.-B. (11 September 2017), *A Treatise on Political Economy* (C.R. Prinsep, trans. and Clement C. Biddle., ed.), 1855. Retrieved from Library of Economics and Liberty: http://www.econlib.org/ library/Say/sayT15.html
70. Baker, D., and Rosnick, D. (November 2005), 'Will a Bursting Bubble Trouble Bernanke? The Evidence for a Housing Bubble'. Retrieved from Center for Economic and Policy Research: http:// cepr.net/documents/publications/housing_bubble_2005_11.pdf
71. Baker, D. (27 July 2017), 'How about a little accountability for economists when they mess up?', *The Guardian*.
72. Kocherlakota, N. (22 September 2016), 'Professors Aren't Feeling the Economy's Pain', Bloomberg.com.
73. Bezemer, D. (2011), 'The Credit Crisis and Recession as a Paradigm Test', *Journal of Economic Issues*, 45 (1), pp. 1–18.
74. Stiglitz, J.E. (11 September 2017), 'Where Modern Macroeconomics Went Wrong'. Retrieved from: https://www8.gsb.columbia.

edu/faculty/jstiglitz/sites/jstiglitz/files/Where%20Modern%20 Macroeconomics%20Went%20Wrong_0.pdf

75. Lucas, R. (2009), 'Robert E Lucas Jr', in W. Breit, and B.T. Hirsch (eds), *Lives of the Laureates: Twenty-three Nobel Economists* (Cambridge, MA: MIT Press), p. 276.

76. See: Akerlof, G.A., and Shiller, R.J. (2016), *Phishing for Phools: The Economics of Manipulation and Deception* (Princeton, NJ: Princeton University Press). The authors themselves continue to view the economy as a Pareto-optimal equilibrium system, but include deception in the equilibrium (the word 'equilibrium' is mentioned 45 times in the text).

77. Orrell, D. (2012), *Truth or Beauty: Science and the Quest for Order* (New Haven, CT: Yale University Press).

78. Krugman, P. (2 September 2009), 'How Did Economists Get it So Wrong?', *New York Times.*

79. Cochrane, J. (2011), 'How Did Paul Krugman Get it So Wrong?', *IEA Economic Affairs*, (June), pp. 36–40. Retrieved from University of Chicago Booth School of Business: https://faculty.chicagobooth .edu/john.cochrane/research/papers/ecaf_2077.pdf

80. Eichengreen, B. (May/June 2009), 'The Last Temptation of Risk', *The National Interest.*

81. Ferguson, C. (3 October 2010), 'Larry Summers and the Subversion of Economics', *Chronicle of Higher Education.*

82. Carrick-Hagenbarth, J., and Epstein, G.A. (2012), 'Dangerous interconnectedness: economists' conflicts of interest, ideology and financial crisis', *Cambridge Journal of Economics*, 36 (1), pp. 43–63.

83. Levinovitz, A.J. (4 April 2016), 'The new astrology'. Retrieved from Aeon: https://aeon.co/essays/how-economists-rode-maths-to -become-our-era-s-astrologers

84. For a discussion of ethics in economics, see: DeMartino, G.F. (2010), *The Economist's Oath: On the Need for and Content of Professional Economic Ethics* (Oxford: Oxford University Press); DeMartino, G.F., and McCloskey, D.N. (eds) (2016), *The Oxford Handbook of Professional Economic Ethics* (Oxford: Oxford University Press).

85. Guy Rolnik (27 October 2016), 'It Takes a Village to Maintain a Dangerous Financial System: Q&A with Anat Admati'. Retrieved from ProMarket: https://promarket.org/takes-village-maintain -dangerous-financial-system-qa-anat-admati/

86. Häring, N. (2013), 'The veil of deception over money', *Real World Economics Review*, 63, pp. 2–18.

87. Economic and Social Research Council (20 April 2017), 'Innovative new network will "revolutionise" how we study the economy'. Retrieved from: http://www.esrc.ac.uk/news -events-and-publications/news/news-items/innovative-new -network-will-revolutionise-how-we-study-the-economy/

88. Orrell, D. (17 September 2017), 'Economyths: The Five Stages of Economic Grief'. Retrieved from Evonomics: http://evonomics. com/economyths-five-stages-economic-grief/. This is an extract from *Economyths: 11 Ways Economics Gets It Wrong.*

89. Stiglitz, J.E. (11 September 2017), 'Where Modern Macroeconomics Went Wrong'. Retrieved from: https://www8.gsb.columbia. edu/faculty/jstiglitz/sites/jstiglitz/files/Where%20Modern%20 Macroeconomics%20Went%20Wrong_0.pdf

90. Bernanke, B., Gertler, M., and Gilchrist, S. (1999), 'The financial accelerator in a quantitative business cycle framework', in J. Taylor, and M. Woodford (eds), *Handbook of Macroeconomics* (Vol. 1), pp. 1341–93. Elsevier.

91. Christiano, L.J., Eichenbaum, M.S., and Trabandt, M. (9 November 2017), 'On DSGE Models'. Retrieved from: http://faculty.wcas .northwestern.edu/~lchrist/research/JEP_2017/DSGE_final.pdf

92. Jakab, Z., and Kumhof, M. (2015), 'Banks are not intermediaries of loanable funds – and why this matters', *Bank of England Working Papers* (529), p. ii.

93. Earle, J., Moran, C., and Ward-Perkins, Z. (2016), *The Econocracy: The Perils of Leaving Economics to the Experts* (Manchester: Manchester University Press), p. 178.

94. This means that models are better at fitting the past than making predictions: 'parameters can be adjusted and epicycles added until the model agrees with historical data; but unlike planets, the economy's past is no guide to its future.' Orrell, D. (2007), *Apollo's Arrow: The Science of Prediction and the Future of Everything* (Toronto: HarperCollins).

95. Makridakis, S., and Hibon, M. (2000), 'The M3-Competition: results, conclusions and implications', *International Journal of Forecasting*, 16, pp. 451–76.

96. Stiglitz, J.E. (11 September 2017), 'Where Modern Macroeconomics Went Wrong'. Retrieved from: https://www8.gsb.columbia. edu/faculty/jstiglitz/sites/jstiglitz/files/Where%20Modern%20 Macroeconomics%20Went%20Wrong_0.pdf

97. Benes, J., Kumhof, M., and Laxton, D. (2014), 'Financial Crises in DSGE Models: A Prototype Model', *IMF Working Papers*, 14 (57).

98. Dirac, P. (1934), 'Banquet Speech', in C.G. Santesson (ed.), *Les Prix Nobel en 1933* (Stockholm: Nobel Foundation). Retrieved from: Nobelprize.org

99. Schrödinger, E. (1944), *What is life?* (Cambridge: Cambridge Uniersity Press).

100. As one example, see: Vitali, S., Glattfelder, J.B. and Battiston, S. (2011), 'The network of global corporate control' *PLOS ONE*, 6 (10), e25995.

101. For example, the agent-based approach has been used to show how excessive leverage can lead to instability: Thurner, S., Farmer, D.J. and Geanakoplos, J. (2012), 'Leverage Causes Fat Fails and Clustered Volatility', *Quantitative Finance*, 12 (5): pp. 695–707.

102. Cristelli, M., Tacchella, A., and Pietronero, L. (2015), 'The Heterogeneous Dynamics of Economic Complexity', *PLOS ONE*, 10 (2), e0117174.

103. Haldane, A. (29 October 2014), 'Managing global finance as a system – speech by Andrew Haldane'. Retrieved from Bank of England: http://www.bankofengland.co.uk/publications/Documents/speeches/2014/speech772.pdf

104. Alstadsaeter, A., Johannesen, N., and Zucman, G. (2017), 'Who Owns the Wealth in Tax Havens?', *Macro Evidence and Implications for Global Inequality NBER Working Paper No. 23805* (Cambridge: National Bureau of Economic Research).

105. Haberly, D. and Wójcik, D. (2015), 'Regional Blocks and Imperial Legacies: Mapping the Global Offshore FDI Network', *Economic Geography*, 91 (3), pp. 251–80.

106. Balzli, B. and Schiessl, M. (7 August 2009), 'The Man Nobody Wanted to Hear'. Retrieved from Spiegel Online: http://www.spiegel.de/international/business/the-man-nobody-wanted-to-hear-global-banking-economist-warned-of-coming-crisis-a-635051.html

107. Orrell, D. (2017), 'A Quantum Theory of Money and Value, Part 2: The Uncertainty Principle', *Economic Thought*, 6 (2), pp. 14–26.

108. Goldenfeld, N., and Kadanoff, L. (1999), 'Simple lessons from complexity', *Science*, 284 (5411), pp. 87–9.

109. See: http://www.physiomics-plc.com/services/virtual-tumour-clinical/. One mainstream economist told me that agent-based models are 'methodologically flawed' but I think we will keep using them.

110. Wren-Lewis, S. (9 January 2018), 'Why does economics get so much stick?' Retrieved from: https://mainlymacro.blogspot.ca/2018/01/because-adviceof-economists-is-so.html

111. YouGov (17 February 2017), 'Leave voters are less likely to trust any experts – even weather forecasters'. Retrieved from: https://yougov.co.uk/news/2017/02/17/leave-voters-are-less-likely-trust-any-experts-eve/

112. From the above-cited working paper 'On DSGE Models'. Economist Noah Smith described the 'dilettantes' phrase as a 'bad look' for economists, but on the other hand at least it was honest. Smith, N. (15 November 2017), 'The "cackling cartoon villain" defense of DSGE'. Retrieved from http://noahpinionblog.blogspot.ca/2017/11/the-cackling-cartoon-villain-defense-of.html

113. Smith, N. (17 October 2017), 'Fixing macroeconomics will be really hard', Bloomberg.com.

114. Romer, P. (2015), 'Mathiness in the Theory of Economic Growth', *American Economic Review*, 105 (5), pp. 89–93.

115. Vines, D. and Wills, S. (5 January 2018), 'The rebuilding macroeconomic theory project: an analytical assessment', *Oxford Review of Economic Policy*, 34 (1–2), pp. 1–42.

116. See: Laughlin, R.B. (2005), *A Different Universe: Reinventing physics from the bottom down* (New York: Basic Books).

117. Bouchaud, J.-P. (19 October 2017), 'The workhorse models of central bankers need a radical change', *Financial Times*.

118. Wallace, T. (21 November 2016), 'Economists need to get into the real world, says Bank of England chief economist'. Retrieved from *The Daily Telegraph*: http://www.telegraph.co.uk/business/2016/11/21/economists-need-get-real-world-says-bank-england-chief-economist/

119. Munchau, W. (12 April 2015), 'Macroeconomists need new tools to challenge consensus', *Financial Times*.

Chapter 9

1. Koestler, A. (1967), *The Ghost in the Machine* (London: Hutchinson).

2. Rowe, S. (2001), 'Transcending this Poor Earth – á la Ken Wilber', *The Trumpeter*, 17 (1).

3. Brooks, C.G. (2012), *Chariots for Apollo: The NASA History of Manned Lunar Spacecraft to 1969* (Mineola, NY: Dover Publications).

4. Cashford, J. (2002), *The Moon: Myth and Image* (New York: Four Walls Eight Windows), p. 364.

5. Editors of *Life* (2003), *Life: 100 Photographs That Changed the World* (New York: Life Books).

6. Watson, J.B. (1913), 'Psychology as the Behaviorist Views it', *Psychological Review*, 20, pp. 158–77.

7. Graziano, M. (21 August 2013), 'How the light gets out'. Retrieved from Aeon: https://aeon.co/essays/how-consciousness-works -and-why-we-believe-in-ghosts

8. Dyson, F. (1979), *Disturbing the Universe* (New York: Basic Books).

9. Talbot, M. (2011), *The Holographic Universe: The Revolutionary Theory of Reality* (New York: HarperCollins).

10. Wendt, A. (2015), *Quantum Mind and Social Science: Unifying Physical and Social Ontology* (Cambridge: Cambridge University Press), p. 120.

11. Penrose, R. (1989). *The Emperor's New Mind: Concerning Computers, Minds and The Laws of Physics.* Oxford: Oxford University Press.

12. Ouellette, J. (2 November 2016), 'A New Spin on the Quantum Brain'. Retrieved from Quanta Magazine: https://www.quantamagazine .org/a-new-spin-on-the-quantum-brain-20161102/

13. Ball, P. (16 February 2017), 'The strange link between the human mind and quantum physics'. Retrieved from BBC: http://www.bbc .com/earth/story/20170215-the-strange-link-between-the-human -mind-and-quantum-physics

14. Wendt, A. (2015), *Quantum Mind and Social Science: Unifying Physical and Social Ontology* (Cambridge: Cambridge University Press), p. 258.

15. Laughlin, R.B. (2005), *A Different Universe: Reinventing physics from the bottom down* (New York: Basic Books), p. 80.

16. This contradicts the idea that it should be possible to generate any social phenomenon using an agent-based model. See, e.g., Epstein, J.M. (2011), *Generative Social Science: Studies in Agent-Based Computational Modeling* (Princeton, NJ: Princeton University Press).

17. 'The more severe inequality becomes, the more entitled people may feel and less likely to share resources they become. The wealthier [that] segments of society become then, the more vulnerable communities may be to selfish tendencies and the less charity the least among us can expect'. Miller, L. (1 July 2012), 'The Money-Empathy Gap', *New York*.

18. Feinberg, C. (May 2015), 'The Science of Scarcity', *Harvard Magazine*. Retrieved from: http://harvardmagazine.com/2015/05/ the-science-of-scarcity

19. Cheng, E. (8 July 2017), 'Here's how the opioid epidemic is damaging the US economy', *The Fiscal Times*.

20. Interpreting these emergent behaviours has resulted in 'a confrontation between reductionist and emergent principles that continues

today'. Laughlin, R.B. (2005), *A Different Universe: Reinventing physics from the bottom down* (New York: Basic Books), pp. 89, 97. See also Anderson, P. (1972), 'More Is Different', *Science*, 177 (4047), pp. 393–6.

21. Talbot, M. (2011), *The Holographic Universe: The Revolutionary Theory of Reality* (New York: HarperCollins).

22. MacKenzie, D., and Spears, T. (2014), '"The Formula That Killed Wall Street?" The Gaussian Copula and Modelling Practices in Investment Banking', *Social Studies of Science*, 44, pp. 393–417.

23. Braudel, F. (1982), *Civilization and Capitalism, 15th–18th Century, Vol. I: The Structure of Everyday Life* (Oakland: University of California Press), p. 436.

24. UN Statistics Division (12 November 2017), *The System of National Accounts*. Retrieved from: https://unstats.un.org/unsd/national account/sna.asp

25. Wiles, P. (July 1953), 'The Soviet Economy Outpaces the West', *Foreign Affairs*.

26. Smith, R., Bizikova, L., McDougal, K., and Thrift, C. (2016), *Comprehensive Wealth in Canada – Measuring What Matters in the Long Run* (Winnipeg, MN: International Institute for Sustainable Development). Retrieved from: http://www.iisd.org/library/ comprehensive-wealth-canada-measuring-what-matters-long-run

27. Kubiszewski, I., Costanza, R., Franco, C., Lawn, P., Talberth, J., Jackson, T., and Aylmer, C. (2013), 'Beyond GDP: Measuring and achieving global genuine progress', *Ecological Economics*, 93, pp. 57–68.

28. Block, N. (3 March 2017), 'Toronto's buried history: the dark story of how mining built a city', *The Guardian*.

29. 'The principles and ethics of human law and convention must not run counter to those of thermodynamics.' Soddy, F. (1922), *Cartesian Economics* (London: Hendersons), p. 91.

30. Ravaioli, C. (1995), *Economists and the Environment* (London: Zed Books), p. 32.

31. Hamilton, C. (2010), *Requiem for a Species: Why We Resist the Truth about Climate Change* (London: Earthscan), p. 62.

32. Orrell, D. (2007), *Apollo's Arrow: The Science of Prediction and the Future of Everything* (Toronto: HarperCollins).

33. Lainà, P. (2015), 'Proposals for Full-Reserve Banking: A Historical Survey from David Ricardo to Martin Wolf', *Economic Thought*, 4 (2), pp. 1–19.

34. Transnational Institute (February 2013), 'The Global Land Grab'. Retrieved from: https://www.tni.org/files/download/

landgrabbingprimer-feb2013.pdf. Bollier, D. (2014), *Think Like a Commoner: A Short Introduction to the Life of the Commons* (Gabriola Island, BC, Canada: New Society Publishers).

35. Aristotle (2000), *Politics* (Mineola, NY: Dover Publications).

36. Hardin, G. (1968), 'The Tragedy of the Commons', *Science*, 162 (3859), pp. 1243–8. The title referred to an earlier 1833 parable by William Forster Lloyd.

37. Colman, R., and Messinger, H. (June 2004), 'Economic Performance and the Wellbeing of Canadians'. Retrieved from Canadian Economic Association: https://economics.ca//2004/papers/0295.pdf

38. Ostrom, E., Burger, J., Field, C.B., Norgaard, R.B., and Policansky, D. (9 April 1999), 'Revisiting the Commons: Local Lessons, Global Challenges', *Science*, 284 (5412), pp. 278–82.

39. As one example, see: Lansing, J.S., and Fox, K.M. (2011), 'Niche Construction on Bali: The Gods of the Countryside', *Philosophical Transactions of the Royal Society B: Biological Sciences*, 366 (1566), pp. 927–34.

40. Sandel, M. (2012), *What Money Can't Buy: The Moral Limits of Markets* (London: Allen Lane).

41. Daly, H.E. (1996), *Beyond Growth: The Economics of Sustainable Development* (Boston, MA: Beacon Press).

42. Edgeworth, F.Y. (1881), *Mathematical Psychics: an essay on the application of mathematics to the moral sciences* (London: C.K. Paul), p. 101.

43. Ragan, C.T., and Lipsey, R.G. (2011), *Economics* (13th edn) (Toronto: Pearson Education Canada), p. 121. Mankiw, N.G. (2016), *Principles of Economics* (8th edn) (Boston, MA: Cengage Learning), p. 410.

44. Aldred, J. (2009), *The Skeptical Economist: Revealing the Ethics Inside Economics* (London: Earthscan), p. 22.

45. Blanchard, O. (2006), *Macroeconomics* (Upper Saddle River, NJ: Pearson Prentice Hall).

46. Coyle, D. (2002), *Sex, Drugs and Economics: An Unconventional Introduction to Economics* (New York: Texere).

47. Helliwell, J.F., et al. (2015), *World Happiness Report 2015* (New York: Sustainable Development Solutions Network).

48. Easterlin, R.A. (2005), 'Feeding the Illusion of Growth and Happiness: A Reply to Hagerty and Veenhoven', *Social Indicators Research*, 74 (3), pp. 429–43.

49. Boyce, C., Brown, G., and Moore, S. (2010), 'Money and happiness: Rank of income, not income, affects life satisfaction', *Psychological Science*, 21 (4), pp. 471–5.

50. University of Warwick (22 March 2010), 'Study says money only makes you happy if it makes you richer than your neighbours'. Retrieved from: http://www2.warwick.ac.uk/newsandevents/pressreleases/study_says_money/

51. Mill, J.S. (January 1907), 'On Social Freedom', *Oxford and Cambridge Review*.

52. Daly, M., Boyce, C., & Wood, A. (2015). A Social Rank Explanation of How Money Influences Health. *Health Psychology*, 34 (3), 222–230.

53. Marmot, M., Smith, G., Stansfeld, S., Patel, C., North, F., Head, J., Feeney, A. (1991), 'Health inequalities among British civil servants: the Whitehall II study', *The Lancet*, 337, pp. 1387–93.

54. Wennerlind, C. (2011), *Casualties of Credit: The English Financial Revolution, 1620–1720* (Cambridge, MA: Harvard University Press), pp. 198–9.

55. Noble, D. (18 August 2014), '11% of UK businesses say slavery in their supply chains is "likely"', *The Guardian*. According to a 2017 UN report, some 40 million people are estimated to be living in slavery, with 'money and debt' at the heart of the problem. Kelly, A. (19 September 2017), 'Latest figures reveal more than 40 million people are living in slavery', *The Guardian*.

56. Elliott, L. (16 January 2017), 'World's eight richest people have same wealth as poorest 50%', *The Guardian*. You can argue that the numbers change if factors such as purchasing power parity are taken into account, but the trend is clear.

57. Ostry, J.D., Berg, A., and Charalambos, G.T. (2014), 'Redistribution, Inequality, and Growth' (Washington, DC: International Monetary Fund, Research Department). OECD (2015), 'In It Together: Why Less Inequality Benefits All' (Paris: Organisation for Economic Cooperation and Development). Mainstream economists often call something mainstream if it becomes popular. For example, in the debate discussed in the box in this chapter, neoclassical economist Pieter Gautier said, 'I think Piketty is very mainstream'. Pontus Rendahl also counts Piketty as a mainstream economist. However, Piketty told the Paris-based *Potemkin Review* that 'I do not believe in the basic neoclassical model'. Dolcerocca, A., and Terzioglu, G. (January 2015), 'Interview: Thomas Piketty Responds to Criticisms from the Left', *Potemkin Review*. Gayne, D. (24 November 2017), 'The forward march of pluralists halted', *Varsity*. Retrieved from: https://www.varsity.co.uk/news/14194

58. Rodrik, D. (15 November 2016), 'Straight Talk on Trade'. Retrieved from Project Syndicate: https://www.project-syndicate.org/

commentary/trump-win-economists-responsible-by-dani-rodrik
-2016-11

59. Ossa, F. (24 March 2016), 'The Economist Who Brought You Thomas Piketty Sees "Perfect Storm" of Inequality Ahead', *New York Magazine*.

60. One problem is that, as Paul Krugman noted in 2016, 'we really don't know how to model personal income distribution'. Krugman, P. (8 January 2016), 'Economists and Inequality'. Retrieved from nytimes.com. Olivier Blanchard wrote the same year that the derivation of distributional effects 'depends on the way distortions are introduced in the model. And, often, for reasons of practicality, these distortions are introduced in ways that are analytically convenient but have unconvincing welfare implications.' Blanchard, O. (2016), 'Do DSGE Models Have a Future? Policy Brief 16-11' (Washington, DC: Peterson Institute for International Economics). Retrieved from: https://piie.com/system/files/documents/pb16-11 .pdf

61. Robbins, L. (1932), *An Essay on the Nature and Significance of Economic Science* (London: Macmillan), p. 125.

62. Lucas, R. (2004), *The Industrial Revolution: Past and Future – 2003 Annual Report Essay* (Minneapolis, MN: Federal Reserve Bank of Minneapolis).

63. Mankiw, N.G. (2013), 'Defending the One Per cent', *The Journal of Economic Perspectives*, 27 (3), pp. 21–34.

64. Duncan, D.E. (July 2003), 'Discover Dialogue: Geneticist James Watson', *Discover*.

65. Johnson, B. (28 November 2013), 'Boris Johnson's speech at the Margaret Thatcher lecture in full', *The Daily Telegraph*.

66. Spencer, H. (1851), *Social statics, or the Conditions essential to human happiness specified and the first of them developed* (London: J. Chapman).

67. Cowen, T. (16 March 2013), 'A Profession With an Egalitarian Core', *New York Times*.

68. As Barad notes, a similar love of symmetry perhaps explains why 'physicists find any suggestion to the effect that the work they are engaged in is in any way partial to one kind of human or another (whether the distinction is drawn on the grounds of nationality, religion, gender, race, class, or eye color) so downright objectionable, even repugnant'. Barad, K. (2007), *Meeting the Universe Halfway: Quantum Physics and the Entanglement of Matter and Meaning* (Durham, NC: Duke University Press), p. 322.

69. Baker, D. (27 July 2017), 'How about a little accountability for economists when they mess up?', *The Guardian*.

70. Baker, D. (2016), 'Rigged: How Globalization and the Rules of the Modern Economy Were Structured to Make the Rich Richer' (Washington, DC: Center for Economic and Policy Research). Retrieved from: https://deanbaker.net/books/rigged.htm

71. Putnam, R.D. (2000), *Bowling Alone: The Collapse and Revival of American Community* (New York: Simon & Schuster), p. 333.

72. Anonymous (4 December 2008), 'Joy to the world is contagious: study'. Retrieved from CBC News: http://www.cbc.ca/news/technology/joy-to-the-world-is-contagious-study-1.712963

73. University of Melbourne (16 June 2017), 'Why chasing happiness could be having the opposite effect'. Retrieved from World Economic Forum: https://www.weforum.org/agenda/2017/06/why-chasing-happiness-could-actually-have-the-opposite-effect

74. Orrell, D., and Chlupatý, R. (2016), *The Evolution of Money* (New York: Columbia University Press).

75. McGilchrist, I. (2009), *The Master and his Emissary* (London: Yale University Press), p. 70.

76. Ibid., p. 209.

77. Ibid., pp. 432, 430.

78. In a speech published the following year, see: Hayek, F.A. (1937), 'Economics and knowledge', *Economica*, 4 (13), pp. 33–54.

79. Ridley, M. (23 March 2017), 'Friedrich Hayek and the collective brain'. Retrieved from CapX: https://capx.co/friedrich-hayek-and-the-collective-brain/

80. Morson, G.S., and Schapiro, M. (2017), *Cents and Sensibility: What Economics Can Learn from the Humanities* (Princeton, NJ: Princeton University Press).

81. Kumar, M. (2008), *Quantum: Einstein, Bohr and the Great Debate About the Nature of Reality* (London: Icon Books), p. 51. Millikan was later awarded the Nobel Prize for helping to confirm the theory.

82. Lee, F. (2009), *A History of Heterodox Economics: Challenging the Mainstream in the Twentieth Century* (London: Routledge), pp. 5–6.

83. Rethinking Economics NL (19 September 2015), 'VPRO Buitenhof: Rethinking Economics'. Retrieved from YouTube: https://www.youtube.com/watch?v=x7uITEBqQvM

84. Auld, C. (23 October 2013), '18 signs you're reading bad criticism of economics'. Retrieved from chrisauld.com: http://chrisauld.com/2013/10/23/18-signs-youre-reading-bad-criticism

-of-economics/. See also: Orrell, D. (1 July 2015), 'Book burning economists', *World Finance*.

85. Pilling, D. (30 September 2016), 'Crash and learn: should we change the way we teach economics?', *Financial Times*. Ben-Gad, M. (27 September 2017), 'Book review: Marxism and modern economics'. Retrieved from FTAdviser: https://www.ftadviser.com/pensions/2017/09/27/book-review-marxism-and-modern-economics/

86. As climate scientist Stephen Schneider put it back in 1997: 'In essence, they accept the paradigm that society is almost independent of nature.' Quoted in: Clark, B., Foster, J.B., and York, R. (2009), 'Capitalism in Wonderland', *Monthly Review*, 61 (1). Economists have certainly moved on in recent years, but have consistently lagged most scientists, as I argued in *Economyths* (pp. 246–8).

87. This is a reference to the 2015 book by an author who did speak with bankers: Luyendijk, J. (2015), *Swimming with Sharks: My Journey Into the World of the Bankers* (London: Guardian Faber).

88. Lucas, R. (2009), 'Robert E. Lucas Jr', in W. Breit, and B.T. Hirsch (eds), *Lives of the Laureates: Twenty-three Nobel Economists* (Cambridge, MA: MIT Press), p. 279.

89. Lee, F. (2009), *A History of Heterodox Economics: Challenging the Mainstream in the Twentieth Century* (London: Routledge), pp. 5–6.

90. For an example from a different context of how a simple model can beat a complicated reductionist model at prediction, see: Mistry, H.B. (2018), 'Complex versus simple models: ion-channel cardiac toxicity prediction', *PeerJ*, 6, e4352.

Chapter 10

1. For critiques, see Woit, P. (2006), *Not Even Wrong: The Failure of String Theory and the Search for Unity in Physical Law* (London: Vintage), pp. 151–2; Lederman, L. and Teresi, D. (1993), *The God Particle: If the Universe Is the Answer, What Is the Question?* (New York: Houghton Mifflin), pp. 189–91.

2. Orrell, D. (12 January 2018), '*Aeon* piece on quantum economics – responses'. Retrieved from: https://futureofeverything.wordpress.com/2018/01/12/aeon-piece-on-quantum-economics-responses/

3. Rand, A. (1938), *Anthem* (London: Cassell).

4. Salmieri, G. (2009), '*Atlas Shrugged* on the Role of the Mind in Man's Existence', in R. Mayhew (ed), *Essays on Ayn Rand's Atlas Shrugged* (Lanham, MD: Lexington Books).

5. Rand, A. (1961), *For the New Intellectual: The Philosophy of Ayn Rand* (New York: Signet).

6. Levine, B.E. (10 December 2014), 'How Ayn Rand Helped Turn the US Into a Selfish, Greedy Nation'. Retrieved from AlterNet: www.alternet. org/culture/how-ayn-rand-helped-turn-us-selfish-greedy-nation

7. Greenspan, A. (2007), *The Age of Turbulence: Adventures in a New World* (New York: Penguin).

8. Ramo, J.C. (15 February 1999), 'The Three Marketeers', *Time*.

9. Greenspan, A. (23 October 2008), 'Testimony of Dr Alan Greenspan', House Committee of Government Oversight and Reform, Washington, DC.

10. Greenspan, A. (29 March 2011), 'Dodd-Frank fails to meet test of our times', *Financial Times*.

11. Coll, S. (11 December 2016), 'Rex Tillerson, from a Corporate Oil Sovereign to the State Department', *The New Yorker*.

12. Reeve, E. (30 April 2012), 'Audio Surfaces of Paul Ryan's Effusive Love of Ayn Rand', *The Atlantic*.

13. Cummins, D. (16 February 2016), 'This is what happens when you take Ayn Rand seriously'. Retrieved from PBS: http://www. pbs.org/newshour/making-sense/column-this-is-what-happens -when-you-take-ayn-rand-seriously/

14. Bilton, N. (November 2016), 'Silicon Valley's Most Disturbing Obsession', *Vanity Fair*.

15. Mayer, J. (27 March 2017), 'The Reclusive Hedge-Fund Tycoon Behind The Trump Presidency', *The New Yorker*.

16. This might explain why in 2018 he launched a Tesla Roadster into space sporting a sign saying 'Don't Panic!' like the one on the book's cover. Ward, M. (6 June 2017), 'Elon Musk says reading this science-fiction classic changed his life'. Retrieved from CNBC: https://www .cnbc.com/2017/06/06/elon-musk-says-this-science-fiction-classic -changed-his-life.html

17. Nietzsche wrote: 'we might call Apollo himself the glorious divine image of the *principium individuationis*, through whose gestures and eyes all the joy and wisdom of "illusion," together with its beauty, speak to us.' Nietzsche, F. (1967), *The birth of tragedy, and the case of Wagner* (W. Kaufmann, trans.) (New York: Vintage Books), p. 36.

18. Harwood Group (1995), *Yearning for balance: Views of Americans on consumption, materialism, and environment* (Takoma Park, MD: Merck Family Fund).

19. Hoff, K., and Stiglitz, J.E. (2016), 'Striving for balance in economics:

Towards a theory of the social determination of behavior', *Journal of Economic Behavior & Organization*, 126, pp. 25–57.

20. Tuan, Y.-F. (1982), *Segmented World and Self* (Minneapolis, MN: University of Minnesota Press), p. 139.

21. Jensen, K., Vaish, A., and Schmidt, M.F. (2014), 'The emergence of human prosociality: aligning with others through feelings, concerns, and norms', *Frontiers in Psychology*, 5, p. 822.

22. Stiglitz, J.E. (11 September 2017), 'Where Modern Macroeconomics Went Wrong'. Retrieved from: https://www8.gsb.columbia. edu/faculty/jstiglitz/sites/jstiglitz/files/Where%20Modern%20 Macroeconomics%20Went%20Wrong_0.pdf. See also Hoff, K., and Stiglitz, J.E. (2016), 'Striving for balance in economics: Towards a theory of the social determination of behavior', *Journal of Economic Behavior & Organization*, 126, pp. 25–57.

23. Wendt, A. (2015), *Quantum Mind and Social Science: Unifying Physical and Social Ontology* (Cambridge: Cambridge University Press), p. 171.

24. Lovelock, J. (1979), *Gaia: A New Look at Life on Earth* (Oxford: Oxford University Press).

25. Descartes, R. (1984), *The philosophical writings of Descartes (Vol. 2)* (J. Cottingham, R. Stoothoff, and D. Murdoch, trans.) (Cambridge: Cambridge University Press), p. 59.

26. From this perspective, as Danah Zohar and Ian Marshall write, 'identity, the very core of the self, has both a particle and a wave aspect. The particle aspect of my self is my "I-ness", that part of me that is a unique and identifiable pattern with my own peculiar characteristics, my own "voice", my own style. It is that aspect of me that makes me a soloist in my own right. The wave aspect of my self is my "we-ness", the part of me that is evoked through my relationship to others and that is literally interwoven with the beings of others. My wave aspect is my public aspect, the dance to which my solo movements contribute and through which they both take on a larger meaning and through which they evolve.' Zohar, D., and Marshall, I. (1993), *The Quantum Society* (London: Flamingo), p. 151.

27. Fourcade, M., Ollion, E., and Algan, Y. (2015), 'The Superiority of Economists', *Journal of Economic Perspectives*, 29 (1), pp. 89–114.

28. Friedman, M. (1953), *Essays in Positive Economics* (Chicago : University of Chicago Press).

29. Doherty, B. (1 June 1995), 'Best of Both Worlds: An Interview with Milton Friedman'. Retrieved from Reason.com: https://reason.com/ archives/1995/06/01/best-of-both-worlds/print

30. Aristotle (2000), *Politics* (Mineola, NY: Dover Publications), p. 46.
31. Robinson, J.M. (1968), *An Introduction to Early Greek Philosophy* (Boston, MA: Houghton Mifflin), p. 202.
32. Descartes, R. (1988), *Descartes: Selected Philosophical Writings* (Cambridge: Cambridge University Press), p. 85.
33. Curtis, A. (director), Kelsall, L. (producer) (2011), *All Watched Over by Machines of Loving Grace* (motion picture).
34. Colander, D., Holt, R., and Rosser, B., Jr. (2004), 'The Changing Face of Mainstream Economics', *Review of Political Economy*, 16 (4), pp. 485–99.
35. Arnsperger, C., and Varoufakis, Y. (2006), 'What is Neoclassical Economics? The three axioms responsible for its theoretical oeuvre, practical irrelevance and, thus, discursive power', *Panoeconomicus*, 1, pp. 5–18.
36. Boerger, L. and the Exploring Economics team (18 December 2016), 'Neoclassical Economics'. Retrieved from Exploring Economics: https://www.exploring-economics.org/en/orientation/neoclassical-economics/
37. Keynes, J.M. (1933), 'National Self-Sufficiency', *The Yale Review*, 22 (4), pp. 755–69.
38. Rodrik, D. (2015), *Economics Rules: The Rights and Wrongs of the Dismal Science* (New York: W.W. Norton & Company).
39. Smith, N. (8 August 2016), 'Economics Without Math Is Trendy, But It Doesn't Add Up'. Retrieved from Bloomberg.com: https://www.bloomberg.com/view/articles/2016-08-08/economics-without-math-is-trendy-but-it-doesn-t-add-up
40. Rethinking Economics NL (19 September 2015), 'VPRO Buitenhof: Rethinking Economics'. Retrieved from YouTube: https://www.youtube.com/watch?v=x7uITEBqQvM
41. Pilling, D. (30 September 2016), 'Crash and learn: should we change the way we teach economics?', *Financial Times*.
42. Hume, D. (1777), *An Enquiry Concerning Human Understanding* (London: A. Millar).
43. Leontief, W. (1971), 'Theoretical Assumptions and Nonobserved Facts', *American Economic Review*, 61 (1), pp. 1–7.
44. Wilmott, P., and Orrell, D. (2017), *The Money Formula: Dodgy Finance, Pseudo Science, and How Mathematicians Took Over the Markets* (Chichester: Wiley).
45. Laughlin, R.B. (2005), *A Different Universe: Reinventing physics from the bottom down* (New York: Basic Books), p. 209.

46. Aristotle (2017), *Nicomachean Ethics* (W.D. Ross, trans.). Retrieved from: http://classics.mit.edu/Aristotle/nicomachaen.mb.txt

47. Haldane, A. and Turrell, A.E. (November 2017), 'An interdisciplinary model for macroeconomics', Staff Working Paper No. 696. Retrieved from Bank of England: http://www.bankofengland.co.uk/research/Documents/workingpapers/2017/swp696.pdf

48. Von Mises, L. (1998), *Human Action: A Treatise on Economics* (Auburn, AL: Ludwig von Mises Institute), p. 874.

49. Heisenberg, W. (1990), *Physics and Philosophy: The Revolution in Modern Science* (London: Penguin), p. 194.

50. Bohm, D. (1980), *Wholeness and the Implicate Order* (London: Routledge), p. 7.

51. Lemos, G.B., and Schaffer, K. (5 February 2018), 'Obliterating Thingness: an Introduction to the "What" and the "So What" of Quantum Physics'. Retrieved from: http://www.kathrynschaffer.com/documents/obliterating-thingness.pdf

52. An example was Frederick Soddy, who according to the *New York Times* was 'roundly dismissed as a crank'. Zencey, E. (12 April 2009), 'Mr Soddy's Ecological Economy', *The New York Times*. More recently, Paul Krugman wrote on his blog in 2015 that the 'intellectual strategy' of treating money 'a lot like ordinary goods ... doesn't come naturally to many people, so there's always a constituency for monetary cranks'. Krugman, P. (10 February 2015), 'There's Something About Money (Implicitly Wonkish)'. Retrieved from: http://krugman.blogs.nytimes.com/2015/02/10/theres-something-about-money-implicitly-wonkish/

53. Friedman, M. (1975), *There's No Such Thing as a Free Lunch* (LaSalle, IL: Open Court).

54. Sutter, A.J. (2010), 'Unlimited Growth and Innovation: Paradise or Paradox?'. Retrieved from SSRN: https://ssrn.com/abstract=1709285. Extracted from: Sutter, A.J. (2012), *Keizai seichou shinwa no owari* [The end of the myth of economic growth] (Y. Nakamura, trans.) (Tokyo: Kodansha Gendai Shinsho), pp. 93-4.

55. Rand, A. (1982), 'The Metaphysical Versus the Man-Made', in A. Rand, and L. Peikoff (ed.), *Philosophy: Who Needs It?* (New York: New American Library), pp. 23-34, p. 25. Quoted in Ibid.

56. Kurtzman, J. (1997), 'An Interview with Paul M. Romer', *Strategy + Business* (6).

57. Paine, A.B. (19 August 2016), 'Mark Twain, A Biography, 1835-1910'. Retrieved from Project Gutenberg: https://www.gutenberg.org/files/2988/2988-h/2988-h.htm

58. Hawking, S. (1988), *A Brief History of Time: from the Big Bang to Black Holes* (New York: Bantam Books), p. 129.

59. Brand, S. (1987), *The Media Lab: Inventing the Future at MIT* (New York: Viking), p. 202.

60. Derman, E., and Wilmott, P. (8 January 2009), 'Financial Modelers' Manifesto'. Retrieved from Wilmott.com: https://www.wilmott.com/financial-modelers-manifesto/

61. Reisz, M., Auld, C., Bateman, V., Keen, S., and Oswald, A. (6 July 2017), 'New horizons: economics in the 21st century', *Times Higher Education.*

62. Milton Friedman, for example, said that 'criticism of this type is largely beside the point unless … the theory being criticised yields better predictions for as wide a range of phenomena', though one could argue that his own theories only became scripture after they were endorsed by Thatcher and Reagan. Friedman, M. (1953), *Essays in Positive Economics* (Chicago : University of Chicago Press).

63. Orrell, D. (2012), *Truth or Beauty: Science and the Quest for Order* (New Haven, CT: Yale University Press).

64. Gayne, D. (24 November 2017), 'The forward march of pluralists halted', *Varsity*. Retrieved from: https://www.varsity.co.uk/news/14194

65. Keynes, J.M. (1926), 'Francis Ysidro Edgeworth, 1845–1926', *Economic Journal*, 36, pp. 140–53.

66. Galbraith, J. (1994), 'Keynes, Einstein, and Scientific Revolution', *The American Prospect* (Winter).

67. McLuhan, M., and McLuhan, E. (1988), *Laws of Media* (Toronto: University of Toronto Press).

Acknowledgements

A number of people helped me with this book, by reading and critiquing chapters or related articles, pointing me towards related research, and clarifying specific issues in economics or physics or both. My profound thanks to (in alphabetical order, and without implying any endorsement on their part of the ideas herein) Hilliard MacBeth, Robert Matthews, Asghar Qadir, Michael Raymer, Jack Sarkissian, Kathryn Schaffer, Michael Schnabel, Didier Sornette, Andrew J. Sutter, Alexander Wendt, and Paul Wilmott. The book also benefited from interactions during two workshops in 2018, one held by the UK's Economic and Social Research Council on Rebuilding Macroeconomics, and another on 'Quantum Theory and the International' at the Mershon Center for International Security Studies. Thanks also to everyone at Icon Books, especially Duncan Heath for his detailed and skilful editing of the manuscript. Finally, thanks as always to my wife Beatriz, and children Isabel and Emma, for whom the question *how much* has no answer.

The book is dedicated to three mentors who inspired me to follow a career in applied mathematics: James Muldowney, Vera Zeidan, and Leonard Smith.

INDEX